T0184051

A Practical Approach to High-Performance Computing

Sergei Kurgalin • Sergei Borzunov

A Practical Approach to High-Performance Computing

 Springer

Sergei Kurgalin
Department of Digital Technologies
Voronezh State University
Voronezh, Russia

Sergei Borzunov
Department of Digital Technologies
Voronezh State University
Voronezh, Russia

ISBN 978-3-030-27560-0   ISBN 978-3-030-27558-7   (eBook)
https://doi.org/10.1007/978-3-030-27558-7

© Springer Nature Switzerland AG 2019
This work is subject to copyright. All rights are reserved by the Publisher, whether the whole or part of the material is concerned, specifically the rights of translation, reprinting, reuse of illustrations, recitation, broadcasting, reproduction on microfilms or in any other physical way, and transmission or information storage and retrieval, electronic adaptation, computer software, or by similar or dissimilar methodology now known or hereafter developed.
The use of general descriptive names, registered names, trademarks, service marks, etc. in this publication does not imply, even in the absence of a specific statement, that such names are exempt from the relevant protective laws and regulations and therefore free for general use.
The publisher, the authors, and the editors are safe to assume that the advice and information in this book are believed to be true and accurate at the date of publication. Neither the publisher nor the authors or the editors give a warranty, express or implied, with respect to the material contained herein or for any errors or omissions that may have been made. The publisher remains neutral with regard to jurisdictional claims in published maps and institutional affiliations.

This Springer imprint is published by the registered company Springer Nature Switzerland AG.
The registered company address is: Gewerbestrasse 11, 6330 Cham, Switzerland

Preface

This book discusses the fundamentals of high-performance computing. The study and mastery of these are essential for solving current problems in fundamental and applied science, and will allow the growing demands of researchers for increased processing speed of large data volumes to be satisfied. In this book, we have attempted to combine visualization, comprehensibility, and rigor of the presentation of the material, with an orientation towards practical applications and training to solve real computing problems.

The book is based on the authors' experience of many years of teaching at Voronezh State University of courses with titles such as "Parallel Programming," "Technologies for Parallel Computing," "Parallel and Grid Technologies," and "Parallel Data-Processing Algorithms" for bachelor's and master's degree students, as well as a course entitled "Information and Communication Technologies" for upgrading the qualifications of university teachers and research fellows. Since 2002, when it launched its first high-performance parallel computer cluster, the university has been providing teaching in the field of supercomputing.

The book is intended for a wide range of levels of readers, from juniors beginning to familiarize themselves with the subject to master's degree students, postgraduates, research fellows, and specialists.

The material of the book has been thoroughly selected and consistently presented to give an idea of various aspects of high-performance computation. The book contains basic theoretical insight into the methods of parallel programming and information about the techniques for parallelizing.

The material is presented at a rather rigorous mathematical level; all statements (lemmas and theorems) are provided with proofs, or, in rare instances, with references to the specialized literature on the topic being discussed.

Each chapter begins with a theoretical part, where the relevant terminology is introduced along with the basic theoretical results and methods of parallel programming. Apart from the basic definitions, theoretical provisions, and computing models, the text contains instructions for their use when developing parallel programs. Furthermore, several standard problems are analyzed in detail. When an example is provided in the text, its end is marked with a square. Each chapter is concluded by a list of test questions for checking and consolidation of the theoretical material; then follow problems to be solved in the lecture hall or computer classroom. These problem can also be used for individual study. The exercises differ considerably in their complexity. The most difficult ones are marked with an asterisk in front of the number.

Many problems are provided with answers, hints, and solutions, including sample program code. The texts of programs demonstrating the solutions of both standard and more complex problems are usually provided in full and unabridged form, which is especially important for first acquaintance with the book's material. The programs are written with plenty of explanatory comments.

There exist two main approaches to the programming of modern computing systems: multithreading-based parallelizing in shared-memory systems and the application of message-passing technologies in distributed systems. Both of these approaches are discussed in the book.

Most of the parallel programs used as examples are supplemented with speedup curves for the computational part of the program code as a function of the number of threads in a shared-memory system. The speedup values were calculated for the supercomputer at Voronezh State University. Visualization of the dependence of the speedup on the number of threads allows students to gain a deeper understanding of the operating principles of parallel algorithms.

The examples and problems provided in the book pay much attention to ensuring the required computational accuracy. In all cases, the computational error bounds required from the program are strictly defined.

The inclusion of reference information in the book allows the reader to consult the specialized literature less often than would otherwise be necessary. The appendices accomplish the methodological task of providing students with the skills required for working with the command shell responsible for communication between the user and the supercomputer system. The book also provides training materials covering the construction and analysis of parallel algorithms. As a result, working with the book should require very little resort to additional resources. The inclusion of extensive reference material and recommendations on the installation of parallel environments and the starting of programs on a supercomputer allows the reader to obtain skills in parallel programming even with minimal knowledge in the field of information and communication technologies. It is only necessary to know the basic constructs of the algorithmic language C, which is used to realize the algorithms and describe the problem solutions presented in the book. The C language was chosen because this language, on the one hand, is widely known and, on the other hand, is one of the main languages for supercomputer computations.

The book includes many illustrations visualizing the objects being studied and their interconnections.

The book consists of six chapters and four appendices.

Chapter 1 offers an overview of the basic methods of parallel programming and discusses the classification of computing system architectures.

Chapter 2 looks into the basic topologies of data-passing networks. It is shown that the network topology has a considerable influence on the performance of the computing system as a whole.

Chapter 3 is devoted to the basic laws of parallel computing. Within the PRAM model, the quantitative characteristics of the efficiency of parallel algorithms are discussed. Here, the notion of an "operations–operands" graph is introduced and Bernstein's conditions are formulated.

The next two chapters contain descriptions of widely used parallel programming technologies.

Chapter 4 is devoted to a description of the distributed-memory-system programming technology MPI. The essential functions of MPI, the operations of pairwise message exchange in blocking and nonblocking modes, and collective data-passing operations are discussed.

Chapter 5 considers the shared-memory computing system programming environment OpenMP, and the computing model used when working with this environment.

Chapter 6 contains implementations of basic parallel algorithms using the OpenMP technology as an example. Algorithms for array element summation, data sorting, basic matrix operations, and Monte Carlo static tests are discussed here.

Appendices A, B, C offer reference material, including methods for analysis of algorithms, a description of working with the Linux shell, and the theoretical fundamentals of Fourier analysis.

Appendix D contains answers, hints, and solutions to the problems. This appendix is rather long, because in many cases it provides detailed solutions and sample program code. This should help students with little programming experience to develop the basic skills of using multiprocessor computer systems.

At the first reference in the book to the names of scientists and researchers, footnotes provide brief bibliographic information about them, taken from Wikipedia.

The notation list contains definitions of the most frequently used symbols.

The text is complemented with a detailed reference list.

Name and subject indexes conclude the book.

Thus, the availability in the book of both theoretical material and examples of solutions to computing problems, discussed in detail, as well as tasks for individual work, will make the book useful for both teaching parallel programming in higher education institutions and for use by researchers and programmers for computation on high-performance computer systems.

Voronezh, Russia   Sergei Kurgalin
Voronezh, Russia   Sergei Borzunov
July 2018

Contents

Notation

$\mathbb{N}$ The set of integers

$\mathbb{R}$ The set of real numbers

$|A|$ Cardinality of set A

$G(V, E)$ G is a graph with vertex set V and edge set E

$d(v)$ Degree of vertex v of a graph

$D(V, E)$ Digraph

$d^+(v)$ Outdegree of vertex v in a digraph

$d^-(v)$ Indegree of vertex v in a digraph

$\lfloor x \rfloor$ Floor function of x, i.e., the greatest integer less than or equal to the real number x

$\lceil x \rceil$ Ceiling function of x, i.e., the smallest integer greater than or equal to the real number x

A **and** B Conjunction of logical expressions A and B

A **or** B Disjunction of logical expressions A and B

$T_p(N)$ Time spent by a parallel algorithm executed on p processors on data of size N

$T_\infty(N)$ Time spent by a paracomputer on data of size N

$O(g(n))$ Class of functions growing not faster than $f(n)$

$\Omega(g(n))$ Class of functions growing at least as fast as $f(n)$

$\Theta(g(n))$ Class of functions growing at the same speed as $f(n)$

$S_p(N)$ Performance speedup using p processors on data of size N

$E_p(N)$ Efficiency of parallel computation using p processors on data of size N

$C_p(N)$ Cost of a parallel algorithm for p processors on data of size N

f Proportion of code that is intrinsically sequential

$R(u)$ Set of input objects for statement u

$W(u)$ Set of output objects for statement u

$u \perp v$ Statements u and v are in a data dependency

$u \, \delta^0 \, v$ Data output dependency of statements u and v

$u \, \delta \, v$ Data flow dependency of statements u and v

$u \, \bar{\delta} \, v$ Data antidependency of statements u and v

Chapter 1
Classification of Computing System Architectures

The development of programs for multiprocessor computing systems, also referred to as parallel programming, has been attracting more and more attention from both researchers and application programmers. This is due to the following reasons.

First, in the world at large, new supercomputer centers have been arising, equipped with multiprocessor computing systems that use parallel programming methods. These supercomputer centers are used for solving the most complex problems, and in higher education institutions they are also used for training high-end, modern specialists in the field of information technology. Second, most computer systems in general use are equipped with multicore processors; moreover, they use several (two, four, eight, or more) processors. Third, the problems encountered by programmers are tending to dramatically increase the requirements on the resources of computing systems, with respect to both computational complexity and memory capacity.

For these reasons, the development of modern supercomputers means that maximally utilizing the resources provided by parallelism has become a pressing need.

The difficulties encountered when developing regular (sequential) versions of software definitely persist when one is creating parallel versions of such programs. Apart from this, additional problems are added that reflect the peculiarities of problem-solving with multiprocessor computing systems. Of course, it is advisable to be able to use standard methods of parallelization, but as it will be shown below, these have a series of drawbacks, the greatest of them being the rather low efficiency of the resulting programs. Also, problems arise associated with support for and portability of software suites. Fortunately, such methods have been developed for many parallel architectures. For further consideration of these issues, we need a classification of parallel computing system architectures.

© Springer Nature Switzerland AG 2019   1
S. Kurgalin, S. Borzunov, *A Practical Approach to High-Performance Computing*,
https://doi.org/10.1007/978-3-030-27558-7_1

1.1 Flynn's Taxonomy

Nowadays, the existence of labor-consuming computing tasks, as well as the dynamic development of multiprocessor computer systems, is bringing the problems of developing and analyzing parallel algorithms into focus. The great variety of existing computer system architectures leads to the necessity for a classification of them with respect to various parameters. Historically, one of the first ways of dividing architectures, based on the criteria of multiple instruction streams and data streams, was proposed by Flynn.[1]

A *stream* is defined as a sequence of instructions or data executed or processed by a processor [31, 73]. From this point of view, a program provides a processor with a stream of instructions for execution; the data for processing also come in the form of a stream. In Flynn's taxonomy, instruction streams and data streams are assumed to be independent. Thus, computing systems are divided into the following classes.

1. *Single instruction stream, single data stream* (SISD). These characteristics are found in standard computers with a single-core processor, which can perform only one operation at a time.
2. *Single instruction stream, multiple data stream* (SIMD). In such systems, the same operation is performed simultaneously on different data. This class includes, for example, vector computer systems, in which a single instruction can be performed on a set of data elements.
3. *Multiple instruction stream, single data stream* (MISD). Despite the lack of practical significance of this approach, MISD machines can be useful for some highly specialized tasks.
4. *Multiple instruction stream, multiple data stream* (MIMD). MIMD systems are the most extensive and diverse group in Flynn's classification. Most modern multiprocessor computer systems belong to this class.

The properties of the computer system classes considered above are schematically presented in Fig. 1.1. The boxes contain examples of the arithmetic operations available for simultaneous execution by the corresponding systems.

There is a widely used refinement of Flynn's taxonomy, according to which the category MIMD is divided according to the method of memory organization in the computer system. Among MIMD systems, we single out *multiprocessors* (uniform memory access, UMA) and *multicomputers* (no remote memory access, NORMA). The interaction between processors in multicomputers is executed using the message-passing mechanism [59]. The principal division of computer system architectures for the purposes of parallel programming is into shared-memory systems, distributed-memory systems, and hybrid systems combining the basic elements of the two previous classes.

---

[1]Michael J. Flynn (b. 1934), an American researcher, is an expert in the field of computer system architectures.

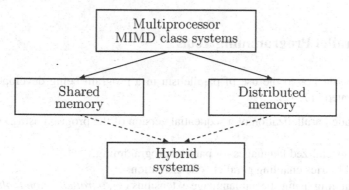

		Data stream	
		Single	Multiple
Instruction stream	Single	SISD $\overline{a_1 + b_1}$	SIMD $\begin{array}{l} a_1 + b_1 \\ a_2 + b_2 \\ a_3 + b_3 \end{array}$
	Multiple	MISD $\begin{array}{l} a_1 + b_1 \\ a_1 - b_1 \\ a_1 * b_1 \end{array}$	MIMD $\begin{array}{l} a_1 + b_1 \\ a_2 - b_2 \\ a_3 * b_3 \end{array}$

Fig. 1.1 Flynn's taxonomy of computer systems

Fig. 1.2 Classification of MIMD class multiprocessor systems based on memory organization principle

The classification of MIMD class multiprocessor systems based on their memory organization principle is shown in Fig. 1.2.

Note Recently, computing systems using graphics processing units (GPUs) have been attracting increasing attention. The programming of such systems has its own peculiarities since today's GPUs, unlike central processors, are massively parallel computing devices with many computing cores and hierarchically organized private memory [64, 72]. For this reason, the use of GPUs is usually studied only after one has obtained some basic knowledge in the field of multiprocessor and/or multicomputer programming.

In shared-memory systems, several physical processors or processor cores (referred to as *computational nodes*) can share a common memory space. This situation corresponds to the *shared-memory model*. The issues of simultaneous access of several computational nodes to memory areas occupy a central position in this model and are resolved with the help of *synchronization* mechanisms, which include the following:

- barriers,
- locks,
- semaphores

(see below and [3, 17]).

In distributed-memory systems, each computational node has access only to the memory area belonging to it, the local memory. In this case, for interprocessor data exchange, the possibility is provided of sending and receiving messages via the communication network that unites the computing system. The respective programming model is called the *message-passing model*.

Hybrid-system programming is based on the use of the above-listed models or combinations of them.

1.2 Parallel Programming Tools

Several approaches to the use of parallelism in a program being developed have been presented [17, 72]:

1. Automatic parallelization of a sequential version of the program using compiler tools.
2. Use of specialized languages for parallel programming.
3. Use of libraries enabling parallel code execution.
4. Programming using special language extensions i.e., *parallelization tools*.

Each of these approaches has both advantages and drawbacks.

For example, automatic program parallelization (the first approach) is very useful for application programmers, but its results, especially for complex algorithm based programs, often turn out to be unsatisfactory.

The second and third approaches have a positive side in that the code is unchanged compared with the sequential version.

Among the drawbacks of these three approaches, we should mention the absence of any possibility for the compiler to optimize the code executed, the rather high overhead costs of referring to library procedures and functions, and the lower portability of the program's source code compared with its sequential version.

The greatest potential for the use of parallelism resources is provided by the fourth approach—the use of special language extensions (*parallelization tools*). This approach will be considered in detail in this book.

1.3   Test Questions

1. Describe Flynn's classification of computing system architectures.
2. On the basis of which criterion are MIMD systems divided into multiprocessors and multicomputers?
3. Present a classification of multiprocessor computing systems by their memory organization principle.
4. Describe the advantages and drawbacks of various approaches to the use of parallelism resources.

Chapter 2
Topologies of Computer Networks

Computer systems that use many simultaneously operating processors can be built based on *data transmission networks*, also referred to as *communication networks* [25, 27, 74].

A system of independent computational nodes combined into a network is called a *distributed computer system*. Unlike multicomputers, distributed systems are usually constructed based on standard hardware and, as a rule, fall within a lower price range. Another difference consists in the spatial separation of the computational nodes; they can be rather far apart. The upper limit on the distance between nodes is defined only by the maximum allowable length of the communication line being used.

However, multicomputers and distributed computer systems have a lot in common, not only in the architecture but also in the peculiarities of the programming methods applied. At present, the message-passing-based approach is a de facto standard in the programming of both multicomputers and distributed systems.

In order to ensure coordinated operation of a system consisting of many modules, the data exchange between them is performed with the help of a communication network. The communication network ensures data transmission between the system's modules [27].

For each network, the format of *packets*, indivisible ordered data sets of a certain size, is defined. Apart from the actual information meant to be transmitted between the modules, the packet also contains the sender's address and the destination.

To obtain a quantitative estimate of the data transfer rate over a communication line, a standard assumption is introduced, stating that a formed packet is sent between two directly interconnected nodes of the computer system in one cycle of the system's operation in a parallel mode. In other words, the packet transmission time between such nodes is considered to have a constant value.

Models of communication networks are usually built using *graph theory*. The computational nodes are represented by the vertices of an undirected or directed

© Springer Nature Switzerland AG 2019
S. Kurgalin, S. Borzunov, *A Practical Approach to High-Performance Computing*,
https://doi.org/10.1007/978-3-030-27558-7_2

graph, and the communication lines that connect them are represented by edges or arcs.

The communication lines can be either bidirectional or unidirectional. In the latter case, the network model is a directed graph, connections between the vertices of which are assigned certain directions.

In this chapter, we will discuss only bidirectional communication line networks, as they are the most common ones in reality. Most parallel computing systems are built using bidirectional communication lines [59].

Let us recall the basic definitions of graph theory that will be required in the following discussion.

A *graph* is a pair $G = (V, E)$, where V is a set of vertices, and E is a set of edges connecting some pairs of vertices [16, 28].

A graph is said to be *simple* if it contains no *loops* (edges beginning and ending at the same vertex) or *multiple edges* (multiple edges are several edges connecting the same pair of vertices), and the sets V and E are finite.

A drawing where the vertices of a graph are represented by points and edges are represented by segments or arcs is called a *graph diagram*.

Two vertices u and v of a graph are *adjacent* if they are connected by an edge $r = uv$. In this case it is said that the vertices u and v are the *endpoints* of the edge r. If a vertex v is an endpoint of an edge r, then v and r are *incident*.

The *size* of a graph $G(V, E)$ is understood to mean the number of its vertices, $p = |V|$.

The *degree* $d(v)$ of a vertex v is the number of edges incident to that vertex. If the degrees of all vertices are equal to α, then the graph is called a *regular graph of degree* α.

A *path* of length k in a graph G is a sequence of vertices $v_0, v_1, \ldots, v_k$ such that, $\forall i = 1, \ldots, k$, the vertices v_{i-1} and v_i are adjacent. The *length* of the path is understood to mean the number of edges in it, taking into account iterations.

The *distance* between two vertices in a graph is the length of the shortest path connecting those vertices.

The *diameter* of a graph is the maximum distance between two vertices in the graph.

A *cycle* in a graph G is a closed path $v_0, v_1, v_2, \ldots, v_0$ where all the vertices except the first and the last are different.

A graph is referred to as *connected* if each pair of its vertices is connected by some path.

The *connectivity* is the minimum number of edges whose removal will result in the formation of a disconnected graph.

Two graphs $G_1 = (V_1, E_1)$ and $G_2 = (V_2, E_2)$ are called *isomorphic* (denoted $G_1 \sim G_2$) if there exists an unambiguous mapping (in other words, a bijection) of the vertices and edges of one of these graphs to the vertices and edges, respectively, of the other graph, and the incidence relation is preserved.

Isomorphic graphs have the same properties and are usually not distinguished.

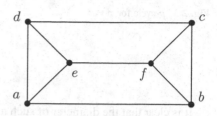

Fig. 2.1 The graph $G(V, E)$ of Example 2.1

Example 2.1 Consider the graph $G(V, E)$ whose sets of vertices and edges are defined as follows:

$$V = \{a, b, c, d, e, f\},$$

$$E = \{ab, ad, ae, bc, bf, cd, cf, de, ef\}.$$

Enumerate the main properties of the graph $G(V, E)$.

Solution A diagram of the graph $G(V, E)$ is shown in Fig. 2.1. This graph, as can be seen from the figure, is connected and regular. The degree of each vertex is equal to 3.

Any two vertices in G are connected by a path consisting of no more than two edges. Hence, the diameter of the graph is equal to 2.

In other to divide the graph G into two disconnected parts, at least three edges need to be removed from the set E; therefore the connectivity of the graph is equal to 3.

□

The *network topology* is determined based on its representation in the form of a graph [8].

Note In mathematics, topology is the science of the most general and universal properties of objects, for example the properties of connectivity, directionality, and continuity. The use of this term in the theory of computer system construction is connected with the study of the properties of the graphs representing communication network models.

2.1 Complete Graph Topology

If any two nodes in a computer system are interconnected directly, then the system is said to have a *complete graph topology* (Fig. 2.2).

Fig. 2.2 Complete graph with eight vertices ($p = 8$)

Fig. 2.3 p-cycle for $p = 8$

It is clear that the diameter of such a graph is equal to one. The number of edges is found from the formula

$$|E| = \frac{1}{2}p(p - 1) = O(p^2).$$

The notation $O(f(n))$ is used to express estimates of the growth rate of the function $f(n)$ for sufficiently large values of n, and such estimates are called *asymptotic estimates* [13]. In particular, the notation $|E| = O(p^2)$ means that there exists a nonnegative constant c and a natural number p_0 such that, for all $p \geqslant p_0$, the inequality $f(p) \leqslant cp^2$ is valid. Reference information about asymptotic estimates is provided in Appendix A.

2.2 Ring Topology

The arrangement of a network in the form of a ring is a simple and very common method of defining a network topology. A ring topology is built on the basis of a p-cycle, i.e., a graph representing a cycle of p edges with $p \geqslant 3$ (Fig. 2.3).

It is easy to see that in this case the diameter is equal to $\lfloor p/2 \rfloor$. Here, $\lfloor x \rfloor$ is the integer part of the real number x, i.e., the greatest integer that is less than or equal to x:

$$\lfloor x \rfloor : \mathbb{R} \to \mathbb{Z}, \quad \lfloor x \rfloor = \max(n \in \mathbb{Z}, n \leqslant x).$$

The integer part of a number is also called the *floor*.

The connectivity of a p-cycle for all $p \geqslant 3$ is equal to 2.

2.3 Hypercube Topology

A *hypercube* Q_d of size d, where d is a nonnegative integer, is a graph containing 2^d vertices. It is built as follows. To the vertices of the graph Q_d are assigned bit strings $\mathbf{b} = (b_1, \ldots, b_t, \ldots, b_d)$, where $\forall t \; b_t \in \{0, 1\}$. Then, vertices v_i and v_j are adjacent if and only if $\mathbf{b}(v_i)$ and $\mathbf{b}(v_j)$ differ in only one component.

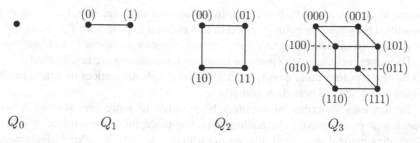

Fig. 2.4 Hypercubes Q_d of size $d = 0, 1, 2, 3$

The main property of a hypercube of size d is that it can be obtained by connecting with edges the corresponding vertices of two copies of a hypercube of size $d - 1$ (see Fig. 2.4, where the hypercubes Q_d are represented for $d \leqslant 3$). Each vertex of the hypercube Q_d is directly connected by edges to exactly d other vertices.

Now let us consider a computer network in the form of a hypercube.

Let the vertices of the graph be numbered with pairwise different natural numbers from the range $[1, N]$, and the i-th vertex of the hypercube correspond to processor P_i. In order to transmit a message from processor P_i to processor P_j, where $1 \leqslant i, j \leqslant N$ and $i \neq j$, the following is done. The binary representations of the numbers i and j are compared starting from the lower-order bit. Since $i \neq j$, there exists at least one difference, for example in the bit of order q. Processor P_i sends a message to a processor P_s, located at an adjacent vertex with the number s, which in the binary representation differs from i in the bit of order q. Then processor P_s transmits the data over the communication line to an adjacent processor, repeating the operations described above. As a result, the resulting recursive algorithm completes the data transmission operation in a finite number of steps.

The message transmission time $T(i, j)$ between two vertices of a hypercube is proportional to the number of differing bits in the binary representations of the numbers i and j. Hence, $\forall i, j \; T(i, j) = O(\log_2 N)$.

2.4 Grid and Torus Topologies

Let us place the processors at points in a Cartesian plane with integer coordinates in the range $x \in [0, q_1 - 1]$, $y \in [0, q_2 - 1]$, where q_1 and q_2 are the numbers of vertices in the horizontal and vertical directions, respectively. Such a method of network arrangement is called a *grid topology* (or *mesh topology*).

Transmission of a message in the grid topology from a processor P_i to a processor P_j, where $1 \leqslant i, j \leqslant q_1 \times q_2$, and $i \neq j$, is performed in two steps. In the first step, the data are transmitted between two processors located in the same row to the column where processor P_j is located. In the second and final step, the message is transmitted between processors located in this column to processor P_j.

Figure 2.5(b), illustrates message transmission from a processor P_a to a processor P_b. The edges included in the path for message transmission are highlighted.

The grid topology corresponds to an irregular graph, all vertices of which can be divided into inner and boundary vertices.

The topology described above may be referred to more precisely as a *two-dimensional grid topology*. If, analogously, we place the processors at points of a three-dimensional space with integer coordinates, we obtain a *three-dimensional grid topology*.

Based on a two-dimensional grid topology, a *torus topology* can be constructed. To do this, we connect with edges, pairwise, those vertices that are located on opposite sides of the grid. In particular, for the grid shown in Fig. 2.6(a), the following pairs of vertices need to be connected:

$$(1, 5), (6, 10), (11, 15), (1, 11), (2, 12), (3, 13), (4, 14), (5, 15).$$

The torus topology, unlike the grid one, has the property of regularity, and the degree of any vertex here is equal to 4 (see Fig. 2.6(b)).

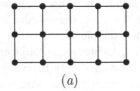
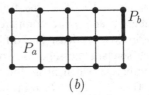

(a)   (b)

Fig. 2.5 (a) $q_1 \times q_2$ grid topology for $q_1 = 5$, $q_2 = 3$; (b) path of length 4, connecting processors P_a and P_b

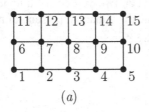
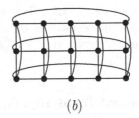

(a)   (b)

Fig. 2.6 (a) Vertices of a 5×3 grid, numbered with natural numbers from 1 to 15; (b) 5×3 torus topology

2.5   Tree Topology

A connected acyclic graph $G = (V, \ E)$ is called a *tree*.

Assume that $G = (V, \ E)$ is a graph with p vertices and m edges. There is a series of propositions, each of which is a necessary and sufficient condition for a graph G to be a tree:

- any pair of vertices of G is connected by only one path;
- G is acyclic, but if just one edge is added, a cycle arises;
- G is connected and $m = p - 1$;
- G is connected, and removal of just one edge violates this property.

Tree-topology-based networks are used to arrange a computer network in a hierarchical structure. It is convenient to single out one of the tree's vertices and call it the *root*. The root of the tree occupies the upper level of the hierarchy, the processors that are directly subordinate to the root node form the level below, and so on (Fig. 2.7(a)).

Other types of tree used for the construction of communication networks are shown in Fig. 2.7(b) and (c). In the star topology, there is one computational node with which all other processors are directly connected (Fig. 2.7(b)). In the linear topology, each inner processor has two communication lines with neighboring nodes, but the boundary elements have only one communication line each (Fig. 2.7(c)).

The drawback of all types of tree topology consists in the small value of connectivity, and a fault in just one communication line results in the partitioning of the computing network into noninteracting subnetworks. At the same time, the diameter of the tree may be rather large. For example, for the tree shown in Fig. 2.7(c), the diameter is equal to $p - 1$.

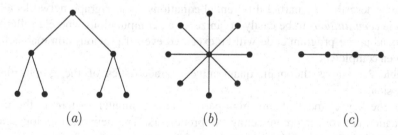

(a) (b) (c)

Fig. 2.7 Various types of tree topology: (**a**) complete binary tree topology, (**b**) star topology, (**c**) linear topology (or linear array)

Table 2.1 Properties of some simple graphs

Name	Number of vertices	Diameter	Connectivity	Number of edges
Complete graph	p	1	$p-1$	$p(p-1)/2$
Ring	p	$\lfloor p/2 \rfloor$	2	p
Grid	$q \times q$	$2(q-1)$	2	$2q(q-1)$
Torus	$q \times q$	$2\lfloor q/2 \rfloor$	4	$2q^2$
Hypercube	$p = 2^d$	$\log_2 p$	$\log_2 p$	$(p \log_2 p)/2$

2.6 Comparison of Different Topologies

Above, we discussed several types of computer network topology. Each topology has both advantages and disadvantages. For example, to connect p computational nodes in a ring topology, only p communication lines are needed, but the diameter in this case grows linearly with the parameter p. On the other hand, the diameter of the other types of network, in particular for a star topology, remains limited for any size of the graph. However, for star-like graphs, the connectivity is equal to one, which is less than that for the other types of graph discussed in this chapter.

There is no "universal" topology suitable for solving the entire range of computational problems, just as, for example, there is no sorting algorithm that can solve a random data-ordering problem with minimum computational and time costs.

Of course, a complete graph network topology ensures direct connection between any nodes, thus allowing faster data transmission, but for many problems the availability of the complete set of pairwise connections is redundant and is unacceptable from the point of view of cost.

A star topology is usually applied in centralized computation schemes. Grid topologies are quite easy to implement and are very suitable for solving grid problems described by partial differential equations. Linear graph networks allow *pipeline computations* to be easily organized, i.e., computations where a following command in the program code will be executed even if previous commands have not been completed.

Table 2.1 shows the main quantitative characteristics of the graphs under discussion.

So, the key element of any high-performance computer system is the communication network interconnecting the processors. The network topology has a considerable influence on the performance of the system on the whole.

2.7 Test Questions

1. Give a definition of a distributed computer system.
2. Enumerate the similarities and differences between distributed computer systems and multicomputers.

3. Apart from the information to be transmitted, what should a data packet contain?
4. Define the following notions: graph, simple graph, graph diagram, diameter, cycle.
5. What are adjacent vertices?
6. What is a path in a graph, and how is its length determined?
7. What are isomorphic graphs?
8. Give a definition of a network topology.
9. Enumerate the main properties of a complete graph, a ring topology, and a hypercube topology.
10. What is the difference between grid and torus topologies?
11. Enumerate the criteria for a graph to be a tree.

2.8 Problems

2.1. Show that the hypercube Q_3 is isomorphic to a torus of size 4×2.
2.2. Draw a diagram of the hypercube Q_4.
2.3. Show that the hypercube Q_4 and the torus of size 4×4 are isomorphic graphs.
2.4. Find the length of the shortest path between the i-th and j-th vertices in a p-cycle.
2.5. Find the length of the shortest path between two random vertices in a torus of size $q \times q$.

Chapter 3
Fundamentals of Parallel Computing

This chapter is devoted to the basic parallel computing laws.

3.1 The RAM and PRAM Models

A computing system model called the *random access machine* (RAM) [10, 45] is widely used for the analysis of program performance. We list here the main properties of the RAM.

The system running in the RAM model consists of a processor, a memory access device (a system bus), and a memory consisting of a finite number of cells (Fig. 3.1). The processor executes successively the instructions of a program Π; in doing so, it executes arithmetic and logical operations and reads and writes data to and from the memory. It is postulated that each instruction is executed in a fixed interval of time.

A random access operation of the processor consists of three stages:

1. Reading of data from the memory into one of its registers r_i, where $1 \leqslant i \leqslant N$.
2. Executing an arithmetic or logical operation on the contents of its registers.
3. Writing of data from a register r_j, where $1 \leqslant j \leqslant N$, into some memory cell.

It is assumed that the execution of the three above steps takes time $\Theta(1)$. (The function $\Theta(f(n))$ is used for estimation of the execution time of an algorithm as a function of the size n of its input data [13, 22]. Thus, for example, $\Theta(n^2)$ indicates a quadratic dependence, $\Theta(\log_2 n)$ indicates a logarithmic dependence, and $\Theta(1)$ indicates the absence of a dependence on the input data size. The estimation of the execution time of algorithms is described in more detail in Appendix A.)

One of the most widely used models of parallel computer systems is the *parallel random access machine* (PRAM) [45, 59]. The PRAM combines p processors, a shared memory, and a control device that transmits instructions from a program Π to the processors (Fig. 3.2).

© Springer Nature Switzerland AG 2019
S. Kurgalin, S. Borzunov, *A Practical Approach to High-Performance Computing*,
https://doi.org/10.1007/978-3-030-27558-7_3

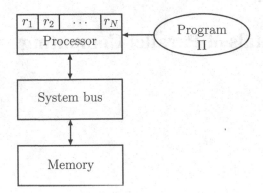

Fig. 3.1 The RAM model

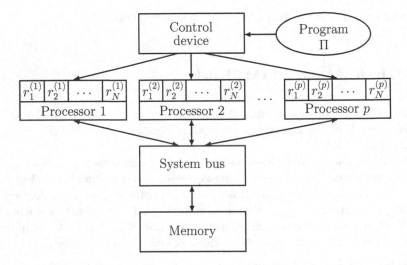

Fig. 3.2 The PRAM model

An important feature of the PRAM is the limited access time of any of the system's processors to a random memory cell. As in the case of the RAM, a step of an algorithm corresponds to three processor operations:

1. Reading by a processor P_i from the j-th memory cell.
2. Executing an arithmetic or logical operation by processor P_i on the contents of its registers.
3. Writing of data into the k-th memory cell.

We emphasize once again that a step of an algorithm is executed in time $\Theta(1)$.

Simultaneous access of two or more processors to the same memory cell leads to *access conflicts*. These are subdivided into *read* and *write conflicts*.

If multiple processors attempt to read data from one cell, then two options for further operations are possible:

1. *Exclusive read* (ER). Only one processor is allowed to read at a given time, otherwise an error occurs in the program.
2. *Concurrent read* (CR). The number of processors accessing the same memory cell is not limited.

If more than one processor attempts to write data to one address, then two options exist:

1. *Exclusive write* (EW). Only one processor is allowed to write to a given cell at a particular moment in time.
2. *Concurrent write* (CW). Multiple processors have simultaneous access to a single memory cell.

The following are the options for what rule a processor (or processors) follows to write a record in the latter case [37, 45, 59]:

- *Record of a general value.* All processors ready to make a record in a single memory cell must record the same value for all of them, otherwise the recording instruction is considered to be erroneous.
- *Random choice.* The processor that executes the recording operation is chosen randomly.
- *Prioritized recording.* Each of the competing processors is assigned a certain priority, such as the value of its computation, and only the value that comes from the processor with the highest or lowest priority (as determined in advance) is retained.
- *Mixed choice.* All processors provide values for the recording, from which by some operation a result (e.g., the sum of the values or the maximum value) is created, which is then recorded.

The classification of PRAM models by conflict resolution method is shown in Fig. 3.3. EREW systems have significant limitations imposed on the work that they can do with memory cells. On the other hand, and CREW, ERCW, and CRCW systems with a large number of processors are difficult to construct for technical reasons, since the number of cores that can simultaneously access a certain memory segment is limited. However, there is an important and somewhat unexpected result that makes it possible to simulate the work of a CRCW machine on a system built in accordance with the EREW principle [71].

Fig. 3.3 Conflict resolution methods for PRAM

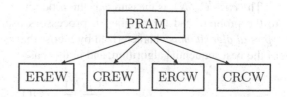

Emulation Theorem *Let there be an algorithm for a CRCW machine that solves a certain problem with a parameter of size N in time T(N), using p processors. Then there exists an algorithm for the same problem on an EREW system with p processors which can be executed in time $O(T(N) \log_2 N)$. (The size of the memory of the PRAM must be increased by $O(p)$ times.)*

Unlike the case for the RAM model, the main measure of the complexity of algorithms for multiprocessor computer systems is the execution time of the algorithm. We introduce the following notation: $T_1(N)$ is the time required by a sequential algorithm to solve a problem, the complexity of which is estimated by the parameter N; and $T_p(N)$ is the time required by a parallel algorithm on a machine with p processors, where $p > 1$. Since it follows from the definition of the RAM that each operation requires a certain time, the value of $T_1(N)$ is proportional to the number of computational operations in the algorithm used.

Note that the minimum execution time of an algorithm is observed in the case $p \to \infty$. A hypothetical computer system with an infinitely large number of available processors is called a *paracomputer*. The asymptotic complexity of an algorithm for a paracomputer is denoted by $T_\infty(N)$.

Note Brief information about methods of mathematical estimation of the properties of algorithms is provided in Appendix A.

In the analysis of parallel algorithms, the concepts of *speedup*, *efficiency*, and *cost* are widely used. First of all, we need to pay attention to how quickly the problem can be solved by comparison with solution on a single-processor machine.

The *speedup*, $S_p(N)$, obtained by using a parallel algorithm on a machine with p processors is given by

$$S_p(N) = \frac{T_1(N)}{T_p(N)}.$$

This is a measure of the productivity gain compared with the *best* sequential algorithm. The greater the speedup, the greater the difference in the problem-solving time between a system with a single processor and a multiprocessor system.

The *efficiency*, $E_p(N)$, of the use of the processors by a particular parallel algorithm is

$$E_p(N) = \frac{T_1(N)}{p T_p(N)} = \frac{S_p(N)}{p}.$$

The *cost*, $C_p(N)$, is measured as the product of the time for the parallel solution to the problem and the number of processors used: $C_p(N) = p T_p(N)$. A *cost-optimal algorithm* is characterized by a cost that is proportional to the complexity of the best sequential algorithm, and in this case

$$\frac{C_p(N)}{T_1(N)} = \Theta(1).$$

Example 3.1 The running time of a sequential version of some algorithm $\mathcal{A}$ is $T_1(N) = 2N\log_2(N)\tau$, where N is the input data size and τ is the execution time for one computing operation. Assuming that the algorithms allows maximal parallelization, i.e., the running time on a computing system with p processors is $T_p(N) = T_1(N)/p$, calculate the running time of algorithm $\mathcal{A}$ in the case $N = 64$, $p = 8$.

Solution The problem is solved by direct substitution of the given data into the relation $T_p(N) = T_1(N)/p$:

$$T_p(N) = \frac{2N\log_2(N)\tau}{p}.$$

Using the numerical values, we obtain

$$T_p(N) = \frac{2 \times 64\log_2(64)\tau}{8} = 96\tau.$$

$\square$

The limiting values of the speedup and efficiency, as follows directly from their definitions, are $S_p = p$ and $E_p = 1$. The maximum possible value of S_p is achieved when it is possible to uniformly distribute the computation across all processors and no additional operations are required to provide communication between the processors during the running of the program and to combine the results. Increasing the speedup by increasing the number of processors will reduce the value of E_p, and vice versa. Maximum efficiency is achieved by using only a single processor ($p = 1$).

We will not discuss here the superlinear speedup effects that may arise in models other than the PRAM for several reasons [81]:

- the sequential algorithm used for comparison in those models is not optimal;
- the multiprocessor system architecture has specific features;
- the algorithm is nondeterministic;
- there are significant differences in the volume of available main memory when the sequential algorithm is required to access a relatively "slow" peripheral memory, and the parallel algorithm uses only "fast" memory.

Many of the algorithms described below require the presence of a sufficiently large number of processors. Fortunately, this does not limit their practical application, since for any algorithm in the PRAM model there is the possibility of modification of it for a system with a smaller number of processors. The latter statement is called Brent's[1] lemma [9, 13, 43].

Brent's Lemma *Let a parallel algorithm $\mathcal{A}$ to solve some problem be executed on a RAM in a time T_1, and on a paracomputer in a time T_∞. Then there exists an algorithm $\mathcal{A}'$ for the solution of the given problem such that on a PRAM with p processors it is executed in a time $T(p)$, where $T(p) \leqslant T_\infty + (T_1 - T_\infty)/p$.*

The proof of Brent's lemma is given in the solution to Problem 3.8.

Any parallel program has a sequential part which is made up of input/output operations, synchronization, etc. Assume that, in comparison with the sequential method of solution, the following are true:

1. When the problem is divided into independent subproblems, the time required for interprocessor communication and union of the results is negligibly small.
2. The running time of the parallel part of the program decreases in proportion to the number of computational nodes.

Under these assumptions, an estimate of the value of S_p is known.

Amdahl's[2] Law *Let f be the proportion of sequential calculations in an algorithm $\mathcal{A}$. Then the speedup when $\mathcal{A}$ is run on a system of p processors satisfies the inequality*

$$S_p \leqslant \frac{1}{f + (1 - f)/p}.$$

To prove this, we calculate the time required for executing the algorithm on a multiprocessor. This time consists of the time for sequential operations, fT_1, and the time for operations that can be parallelized, and is equal to $T_p = fT_1 + ((1 - f)/p)T_1$. Therefore, the upper limit on the speedup can be represented as

$$(S_p)_{max} = \frac{T_1}{fT_1 + (1 - f)T_1/p} = \frac{1}{f + (1 - f)/p},$$

which proves Amdahl's law.

The inequality $S_p \leqslant (S_p)_{max}$ shows that the existence of sequential computations that cannot be parallelized imposes a restriction on S_p. Even when a paracomputer is used, the speedup cannot exceed the value $S_\infty = 1/f$.

Figure 3.4 shows the dependence of S_p on the number of processors p for typical values of the parameter f in computing tasks.

---

[1] Richard Peirce Brent (b. 1946), Australian mathematician and computer scientist.
[2] Gene Myron Amdahl (1922–2015), American computer scientist and computer technology expert.

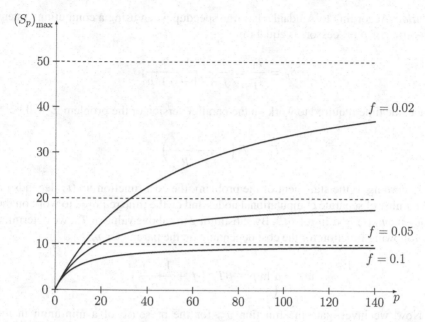

Fig. 3.4 Illustration of Amdahl's law, showing the dependence of the maximum speedup value $(S_p)_{max}$ on the number of processors p for different proportions f of sequential computations

It is found empirically that, for a wide class of computing tasks, the proportion of sequential computations decreases with increasing size of the input data of the task. Therefore, in practice, the speedup can be increased by increasing the computational complexity of the task being performed.

Despite the fact that the PRAM model is in widespread use, we should not forget its limitations. In particular, the possibility of different data transfer rates for different processors in specific computer system architectures is completely ignored.

Let us consider an example that illustrates Amdahl's law.

Example 3.2 Suppose that a researcher needs to solve a resource-intensive computing problem $\mathcal{Z}$. A sequential version of a program that solves the problem $\mathcal{Z}$ is executed in time T_1. A parallel version of the program contains a fraction f of sequential computations, $0 < f < 1$. A third-party organization provides access to a computing system consisting of p processors ($1 < p < 512$), and the cost of access to the system is $w_p(t) = \alpha \ln p + \beta t^\gamma$, where α, β, γ are constants, and t is the time that the system works on the researcher's problem. How many processes should be used in order to minimize the cost of working on the problem $\mathcal{Z}$? Let us perform computations for the following values of the parameters:

$$f = 0.1, T_1 = 10.0, \alpha = 1.21, \beta = 5.37, \gamma = 1.5.$$

Solution According to Amdahl's law, the speedup when using a computing system consisting of p processors is equal to

$$S_p = \frac{T_1}{T_p} = \frac{1}{f + (1-f)/p};$$

hence, the time required to work on the parallel version of the problem $\mathcal{Z}$ will be

$$T_p = T_1\Big(f + \frac{1-f}{p}\Big).$$

According to the statement of the problem, the cost function $w_p(t)$ depends on the number of separate computational nodes and on the time required to work on the problem: $w_p(t) = \alpha \ln p + \beta t^\gamma$. By substituting the above value of T_p, we determine the following function for the cost depending on the parameter p:

$$w_p = \alpha \ln p + \beta T_1^\gamma \Big(f + \frac{1-f}{p}\Big)^\gamma.$$

Now, we investigate the function w_p for the presence of a minimum in the interval $(1, 512)$. As is well known from any course in mathematical analysis, the minimum points should be sought from among the roots of the equation $dw_p/dp = 0$. By direct differentiation, we obtain

$$\frac{dw_p}{dp} = \frac{\alpha}{p} - \beta \gamma\, T_1^\gamma \frac{1-f}{p^2}\Big(f + \frac{1-f}{p}\Big)^{\gamma-1}.$$

Because the equation $dw_p/dp = 0$ cannot be solved analytically, numerical methods must be used. We can show that there is only one minimum for $p \in (1, 512)$. We can find its abscissa by a bisection method (see Problem 3.9).

A program in the language C that performs a computation of the minimum of the cost function is shown in Listing 3.1.

Listing 3.1

```
1   #include <stdio.h>
2   #include <stdlib.h>
3   #include <math.h>
4
5   #define PMIN 1.0        // PMIN and PMAX
6   #define PMAX 512.0      // are endpoints
7                           // of the interval
8   #define EPS  1.0e-14    // zero of function
9                           // determination accuracy
10
11  double f,T1,alpha,beta,gamma;// cost function
```

```
12                                    // parameters
13
14  double fprime(double p)          // derivative
15                                    // of cost function
16  {
17    double temp = pow(f+(1-f)/p,gamma-1.0);
18    return alpha/p - \
19      beta*gamma*pow(T1,gamma)*(1-f)*temp/(p*p);
20  }
21
22  double bisection(double func(double), \
23                    double x1, double x2,\
24                    const double epsilon)
25  {
26    double xmid;
27    while ( fabs(x2 - x1) > epsilon )
28      {
29        xmid = (x1 + x2) / 2;
30        if (func(x2) * func(xmid) < 0.0)
31          x1 = xmid;
32        else
33          x2 = xmid;
34      }
35    return (x1 + x2) / 2;
36  }
37
38  int main(void)
39  {
40    int pz;      // zero of function fprime(p)
41    FILE * fp;
42
43    if ((fp = fopen("input.txt","r")) == NULL)
44      {
45        perror("\nError opening file " \
46                "\"input.txt\"");
47        exit(EXIT_FAILURE);
48      }
49    fscanf(fp,"%lf %lf %lf %lf %lf", \
50            &f,&T1,&alpha,&beta,&gamma);
51    fclose(fp);
52
53    pz = \
54      (int)round(bisection(fprime,PMIN,PMAX,EPS));
55    if ( pz<PMIN || pz>PMAX )
```

```
56    {
57        perror("\nError determining zero " \
58                "of function fprime(p)");
59        exit(EXIT_FAILURE);
60    }
61    if ((fp = fopen("output.txt","w")) == NULL)
62    {
63        perror("\nError opening file " \
64                "\"output.txt\"");
65        exit(EXIT_FAILURE);
66    }
67    else
68      if (fprintf(fp,"%d",pz)<=0)
69        // fprintf returns the number of written
70        // characters
71      {
72          perror("\nError writing to file " \
73                  "\"output.txt\"");
74          fclose(fp);
75          exit(EXIT_FAILURE);
76      }
77    fclose(fp);
78    printf("The answer is written to file " \
79            "\"output.txt\"");
80    return 0;
81 }
```

The program reads the parameters f, T_1, α, β, γ from a text file input.txt. The function bisection() realizes the binary division algorithm and finds a zero of the function func() in the interval (x_1, x_2) with an accuracy of epsilon. Into the file output.txt, after execution of the program, the number 64 will be written; i.e., with a number of processors $p = 64$, the cost function with the parameters listed in the example will be minimized.   □

Note Notice the method of organizing the data streams in the program when the data are read from a text file, for example input.txt, and when the result of the program is put into a text file, for example output.txt (or into several files, where necessary). The method described is generally accepted for high-performance computations since it is convenient when working with remote computational resources. Moreover, when a program is used as part of a suite of programs, storing the results of the computation in a file allows one, when necessary, to visualize the data and to pass them as input data to another program for processing.

3.2 The "Operations–Operands" Graph

Let us recall some definitions from graph theory that we require for the following presentation [2, 6].

A *directed graph*, or *digraph*, is a pair $D = (V, E)$, where V is a finite set of vertices and E is a relation on V. The elements of the set E are called *directed edges* or *arcs*. An arc that connects a pair (u, v) of vertices u and v of a digraph D is denoted by uv.

A *path* of length n in a digraph is a sequence of vertices $v_0, v_1, \ldots, v_n$, each pair $v_{i-1}v_i$ $(i = 1, \ldots, n)$ of which forms an arc. A sequence of vertices $v_0, v_1, \ldots, v_n$ where the first vertex v_0 coincides with the last one, i.e., $v_0 = v_n$, and where there are no other repeated vertices forms a *circuit*.

The *outdegree* of a vertex v of a digraph D is the number of arcs $d^+(v)$ of the digraph going out from v, and the *indegree* of that vertex is the number of arcs $d^-(v)$ going into it.

For example, for the directed graph D with five vertices a, b, c, d, and e whose diagram is presented in Fig. 3.5, the following relations are fulfilled:

$$d^+(a) = d^+(b) = 1, \ d^+(c) = 2, \ d^+(d) = 0, \ d^+(e) = 3,$$

$$d^-(a) = d^-(c) = d^-(e) = 1, \ d^-(b) = d^-(d) = 2.$$

The structure of an algorithm for solving a problem may be graphically represented as a directed graph called an "operations–operands" graph. It is an acyclic digraph. We denote it by $D = (V, E)$, where V is a set of vertices representing the operations performed in the algorithm, and E is a set of edges. An edge $v_i v_j \in E$ if and only if the operation numbered j uses the result of the operation numbered i. Vertices $v_k^{(in)}$, where $k \in \mathbb{N}$, with indegree $\forall k \ d^-(v_k^{(in)}) = 0$ are used for data input operations, and vertices $v_l^{(out)}$, $l \in \mathbb{N}$, with outdegree $\forall l \ d^+(v_l^{(out)}) = 0$ correspond to output operations (Fig. 3.6).

Fig. 3.5 Example of a directed graph with five vertices

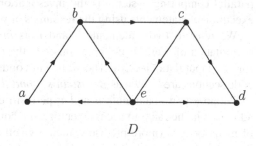

D

Fig. 3.6 Example of an
"operations–operands"
digraph

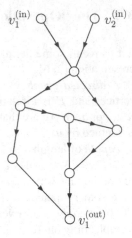

If we assume that the computations at each vertex of the digraph D using a RAM take a constant time τ, the algorithm execution time on a paracomputer is equal to

$$T_\infty = \tau \times \max_{(i,j)} \left(|C^{(i,j)}| \right),$$

where $C^{(i,j)}$ is the path $v_i^{(in)}, \ldots, v_j^{(out)}$, and the maximum is taken with respect to all possible pairs (i, j). In other words, the time T_∞ is proportional to the number of vertices in the maximal path connecting vertices $v_i^{(in)}$ and $v_j^{(out)}$ for all i and j.

3.3 Bernstein's Conditions

In most programming languages, as is well known, the program code consists of a sequence of statements. One of the principal tasks that arises when working with parallel computing systems is the investigation of the possibility of independent execution of statements using the resources of parallelism.

We refer to two statements u and v as *independent* or *commutative* if after permutation of them in the program code the program output remains unchanged for any input data [19, 20]. The sufficient conditions for independence of program code sections are known as *Bernstein's*[3] *conditions*.

Suppose that statements u and v perform data reading and writing at known addresses in the random access memory of a computing system. Let $R(u)$ be the set of memory cells (more precisely, memory cell addresses) from which information is read during execution of the statement u. Further, let $W(u)$ be the set of memory

---

[3] Arthur Jay Bernstein, an American researcher, is a specialist in the field of computing systems.

cells (more precisely, memory cell addresses) into which data are written. $R(u)$ and $W(u)$ are often called the *input object set* and the *output object set*, respectively, of statement u [54].

Bernstein's Conditions [7, 19] *Two statements u and v are independent and their order does not influence the program output if the following equalities are fulfilled:*

1. $W(u) \cap W(v) = \varnothing$.
2. $W(u) \cap R(v) = \varnothing$.
3. $R(u) \cap W(v) = \varnothing$.

The above equalities are sufficient but not necessary conditions for the commutativity of two statements (see Problem 3.13).

If, for two statements u and v, at least one of the equalities in Bernstein's conditions is violated, the notation $u \perp v$ is used. In this case it is said that u and v have a *dependency relationship*.

Note that the equalities 1–3 forming Bernstein's conditions are fulfilled independently from each other. In this connection, special notation for violation of each of these equalities is used [54]:

1. If the first condition is violated and $W(u) \cap W(v) \neq \varnothing$, then it is said that between statements u and v there exists an *output dependency*, $u\,\delta^0\,v$.
2. If the second condition is violated and $W(u) \cap R(v) \neq \varnothing$, then u and v are in a relationship of *true* or *flow dependency*, $u\,\delta\,v$.
3. If the third condition is violated and $R(u) \cap W(v) \neq \varnothing$, then between statements u and v there exists an *antidependency*, $u\,\bar{\delta}\,v$.

Using this notation, a dependency relationship can be presented symbolically in the form

$$u \perp v \;\Leftrightarrow\; (u\,\delta^0\,v) \text{ or } (u\,\delta\,v) \text{ or } (u\,\bar{\delta}\,v).$$

Example 3.3 Investigate the possibility of parallelizing the following program code sections, for which Bernstein's conditions are violated:

1. o_1: x = y + 1;
   o_2: x = z * 2;
2. p_1: x = y + 1;
   p_2: z = x * x;
3. q_1: x = y + 1;
   q_2: y = z / 2;

Solution

1. For this pair of statements, there exists an input data dependency $W(o_1) \cap W(o_2) = \{x\} \cap \{x\} = \{x\} \neq \varnothing$, i.e., $o_1\,\delta^0\,o_2$. Usually, input dependencies

allow parallelizing after renaming of the variables. In our case, the following pair (o_1', o_2') will satisfy Bernstein's conditions:

```
o'₁:  x1 = y + 1;
o'₂:  x2 = z * 2;
```

2. Since for the pair (p_1, p_2) we have $W(p_1) \cap R(p_2) = \{x\} \cap \{x\} = \{x\} \neq \varnothing$, the program code contains a true dependency $p_1 \delta p_2$, and no parallelizing is possible in this case.
3. One and the same variable in the given code section is used first in q_1 and then in q_2: $R(q_1) \cap W(q_2) = \{y\} \cap \{y\} = \{y\} \neq \varnothing$. There exists an antidependency $q_1 \bar{\delta} q_2$. The code section under consideration can be parallelized if we copy the value of the variable y into the local memories of the computational nodes, and only after that begin execution of the statements q_1 and q_2.   □

Analysis of Example 3.3 shows that dependencies of the type $p_1 \delta^0 p_2$ and $p_1 \bar{\delta} p_2$ appear not because the data are passed from one statement to another, but because the same memory area is used in several places. Output dependencies and antidependencies can often be eliminated by renaming some variables and, additionally, copying data [54].

Example 3.4 Enumerate the dependencies between the statements in the following program code section:

```
o₁:    a = a + 2;
o₂:    b = a + d / 2;
o₃:    c = 2 * c;
o₄:    a = a + c + 1;
```

Solution We write out the output object sets $W(o_i)$ and input object sets $R(o_i)$ for $i = 1, 2, 3, 4$:

$$W(o_1) = \{a\}, \qquad R(o_1) = \{a\},$$
$$W(o_2) = \{b\}, \qquad R(o_2) = \{a, d\},$$
$$W(o_3) = \{c\}, \qquad R(o_3) = \{c\},$$
$$W(o_4) = \{a\}, \qquad R(o_4) = \{a, c\}.$$

For each pair of statements (o_i, o_j), where $i, j = 1, 2, 3, 4$ and $i < j$, we construct the intersections $W(o_i) \cap W(o_j)$, $W(o_i) \cap R(o_j)$, and $R(o_i) \cap W(o_j)$. Those intersections that are not empty sets lead to dependencies between statements:

$$(o_1, o_2): \quad W(o_1) \cap R(o_2) = \{a\};$$
$$(o_1, o_3): \quad \text{no dependencies};$$
$$(o_1, o_4): \quad W(o_1) \cap W(o_4) = \{a\},$$
$$\qquad\qquad W(o_1) \cap R(o_4) = \{a\},$$
$$\qquad\qquad R(o_1) \cap W(o_4) = \{a\};$$

$$(o_2, o_3): \quad \text{no dependencies;}$$

$$(o_2, o_4): \quad R(o_2) \cap W(o_4) = \{a\};$$

$$(o_3, o_4): \quad W(o_3) \cap R(o_4) = \{c\}.$$

As a result, we obtain the following dependencies in the program code section considered:

$$o_1 \delta o_2, \ o_1 \delta^0 o_4, \ o_1 \bar{\delta} o_4, \ o_1 \overline{\delta} o_4, \ o_2 \overline{\delta} o_4, \ o_3 \delta o_4.$$

$\square$

In parallel programming, Bernstein's conditions are used to obtain a mathematically correct proof that after applying a parallelization procedure to a sequential program code the program output remains unchanged. Programs for numerical computation usually require only storing of the final answer; in other words, identity of the output files that are created is needed. However, as can be seen, the set of parallel program suites extends further than just numerical computation programs. There exist continuously functioning programs, for example operating systems, and in this connection a more detailed consideration of data change in the parallel system's random access memory is needed. Not only the information at a fixed moment in time, but also data sets at previous moments in time are of great importance.

Let us introduce the notion of a *memory content history*—a time-ordered set of vectors made up of all the data in the computing system's memory. Using this definition, we can formulate the *statement permutation theorem*, which is the mathematical basis for program code parallelization and optimization [19].

Statement Permutation Theorem *Let a computing device perform sequentially a program made up of an ordered collection of statements* $\mathbf{U} = \{u_1, u_2, \ldots, u_n\}$, *where* $n \in \mathbb{N}$ *is the number of statements, or the program size. We permute the components of the vector* $\mathbf{U}$ *in such a way that all dependent statements preserve their relative order, i.e.,*

$$[(i < j) \text{ and } (u_i \perp u_j)] \text{ and } (u_i = v_{i'}) \text{ and } (u_j = v_{j'}) \Rightarrow (i' < j').$$

Then the memory content history of the computing system will not change as a result of this permutation.

The proof of this theorem is based on the method of mathematical induction (see Problem 3.15).

In practical applications, Bernstein's conditions are relatively easily checked for computational operations with scalar values and arrays. Considerable difficulties in checking arise, however, if the program code uses operations with pointers. In the general case, there is no algorithm able to determine the possibility of parallel execution of two program code sections [7].

Theorem of Undecidability of the Possibility of Parallelism *There exists no algorithm that can determine the possibility of parallel execution of two arbitrary program code sections.*

In order to prove the theorem, we use the method of "proof by contradiction." Suppose that there exists an algorithm as described in the statement of the theorem. We can us show that it entails the solution of an arbitrary Turing[4] machine halting problem [61, 69].

Consider a Turing machine T, whose input tape stores a natural number N. We denote by N_i the number formed by the i highest-order digits of the number N.

Let a program Π execute the following operations:

S_1: The value of N_i is written at the address A. If the Turing machine T halts after N or fewer steps, then the value N_i^2 is stored at the address A; otherwise, the value written in A is stored at the address Z_1.

S_2: The value written in A is stored at the address Z_2.

Let us analyze the operation of the program Π. If T does not halt for any input data N, then S_1 and S_2 can be executed in parallel. Otherwise, for some N, the value of N_i^2 is stored at the address Z_2 during the operation S_2. Then S_1 and S_2 must be executed sequentially, since $S_1 \perp S_2$.

We obtain the result that the problem of determining the possibility of parallel execution of the parts of code S_1 and S_2 is equivalent to the arbitrary Turing machine halting problem, but this problem, as is well known, is undecidable [61, 69]. Hence, the theorem of undecidability of the possibility of parallelism is proved.

The practical importance of Bernstein's conditions is not limited to the field of parallel programming. One of the methods for program code optimization consists in changing the order of execution of some statements or code sections. For example, the use of data located as near as possible to the place of their description in the program increases the performance of the computing system owing to active use of cache memory. As is well known, when the central processor addresses random access memory, the request is first sent to cache memory. If the required data are available, the cache memory sends them quickly, to a processor register. Hence, a change in the order of execution of some statements can increase the speed of the computing system.

---

[4]Alan Mathison Turing (1912–1954), English mathematician and logician.

3.4 Test Questions

1. Describe the RAM model.
2. In what why is the PRAM model a generalization of the RAM model?
3. Define the term "access conflict."
4. How is the PRAM model classified by conflict resolution method?
5. Formulate the emulation theorem.
6. What is the notion of a "paracomputer" introduced for?
7. What values are used for the analysis of parallel algorithms?
8. What are the limiting values of the speedup and efficiency equal to?
9. Formulate Brent's lemma.
10. How is Amdahl's law used for estimation of the speedup?
11. What peculiarities of multiprocessor computing systems are not taken into account in the PRAM model?
12. Describe the "operations–operands" graph.
13. State Bernstein's conditions.
14. Describe clearly the role of the statement permutation theorem in parallel programming.

3.5 Problems

3.1. The execution time of a sequential version of some algorithm $\mathcal{A}$ is $T_1(N) = 2N \log_2(N)\,\tau$, where N is the input data size and τ is the execution time of one computational operation. Supposing that the algorithm allows maximal parallelizing, i.e., the execution time on a computation system with p processors is $T_p(N) = T_1(N)/p$, calculate the execution time of the algorithm $\mathcal{A}$ in the following cases:

(a) $N = 32,\ p = 4$;
(b) $N = 32,\ p = 16$.

3.2. Solve the previous problem for an algorithm $\mathcal{B}$ with an exponential asymptotic complexity $T_1(N) = 2^N \tau$.

3.3. Let the proportion of sequential computation in a program be $f = 1/10$. Calculate the maximum speedup $(S_p)_{max}$ of the program on a computation system with p processors taking into account Amdahl's law.

3.4. Let the proportion of sequential computation in a program be $f = 1/100$. Calculate the maximum speedup S_∞ of the program taking into account Amdahl's law.

3.5. Let the speedup for some parallel algorithm $\mathcal{A}$ executed on a system with p processors be S_p. Taking into account Amdahl's law, calculate the speedup when the algorithm $\mathcal{A}$ is executed on a system with p' processors.

3.6. Consider a computational algorithm $\mathcal{A}$ consisting of two blocks $\mathcal{A}_1$ and $\mathcal{A}_2$, where the second block can start execution only after completion of the first. Let the proportions of sequential computation in $\mathcal{A}_1$ and $\mathcal{A}_2$ be f_1 and f_2, respectively, and let the execution time of $\mathcal{A}_2$ in the sequential mode exceed the sequential execution time of $\mathcal{A}_1$ by η times. Calculate the maximum speedup of the algorithm $\mathcal{A}$ achievable on a computation system with p processors.

3.7. Draw a graph of the maximum efficiency $(E_p)_{max}$ of use of the processors by a parallel algorithm as a function of the number of computational nodes p taking into account Amdahl's law, if the proportion of sequential computation is equal to:

(a) $f = 1/10$;

(b) $f = 1/50$.

*3.8. Prove Brent's lemma.

3.9. Give a detailed explanation of how a numerical solution of the equation $dw_p/dp = 0$ in Example 3.2 can be obtained.

3.10. Suppose that a researcher needs to solve a resource-intensive computing problem $\mathcal{Z}$. A sequential version of a program that solves the problem $\mathcal{Z}$ is executed in time T_1. A parallel version contains a proportion f of sequential computation, $0 < f < 1$. A third-party organization provides access to a computing system consisting of p processors $(1 < p < 512)$, and the cost of access to the system is $w_p(t) = \alpha \ln p + \beta t^\gamma$, where α, β, γ are constants and t is the time that the system works on the researcher's problem. How many processors should be used in order to minimize the cost of working on the problem $\mathcal{Z}$? Perform calculations for the following values of the parameters:

(a) $f = 0.1, T_1 = 10.0, \alpha = 1.70, \beta = 11.97, \gamma = 1.9$;

(b) $f = 0.1, T_1 = 10.0, \alpha = 2.73, \beta = 8.61, \gamma = 1.1$;

(c) $f = 0.1, T_1 = 10.0, \alpha = 2.17, \beta = 35.44, \gamma = 1.7$.

3.11. Solve Problem 3.10 for a cost function of the form $w_p(t) = \alpha p + \beta t^\gamma$. Perform calculations for the following values of the parameters:

(a) $f = 0.1, T_1 = 10.0, \alpha = 1.17, \beta = 3.84, \gamma = 1.9$;

(b) $f = 0.1, T_1 = 10.0, \alpha = 1.08, \beta = 9.31, \gamma = 1.9$;

(c) $f = 0.1, T_1 = 10.0, \alpha = 1.19, \beta = 35.90, \gamma = 1.8$.

3.12. Solve Problem 3.10 for a cost function of the form $w_p(t) = e^{\alpha p} + \beta t^\gamma$. Perform calculations for the following values of the parameters:

(a) $f = 0.1, T_1 = 10.0, \alpha = 0.001, \beta = 10.62, \gamma = 1.9$;

(b) $f = 0.1, T_1 = 10.0, \alpha = 0.002, \beta = 2.70, \gamma = 1.8$;

(c) $f = 0.1, T_1 = 10.0, \alpha = 0.004, \beta = 4.40, \gamma = 1.1$.

3.13. Show that Bernstein's conditions are not necessary conditions for the commutativity of two statements.

3.14. List the dependencies between statements in the following program code section:

o_1: a = c - 1;
o_2: b = a / 2 - 1;
o_3: c = b + c / b;
o_4: b = a * c + 1;

*3.15. Prove the statement permutation theorem.

Chapter 4
The MPI Technology

A significant number of modern multiple-processor computer systems belong to the class of multicomputers. This type of system is characterized by distributed memory organization, i.e., an arbitrary processor cannot directly access the address space of another processor. In order to implement interprocessor communication, an approach is currently being adopted which consists in receiving and passing messages between computational nodes via a communication network.

According to the official description [46], MPI (Message Passing Interface) is a specification of a library programming interface for data transfer. Producers of parallel architectures and software, as well as researchers, take part in the development of MPI.

In the framework of the MPI technology, a single program written in a high-level programming language is run on the processors of a computer system, thus creating a multitude of processes. In other words, an MPI *program* at run time is a set of parallel interacting processes. Each process has a unique index number, its *rank*, which makes it possible to vary the actions performed at different computational nodes. The data exchange required for the functioning of the program is carried out by means of a message-passing mechanism. This mechanism is implemented through library calls that use the capabilities of communication lines.

The MPI standard is made up of message-passing procedures, and additional procedures for organizing input/output that use parallel resources. In MPI-1.0, published in 1994, functions were introduced to pass/receive messages between individual processes, to perform collective communications between processes, to provide implementations of process topologies, and for other purposes. In MPI-2.0, released in 1997, functions for dynamic process control, parallel input and output, one-way communications, etc. were added. MPI-3.0, published in 2012, expanded the standard by adding nonblocking versions of collective operations and new opportunities for individual operations. At the time of writing, the current standard is MPI-3.1, adopted in 2015.

© Springer Nature Switzerland AG 2019
S. Kurgalin, S. Borzunov, *A Practical Approach to High-Performance Computing*,
https://doi.org/10.1007/978-3-030-27558-7_4

As alternative approaches to multicomputer programming, the specialized programming languages HPF (High Performance Fortran), Co-array Fortran, and Unified Parallel C should be noted [59]. Despite some advantages provided by these programming languages (the relative ease of writing program code, and the possibility of parallelizing initially sequential code), the MPI technology has become very popular owing to its extended universality and the possibility of practically full utilization of parallel resources. On the other hand, the factors required for achieving high performance of a program and ease of programming are often incompatible. Because of this, one should note the relative complexity of developing parallel programs in the MPI environment in comparison with the use of specialized parallel languages. Ultimately, the choice of parallelization technology should also take into account the specific target architecture of the multiple-processor computer system and the collection of algorithms used.

An official description of the MPI standard is available on an electronic resource [46]. There are also a number of textbooks [25, 53, 58] which describe programming methods in the MPI environment.

4.1   Compiling and Running a Parallel Program in an MPI Environment: The Most Important MPI Functions

The MPI standard comprises descriptions of hundreds of library functions. In particular, the current version of the MPI-3.1 standard contains more than 440 functions. For many applications, it suffices to use functions from the following list:

- initialization and termination of an application;
- determining the rank of a process and the total number of processes;
- organization of the sending and receiving of messages from one process to another.

A parallel program using the MPI technology must be compiled and run in a special way, determined by the *implementation of the standard*. Open MPI [51] and MPICH [47] are widespread implementations. Let us consider program compilation and application running in Open MPI. This implementation offers the possibility of using all the features of the MPI-3.1 standard. For brief information about installing Open MPI on a user workstation, see Appendix B.

The code of a parallel program appears in the form of a text file with the extension c and must contain a connection to the mpi.h header file in the preamble:

```
#include <mpi.h>
```

Suppose that the program is named task.c. The Open MPI implementation provides a source code compilation via the call

```
>mpicc task.c -o task.out
```

As a result of execution of this command, the file `task.c` is compiled and located in the current directory. The executable file `task.out` is created in the same directory.

Running the file `task.out` with the formation of N processes can be carried out as follows:

```
>mpirun -np N ./task.out
```

where $N = 1, 2, 3, \ldots$ is the number of processes created on startup executing the program `task.out`.

As noted above, an MPI program is a set of parallel interacting processes. Each process is allocated a separate address space, and the interprocessor interaction is performed by means of message receiving and passing.

Let us consider the most important functions of the MPI environment, which occur in any parallel program. All functions described in this chapter, unless mentioned otherwise, were introduced in the first version of the MPI standard.

Immediately after the declaration of variables in the function `main()`, there should follow a call of the function `MPI_Init()`:

```
int MPI_Init(int * argc, char *** argv)
```

where `argc` is a pointer to the number of command line parameters, and `argv` is the address of a pointer to an array of pointers to text strings (this array contains the command line parameters passed to the program on startup from the shell). Using this method, the type of the `MPI_Init()` arguments is selected to pass the parameters `argc` and `argv[]` to all the processes.

Thus the parallel part of the program starts. Note that the `MPI_Init()` function can only be called once in the program. The parallel part of the program is completed by calling the function

```
int MPI_Finalize(void)
```

Outside the parallel region of a program, the calling of MPI functions is prohibited, except for the following four functions:

```
MPI_Get_version();
MPI_Get_library_version();
MPI_Initialized();
MPI_Finalized().
```

The first two functions in this list provide information about the version of the MPI standard supported by the implementation and about the version of the library. The first function is

```
int MPI_Get_version(int * version, int * subversion)
```

where `version` is a pointer to the version number (an integer), and `subversion` is a pointer to the version revision number (another integer, usually located after the decimal point). This function has been available starting from MPI-1.2. The second function is

```
int MPI_Get_library_version(char * version, int *
resultlen)
```

where `version` is a pointer to a text string containing the version information, and `resultlen` is a pointer to the length of the string. This function was introduced relatively recently, in 2012, and has been available starting from MPI-3.0.

Further, the functions `MPI_Initialized()` and `MPI_Finalized()` can be used to verify that the program code is to be executed in parallel. Such checking is often necessary in complex software systems compiled from multiple source files. The call format of the functions considered is

```
int MPI_Initialized(int * flag)
int MPI_Finalized(int * flag)
```

The pointer to an integer variable `flag` acts as the output argument in both cases. `flag` takes a nonzero value if a call of the function `MPI_Init()` or `MPI_Finalize()`, respectively, has been made in the program, otherwise `flag` is equal to zero.

Note that `MPI_Finalized()` is described only in the standards starting from version MPI-2.0. This function cannot be used in the lower versions 1.0–1.3.

Note The reserved names determined by the MPI environment have a prefix `MPI_`. The MPI environment constants are written in uppercase letters, and the names of types and functions include one capital letter immediately after the prefix. In this regard, it is prohibited to enter user names for variables, functions, macros, etc. beginning with `MPI_` in all cases.

The *communicator* is an important concept of the MPI technology. By a communicator we mean a group of processes which is assigned a *descriptor* (a description of a special object).

Immediately after the call of the `MPI_Init()` function, the so-called *global communicator*, denoted by `MPI_COMM_WORLD`, is created in the program and becomes available. The global communicator contains all available processes.

The function `MPI_Comm_size()` defines the number of processes within the communicator `comm` passed as an argument:

```
int MPI_Comm_size(MPI_Comm comm, int * size)
```

where `MPI_Comm` is the type of the input parameter `comm`, and the output parameter `size` is a pointer to an integer variable containing the number of processes. In particular, the call `MPI_Comm_size(MPI_COMM_WORLD, &size)` will create in the memory cell at the address `size` the number of processes executing the program.

Each of the processes of the global communicator is assigned a unique number, a rank. This is a nonnegative integer. To determine this rank, the function `MPI_Comm_rank()` is used:

```
int MPI_Comm_rank(MPI_Comm comm, int * rank)
```

which has two arguments: the communicator `comm` and the address of the variable `rank` for recording the result obtained.

Note All functions of the MPI environment (except for `MPI_Wtime()` and `MPI_Wtick()`; see the description of functions for timer operations on Sect. 4.4) return a value of the standard integer type `int`. Upon successful completion of any function, the value of `MPI_SUCCESS` is returned; if an error occurs, then the returned value depends on the implementation of the MPI standard used.

The "framework" of a parallel program in the C language, developed using the MPI technology, has the following form:

```
...  // including of the required header files
#include <mpi.h>
int main(int argc, char * argv[])
{
  int rank, size;

  ...  // declarations of user variables

  MPI_Init(&argc, &argv);
  MPI_Comm_rank(MPI_COMM_WORLD, &rank);
  MPI_Comm_size(MPI_COMM_WORLD, &size);

  ...  // program code using MPI functions

  MPI_Finalize();
  return 0;
}
```

When user programs are written, this "framework" is filled with real content.

4.2   The Standard Message-Passing Method

By *message* we mean a data vector of fixed type. The data types available in the MPI environment and their analogs in the C language are listed in Table 4.1.

Not all of the types mentioned in the table were available in the first version of standard for the environment. Thus, the following three types,

MPI_UNSIGNED_CHAR,
MPI_UNSIGNED_LONG_LONG,
MPI_WCHAR,

are present only in MPI-2.0 and later versions. The set of types whose names begin with the prefix MPI_C_ have been present starting from MPI-2.2. For the type MPI_LONG_LONG_INT, starting from version 2.1 of the standard, the synonym MPI_LONG_LONG is provided.

Note that for the types MPI_BYTE and MPI_PACKED there is no correspondence with the standard types of the C language.

A value of type MPI_BYTE is made up of eight binary bits, i.e., it consists of one byte. At first sight, it may appear that this is a synonym of the type char available in the C language, which usually consists of eight binary digits. However, on computing systems with different architectures' the representations of a symbol of type char may differ. In particular, more than one byte may be used for this.

Table 4.1 Data types in the MPI environment and their analogs in the C language

MPI environment	C language
MPI_CHAR	char
MPI_SHORT	signed short int
MPI_INT	signed int
MPI_LONG	signed long int
MPI_LONG_LONG_INT	signed long long int
MPI_SIGNED_CHAR	signed char
MPI_UNSIGNED_CHAR	unsigned char
MPI_UNSIGNED_SHORT	unsigned short int
MPI_UNSIGNED	unsigned int
MPI_UNSIGNED_LONG	unsigned long int
MPI_UNSIGNED_LONG_LONG	unsigned long long int
MPI_FLOAT	float
MPI_DOUBLE	double
MPI_LONG_DOUBLE	long double
MPI_WCHAR	wchar_t
MPI_C_BOOL	_Bool
MPI_C_COMPLEX	float _Complex
MPI_C_DOUBLE_COMPLEX	double _Complex
MPI_C_LONG_DOUBLE_COMPLEX	long double _Complex
MPI_BYTE	*No correspondence*
MPI_PACKED	*No correspondence*

Because of this, the type MPI_BYTE was introduced to ensure maximum portability of parallel programs.

The type MPI_PACKED is used for sending messages using packing of data located in various memory areas, and subsequent unpacking.

Consider the simplest message-passing method—sending a data vector from one process (the *sending process*) to another (the *receiving process*), where only two processes interact. Such an operation is called a *point-to-point communication*.

Let us describe the message-passing stages using the so-called *standard*, or blocking asynchronous, method (for the description of other methods, see Sect. 4.5). Message passing in MPI is organized into three sequential stages:

1. The data vector to be sent is complemented with a header containing information about the sending process, the receiving process, the message identifier, and the communicator. The message formed in this way is copied to the system buffer of the MPI environment.
2. The message is actually sent via a communication line.
3. The data vector is copied from the system buffer to the memory area available to the receiving process.

It should be noted that the necessity to allocate and use an additional system buffer is determined by the MPI implementation. In some cases, message copying can be done directly over the communication line, without using a system buffer.

In order to perform point-to-point communication (more strictly, message sending by the blocking asynchronous method), the functions `MPI_Send()` and `MPI_Recv()` are provided in the MPI environment.

The sending process calls the function

```
int MPI_Send(const void * buf, int count,
             MPI_Datatype datatype, int dest, int tag,
             MPI_Comm comm)
```

The following arguments are used:

buf: the address of the memory buffer containing the message being sent;
count: the number of elements in the message;
datatype: the data type of the message;
dest: the rank of the receiving process;
tag: the message identifier (a nonnegative integer);
comm: the communicator including the sending process and the receiving process.

After the function `MPI_Send()` is called, the data determined by the parameters buf, count, and datatype are sent to a recipient with rank dest in the communicator comm. This function can take the current process to a waiting state, which will be active until the receiving process receives the message.

The parameter tag is introduced for the purpose of distinguishing messages formed by the same process. tag is a nonnegative integer in the interval [0, MPI_TAG_UB], where MPI_TAG_UB is a constant defined by the implementation. The standard guarantees that the variable $MPI\_TAG\_UB \geqslant 2^{15} - 1$, and the value of tag will not change during the program's running time.

The completion of operation of the function `MPI_Send()` indicates only that execution of the data-passing operation has begun. No definite information about the message receipt status can be obtained in this connection.

In order to receive the message, the receiving process calls the function

```
int MPI_Recv(void * buf, int count, MPI_Datatype datatype,
             int source, int tag, MPI_Comm comm,
             MPI_Status * status)
```

The following arguments are used:

buf: the address of the memory buffer containing the message being received;
count: the number of elements in the message;
datatype: the data type of the message;
source: the rank of the sending process;
tag: the message identifier;

comm: the communicator including the sending process and the receiving
                    process;
status: a pointer to a structure containing some parameters of the received
                    message.

The function MPI_Recv() ensures reception of the message defined by the
parameters buf, count, datatype. The structure of type MPI_Status stores
information about some parameters of the received message. This structure includes
the following fields:

- MPI_SOURCE, the rank of the sending process;
- MPI_TAG, the message identifier;
- MPI_ERROR, an error code;
- other service fields defined by the implementation.

The size of the received message is not stored in the structure directly; it can be
determined with the help of the function MPI_Get_count():

```
int MPI_Get_count(const MPI_Status * status,
                  MPI_Datatype datatype, int * count)
```

Here, count is the output parameter, which is equal to the number of
received elements in the message, in units of type datatype or the constant
MPI_UNDEFINED if the size of the data vector exceeds the range of the type of
the variable count.

The fields MPI_SOURCE and MPI_TAG are important in the case where
universal parameters are used in the program (see Sect. 4.3).

Often, it is of great importance for organization of the data communication
between processes to have a data exchange operation, when a pair of processes need
to send messages to each other and receive those messages. In other words, it is
necessary to perform a message exchange between the processes. This procedure
can, of course, be performed with the help of the functions MPI_Send() and
MPI_Recv() described above.

For example, let the data exchange be organized between processes of rank 0 and
1 within the communicator comm. Suppose that the identifier of the message being
sent by the rank 0 process is equal to tag0, and that of the message being sent by
the rank' process is equal to tag1 (Fig. 4.1). In this case, the following program
code can be used:

```
int rank;
double sendbuf[MAXN], recvbuf[MAXN];
int count0, count1;
int tag0, tag1;
MPI_Datatype datatype0, datatype1;
MPI_Status status;
MPI_Comm comm;

... // parallel program operators
```

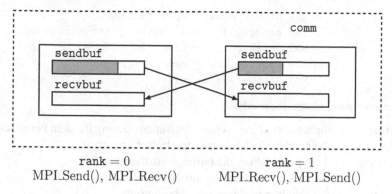

$$\text{rank} = 0 \qquad\qquad\qquad \text{rank} = 1$$
$$\text{MPI\_Send(), MPI\_Recv()} \qquad \text{MPI\_Recv(), MPI\_Send()}$$

Fig. 4.1 A pair of processes with ranks `rank = 0` and `rank = 1` send messages to each other. The correct call order for the data send and receive functions at each of the processes so as not to result in a deadlock state is shown at the bottom of the figure

```
MPI_Comm_rank (comm, &rank);

if ( rank == 0 )
  {
    MPI_Send(sendbuf, count0, datatype0, 1, tag0, comm);
    MPI_Recv(recvbuf, count1, datatype1, 1, tag1, comm, \
            &status);
  }

if ( rank == 1 )
  {
    MPI_Recv(recvbuf, count0, datatype0, 0, tag0, comm, \
            &status);
    MPI_Send(sendbuf, count1, datatype1, 0, tag1, comm);
  }
```

In this region of the program, the zero-ranked process sends a message to another process whose rank is equal to one, and then receives a reply. The process with `rank = 1`, in turn, must first receive the data vector from the process with `rank = 0`, and then send its own message to it.

It should be noted that violation of the order of function calls may result in a "deadlock" situation, where each process is waiting for actions from the other one.

MPI provides a simpler method of organizing the above data exchange between two processes so that it does not result in a deadlock state. Here, the function `MPI_Sendrecv()` combines the actions performed by the functions `MPI_Send()` and `MPI_Recv()`:

```
int MPI_Sendrecv(const void * sendbuf, int sendcount,
```

```
MPI_Datatype sendtype, int dest,
int sendtag, void * recvbuf, int recvcount,
MPI_Datatype recvtype, int source,
int recvtag, MPI_Comm comm,
MPI_Status * status)
```

The following arguments are used:

sendbuf: the address of the memory buffer containing the data being sent;
sendcount: the number of elements in the buffer sendbuf;
sendtype: the type of data in the buffer sendbuf;
dest: the rank of the receiving process;
sendtag: the identifier of the message being sent;
recvbuf: the address of the buffer that receives the data;
recvcount: the maximum number of elements in the buffer recvbuf;
recvtype: the type of data in the buffer recvbuf;
source: the rank of the sending process;
recvtag: the identifier of the message being received;
comm: the communicator including the sending process and the receiving
                process;
status: a pointer to a structure containing some parameters of the received
                message.

For the function MPI_Sendrecv(), the standard prohibits specifying the same values for the input and output buffers. If it is necessary to exchange messages within a single buffer, the function MPI_Sendrecv_replace() is used. In this case, the data being received replace the sent data:

```
int MPI_Sendrecv_replace(void * buf, int count,
                MPI_Datatype datatype, int dest,
                int sendtag, int source, int recvtag,
                MPI_Comm comm, MPI_Status * status)
```

Similarly to the function MPI_Sendrecv(), the application of the function MPI_Sendrecv_replace() requires one to use the following arguments:

buf: the address of the memory buffer for data exchange;
count: the number of elements in the buffer buf;
datatype: the type of data in the buffer buf;
dest: the rank of the receiving process;
sendtag: the identifier of the message being sent;
source: the rank of the sending process;
recvtag: the identifier of the message being received;
comm: the communicator including the sending process and the receiving
                process;
status: a pointer to a structure containing some parameters of the received
                message.

4.3 Group Names and Null Processes

Often, in a parallel program, when executing a message receive operation, it is desirable not to concretize the rank of the sending process; in other words, it is required to receive a message from an arbitrary source. For this purpose, MPI provides a universal parameter, the so-called *group name* MPI_ANY_SOURCE. Thus, a call of the command

```
MPI_Recv(buf, count, datatype, MPI_ANY_SOURCE, tag, comm,
         &status)
```

will ensure the receiving of a message from any sending process. Despite this, the sending of messages without specification of the receiving process's rank is not allowed by the standard; for this reason, there is no universal parameter of the form "MPI_ANY_DEST" in the MPI environment.

To receive a message with any parameter tag, the universal identifier MPI_ANY_TAG is used.

Thus, the meaning of some fields in the structure to which the variable status of the function MPI_Recv() refers should become clear. These fields allow one to determine the parameters of the received message when group names are specified in a program.

In many cases, some simplification of the program code can be achieved by using the number of processes with which there is no real data exchange (so-called *null processes*). The variable MPI_PROC_NULL is used to specify the rank of a null sending or receiving process, and in this case the receiving and sending of the message terminates immediately with the return code MPI_SUCCESS, without change of the buffer parameters.

4.4 Time Measurement

Time measurement is essential for evaluation of the performance of parallel programs. When programming is done on distributed-memory systems, the program's run time is not a representative index of the quality of parallelization. The reason is that the time spent on message exchange between the computational nodes is not taken into account. The MPI standard provides a convenient means of addressing the system timer, which allows one to eliminate the dependence of the program code on the program's runtime environment and, hence, increases the portability of the code.

To work with the timer, MPI uses the functions MPI_Wtime() and MPI_Wtick().

The function MPI_Wtime() returns the number of seconds elapsed from a certain moment in the past:

```
double MPI_Wtime(void)
```

The standard requires that the realization is such that the given moment in the past is not changed while the process is in operation. On the other hand, the time at different computational nodes need not be synchronized. In MPI, the variable MPI_WTIME_IS_GLOBAL is available, which is equal to one if all the processes of the global communicator are synchronized, and is equal to zero otherwise.

The second function for working with the timer,

```
double MPI_Wtick(void)
```

returns the number of seconds between two successive time counts. In other words, this function allows one to determine the resolution of the system timer in seconds.

Measurement of the time spent on the execution of the computational part of a program is usually performed as follows:

```
double t1, t2;
t1 - MPI_Wtime();
... // computational part of the program
t2 = MPI_Wtime();
printf("Computation time is %lf seconds", t2-t1);
```

Note that there is in fact no need to introduce two variables t1 and t2 for time computation. It turns out that one variable of type double is enough for measurement of a time interval (see Problem 4.3).

4.5   Message-Passing Methods

Section 4.2 describes the simplest method of interprocessor communication in the MPI environment.

The implementation may provide for buffering of a message being sent. In such a case it is not improbable that the function MPI_Send() will terminate before the call of MPI_Recv() on the receiver's side. However, on the other hand, the system buffer size is limited and the possibility of using it may be unavailable. Hence, MPI_Send() will not be able to terminate until the receiving process initializes data copying.

In addition to the standard message-passing methods considered above, several other methods of sending data are provided:

- buffered mode;
- synchronous mode;
- ready mode.

Each of these methods (and the standard method) is available in two options, *blocking* and *nonblocking*.

We now describe the various process-to-process message-passing methods.

In the buffered method, the operation on the sending process's side can be terminated before the receiving process calls the receiving function. A user buffer needs to be explicitly allocated in the program; the size of this buffer must be sufficient for working with the data being sent. The buffer can be used again when the message-passing procedure is over or when the send operation is aborted. Note that the execution of the buffered send function does not depend on a call of the message receive procedure.

In the synchronous method, the operation of the message-sending process can only be terminated if the receiving process has reported the beginning of the receiving of the message. The use of the synchronous method may result in temporary delays when programs are executed, but, on the other hand, it allows one to avoid a large number of buffered messages.

The ready data-passing method is characterized by the condition that the message send operation can begin only if the receive procedure has been initiated and is ready to receive. If this condition is not fulfilled, the result of the operation is undefined.

The type of communication method is taken into account in the name of the transfer function by adding the first letter of the name:

- MPI_Bsend(), buffered mode;
- MPI_Ssend(), synchronous mode;
- MPI_Rsend(), ready mode.

The arguments of the functions MPI_Bsend(), MPI_Ssend(), and MPI_Rsend() coincide with the arguments of MPI_Send(). They are all blocking, i.e., they suspend the operation of the process until the message itself and the service data are stored and, thus, the possibility of using the buffer appears again. Receiving of a message formed by any of the methods listed above is available with the help of MPI_Recv(); this function is common to all types of communication between two processes.

The use of the buffered message-passing method-equires that the user should allocate a memory area with the help of the function

```
int MPI_Buffer_attach(void * buffer, int size)
```

The size of the buffer size, to which the variable buffer refers, is used for the operation of MPI_Bsend() and should not be used in the program for other purposes. Note that the buffer size must exceed the size of the message being sent by the value MPI_BSEND_OVERHEAD. The constant MPI_BSEND_OVERHEAD defines the memory space required for placing the service information.

For each process, at any moment in time, only one buffer can be allocated by the above method.

Further, the function

```
int MPI_Buffer_detach(void * buffer_addr, int * size)
```

frees the memory area allocated to the buffer and returns the pointers to its beginning and to its size. The process is blocked until all the messages accumulated in this memory area are sent to the receiving processes.

The message-passing methods available in the MPI environment are schematically presented in Fig. 4.2.

In addition to the message-passing methods considered above, there exist nonblocking functions, whose names contain the suffix "I" (from "Immediate"): MPI_Isend(), MPI_Ibsend(), MPI_Issend(), and MPI_Irsend().

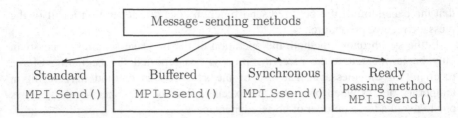

Fig. 4.2 Message-sending methods in the MPI environment

Their use is expedient in systems where the interaction of processes can be executed autonomously with respect to the execution of the computing operations. Only one nonblocking receiving operation is provided, namely `MPI_Irecv()`.

To identify nonblocking data transfers, service objects of the predefined type MPI_Request are used. For example, the function `MPI_Isend()` can be described as follows:

```
int MPI_Isend(const void * buf, int count,
              MPI_Datatype datatype, int dest, int tag,
              MPI_Comm comm, MPI_Request * request)
```

The following arguments are used:

buf: the address of the memory buffer containing the data being sent;
count: the number of elements that form the message;
datatype: the type of data in the buffer buf;
dest: the rank of the receiving process;
sendtag: the identifier of the message being sent;
comm: the communicator including the sending process and the receiving
            process;
request: a service object of type MPI_Request, used for identification of a
            nonblocking send operation.

It is usually known in advance at what moment in time a nonblocking operation will be completed. To wait for termination of such an operation started by `MPI_Irecv()` or `MPI_Isend()` (or a similar function), the following function is used:

```
int MPI_Wait(MPI_Request * request, MPI_Status * status)
```

Here, `request` is a pointer to the operation identifier defined when the nonblocking function was called, and `status` is a pointer to a structure containing the message parameters (it is only defined for the completed operation). The process that called `MPI_Wait()` is blocked until the operation defined by the variable `request` is completed.

To wait for execution of several operations, whose identifiers are listed in an array `requests`, the following function is used:

```
int MPI_Waitall(int count, MPI_Request requests[],
                MPI_Status statuses[])
```

This uses the following arguments:

count: the number of nonblocking receive and send operations;
requests: an array of operation identifiers;
statuses: an array of structures containing the parameters of each message.

The process that called `MPI_Waitall()` is unblocked when all the exchange operations in `requests[]` are completed.

In order to check whether an operation defined by the identifier `request` has been executed, the function `MPI_Test()` is used:

```
int MPI_Test(MPI_Request * request, int * flag,
             MPI_Status * status)
```

The following arguments are used:

request: a pointer to the operation identifier;
flag: an integer, the operation completion flag;
status: a pointer to a structure containing the message parameters.

The output parameter `flag` is set to a nonzero value if the operation is completed, and to zero otherwise.

The result of operation of the function `MPI_Testall()` answers the question of whether all the operations in some set have been completed:

```
int MPI_Testall(int count, MPI_Request requests[],
                int * flag, MPI_Status statuses[])
```

The parameters `count`, `requests`, and `statuses` are similar to the parameters of the function `MPI_Waitall()`. The value of `flag` is nonzero if all the operations characterized by the identifiers in the array `requests[]` have been completed, and `flag = 0` otherwise.

The use of the functions `MPI_Test()` and `MPI_Testall()` allows one to obtain information about message exchange operations without blocking the processes that called these functions.

As follows from the above, the nonblocking exchange options are more complex than the blocking ones, but when they are used correctly they allow the run time of a parallel program to be reduced.

In conclusion, we briefly sum up the peculiarities of the various communication methods. The standard communication mode is widely used and occurs frequently in applications. The buffered mode allows one to manage the buffer space directly, which requires special attention from the program developer to deal with the possibility of buffer overflow. The synchronous mode tells the system that buffering should be avoided when exchanging messages. The ready transfer mode is relatively rare; in this case, MPI realizations reduce the size of the communication protocol of the processes and the overheads of message-passing organization.

4.6   Collective Communications

Collective communications ensure data exchange between all the processes belonging to some communicator [59]. The MPI technology provides the following collective communication functions:

* synchronization;
* data broadcasting (broadcast), gathering data into one process (gather), scattering data from one process (scatter), gathering data into all processes (allgather), and gathering and scattering data into all processes from all processes (alltoall);
* reduction and generalized reduction operations.

All of the collective functions in the previous versions of the standard (up to version MPI-3.0) were blocking. In the latest versions of the MPI descriptions, nonblocking collective operations were introduced. In the present section we will consider only the blocking variants of the most important collective operations. A complete list of the available collective communications is given in [46].

The action of the broadcast, gather, scatter, allgather, and alltoall functions is schematically presented in Fig. 4.3. Note that for the execution of any collective operation, all processes within the communicator need to call that operation.

For the synchronization of processes, the following function is used:

```
int MPI_Barrier(MPI_Comm comm)
```

Its only argument is the communicator comm, all processes of which are subject to synchronization. This command blocks the processes until all the processes in comm have called the function MPI_Barrier().

Note Sometimes it becomes necessary to interrupt the execution of a parallel program. For correct termination of all processes in the communicator comm, the following function should be used:

```
int MPI_Abort(MPI_Comm comm, int errorcode)
```

where errorcode is the code for return from the program. Usually, the function call format is as follows: MPI_Abort(MPI_COMM_WORLD, MPI_ERR_OTHER).

Broadcast consists in transferring a message from a sending process with rank root to all processes within the communicator comm. Such an operation may be useful, for example, for allowing all computational nodes to obtain the input parameters of the problem at the beginning of operation of the parallel program.

The format of the broadcast function call is

```
int MPI_Bcast(void * buffer, int count, MPI_Datatype datatype,
              int root, MPI_Comm comm)
```

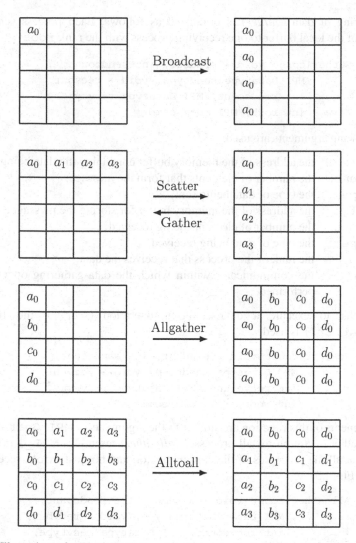

Fig. 4.3 Illustration of execution of the collective operations of broadcast, scatter, gather, allgather, and alltoall. The rows of the matrices indicate the memory areas available to various processes

The following arguments are used:

`buf:` the address of the memory buffer containing the data being sent;
`count:` the number of elements that form the message;
`datatype:` the type of data in the buffer `buf`;
`root:` the rank of the process that is sending data;
`comm:` the communicator within which the broadcast is performed.

Gathering of data (*gather*) is organized as follows. Each process sends the contents of the local buffer to one receiving process with the rank `root`:

```
int MPI_Gather(const void * sendbuf, int sendcount,
               MPI_Datatype sendtype, void * recvbuf,
               int recvcount, MPI_Datatype recvtype,
               int root, MPI_Comm comm)
```

The following arguments are used:

sendbuf: the address of the memory buffer containing the data being sent;
sendcount: the number of elements that form the message;
sendtype: the type of data being sent;
recvbuf: the address of the memory buffer for storing the message;
recvcount: the number of elements being received;
recvtype: the type of data being received;
root: the rank of the process that receives the data;
comm: the communicator within which the data-gathering operation is
               performed.

In order to execute a data-scattering operation (*scatter*), the function `MPI_Scatter()` is used:

```
int MPI_Scatter(const void * sendbuf, int sendcount,
                MPI_Datatype sendtype, void * recvbuf,
                int recvcount, MPI_Datatype recvtype,
                int root, MPI_Comm comm)
```

The arguments of this function are similar to the arguments of `MPI_Gather()`.

The gather operation for all processes (*allgather*) resembles `MPI_Gather()` except that all the processes of the communicator, and not just `root`, receive the data (see Fig. 4.3):

```
int MPI_Allgather(const void * sendbuf, int sendcount,
                  MPI_Datatype sendtype, void * recvbuf,
                  int recvcount, MPI_Datatype recvtype,
                  MPI_Comm comm)
```

The arguments of this function coincide with the arguments of `MPI_Gather()`, except the rank of the process that receives data is absent.

Finally, the collective operation *alltoall* generalizes the allgather operation so that each process sends various data to other processes:

```
int MPI_Alltoall(const void * sendbuf, int sendcount,
                 MPI_Datatype sendtype, void * recvbuf,
                 int recvcount, MPI_Datatype recvtype,
                 MPI_Comm comm)
```

The following arguments are used:

sendbuf: the address of the memory buffer containing the data being sent;
sendcount: the number of elements that form the message;
sendtype: the type of data being sent;
recvbuf: the address of the memory buffer for storing the message;
recvcount: the number of elements being received;
recvtype: the type of data being received;
comm: the communicator within which the collective operation is performed.

The gather, scatter, allgather, and alltoall functions have "vector" options, in which the sizes of the data sets in different processes may differ. The names of such functions are formed by adding the postfix "v" to the names of the original function: MPI_Gatherv, MPI_Scatterv, MPI_Allgatherv, and MPI_Alltoallv. The vector options take as one of their arguments not the size of the message but an array of such sizes.

Here, we provide a list of arguments for the function MPI_Gatherv(); the rest of the functions listed are called similarly:

```
int MPI_Gatherv(const void * sendbuf, int sendcount,
                MPI_Datatype sendtype, void * recvbuf,
                const int recvcounts[], const int displs[],
                MPI_Datatype recvtype, int root, MPI_Comm comm)
```

The following arguments are used:

sendbuf: the address of the memory buffer containing the data being sent;
sendcount: the number of elements that form the message;
sendtype: the type of data being sent;
recvbuf: the address of the memory buffer for the message being received;
recvcounts: an array of integers whose i-th element is equal to the number of elements received from the i-th process;
displs: an array of integers whose i-th element is equal to the offset with respect to the address recvbuf at which the data from the i-th process should be placed;
recvtype: the type of data being received;
root: the rank of the process that receives data;
comm: the communicator within which the collective operation is performed.

The reduction operation MPI_Reduce(), widely used in parallel applications, calculates a function of the data received by one process from all processes in the communicator:

```
int MPI_Reduce(const void * sendbuf, void * recvbuf, int count,
               MPI_Datatype datatype, MPI_Op op, int root,
               MPI_Comm comm)
```

The following arguments are used:

sendbuf: the address of the memory buffer containing the source data;
recvbuf: the address of the memory buffer that receives data;
count: the number of elements in the array addressed by sendbuf;
datatype: the type of data being sent;
op: the function applied to the data;
root: the rank of the process that receives the result;
comm: the communicator within which the reduction operation is per-
              formed.

Let us consider in more detail what happens to the above arguments after a call of the function MPI_Reduce(). The operation op is applied to the elements of the local arrays sendbuf[i], where i = 0, 1, ..., count − 1, following which the elements recvbuf[i] are formed. The result of applying the operation op to the arguments a and b is denoted by $a \otimes b$. Then, the following relations are fulfilled:

$$\mathtt{recvbuf[i]} = {}^{(0)}\mathtt{sendbuf[i]} \otimes {}^{(1)}\mathtt{sendbuf[i]} \otimes \ldots \otimes {}^{(r)}\mathtt{sendbuf[i]} \otimes \ldots$$

$$\ldots \otimes {}^{(\mathtt{count}-1)}\mathtt{sendbuf[i]},$$

where ${}^{(r)}\mathtt{sendbuf[i]}$ denotes the element of the array sendbuf located in the memory of the process with rank $r \in [0, \mathtt{count} - 1]$.

A list of the functions predefined by the MPI environment op is shown in Table 4.2. Let us explain the meanings of the last two functions, namely MPI_MAXLOC and MPI_MINLOC. The first defines the maximum of the arguments and its location. The second defines the minimum and its location.

Table 4.2 Predefined functions for MPI_Reduce()

Function name	Function description
MPI_MAX	Maximum
MPI_MIN	Minimum
MPI_SUM	Sum
MPI_PROD	Product
MPI_LAND	Logical AND
MPI_BAND	Bitwise AND
MPI_LOR	Logical OR
MPI_BOR	Bitwise OR
MPI_LXOR	Logical exclusive OR
MPI_BXOR	Bitwise exclusive OR
MPI_MAXLOC	Maximum and its location
MPI_MINLOC	Minimum and its location

Speaking more formally, these functions compute the *lexicographic maximum* and the *lexicographic minimum* of an arbitrary data set in accordance with the relations

$$\begin{pmatrix} a \\ i \end{pmatrix} \otimes_{\text{MAXLOC}} \begin{pmatrix} b \\ j \end{pmatrix} = \begin{pmatrix} c \\ k \end{pmatrix},$$

where $c = \max(a, b)$ and

$$k = \begin{cases} i & \text{if } a > b, \\ \min(i, j) & \text{if } a = b, \\ j & \text{if } a < b \end{cases}$$

for MPI_MAXLOC, and

$$\begin{pmatrix} a \\ i \end{pmatrix} \otimes_{\text{MINLOC}} \begin{pmatrix} b \\ j \end{pmatrix} = \begin{pmatrix} c \\ k \end{pmatrix},$$

where $c = \min(a, b)$ and

$$k = \begin{cases} i, & \text{if } a < b, \\ \min(i, j), & \text{if } a = b, \\ j, & \text{if } a > b \end{cases}$$

for MPI_MINLOC.

To use the functions MPI_MAXLOC and MPI_MINLOC in a reduction operation, it is necessary to specify correctly the argument datatype. A program in the C language can contain six possible types in this case, as listed in Table 4.3. The traditional use of the functions MPI_MAXLOC and MPI_MINLOC is in computing the global maximum (or minimum), together with the rank of the process that contains the given variable.

Table 4.3 Predefined types for use with the operations MPI_MAXLOC and MPI_MINLOC

Type name	Type description
MPI_FLOAT_INT	float and int
MPI_DOUBLE_INT	double and int
MPI_LONG_INT	long and int
MPI_2INT	Two values of type int
MPI_SHORT_INT	short and int
MPI_LONG_DOUBLE_INT	long double and int

The functions allowable in a reduction operation go beyond those listed in Table 4.2. There is the possibility of constructing user operations. To create new operations, the function `MPI_Op_create()` is used:

```
typedef int MPI_Op_create(MPI_User_function * user_fn,
                          int commute, MPI_Op * op)
```

After a call of the command `MPI_Op_create(user_fn, commute, op)` the user operation `op` is created; it is computed with the help of the function referred to by `user_fn`. The resulting operation needs to be associative, i.e., $\forall a, b, c \ (a \otimes b) \otimes c = a \otimes (b \otimes c)$. All predefined operations in Table 4.2 are also commutative: $\forall a, b \ a \otimes b = b \otimes a$. The user may introduce noncommutative operations. The parameter `commute` should be equal to one (or any integer other than zero) if `op` is commutative, and equal to zero otherwise. If the equality `commute` $= 0$ is fulfilled, then the computations are performed in ascending order of the rank of the processes:

$$\text{recvbuf[i]} = (\ldots((^{(0)}\text{sendbuf}[i] \otimes^{(1)} \text{sendbuf}[i]) \otimes^{(2)} \text{sendbuf}[i]) \otimes \ldots).$$

The user function should have four parameters, `invec`, `inoutvec`, `len`, and `datatype`:

```
typedef void MPI_User_function(void * invec,
void * inoutvec, int * len, MPI_Datatype * datatype)
```

The first parameter, `invec`, forms the first argument of the binary operation `op`; the next parameter, `inoutvec`, forms the second argument of `op`. The result of this binary operation is stored in `inoutvec`. The variable located at the address `len` is equal to the number of elements in the input (and, correspondingly, the output) arrays. The parameter `datatype` specifies the type of the input and output data.

Note An indication of the fact that the operation `op` is commutative will allow the MPI environment to change the order of actions. This may result in different responses in the case of operations that are only approximately commutative (for example, when the addition of real numbers is used).

Upon completion of work with a user operation `op`, the resources allocated for it should be freed with the help of the function

```
int MPI_Op_free(MPI_Op * op)
```

The variable `op` will then be set equal to the predefined constant MPI_OP_NULL.

The MPI standard also provides for operations of *generalized reduction*, described in more detail in [46].

Let us stress one more time that for execution of any collective operation, all of the processes within the communicator must call that operation.

Example 4.1 Consider a parallel program which defines the maximum of some real numbers written in a text file `input.txt`. Into an output file `output.txt`, the program should output the maximum number obtained and its ordinal number in the source file.

Solution We compute the greatest element of the array and its ordinal number with the help of a reduction operation, in which we specify the predefined operation MPI_MAXLOC as the function to be used. In order to execute the reduction operation in the parallel program, it is necessary to use auxiliary structures with two fields to store an array element and the number of this element.

In order to perform comparison of the elements with each other, it is necessary to send the input data to the nodes of the computer system. This distribution of the computing load should, where possible, result in balanced work of the processes.

In our case, the sending of the elements of the source array is organized as follows.

Let the number of elements in the input file be equal to N, and the number of parallel process created be equal to size. We compute the remainder of the division residual = N%size. If N is divisible by size exactly and so residual=0, then all the process receive subarrays of the same size, N/size, for processing. Otherwise, residual > 0, and then the processes with ranks not exceeding residual-1 receive N/size+1 numbers, and the remaining processes receive N/size numbers. Recall that in the C language, notation of the form A/B means integer division.

The sending of the elements is performed using the function MPI_Scatterv(). After its execution, each of the processes determines the local maximum of elements obtained as a result of sending the data subarray from the process with rank root to the executing processes.

In the closing part of the program, using a reduction operation over the set of local maxima the global maximum of the numbers in the file input.txt and the ordinal number of the maximum element in this file are computed. The program code is shown in Listing 4.1. □

Listing 4.1

```
1  #include <stdio.h>
2  #include <stdlib.h>
3  #include <math.h>
4  #include <mpi.h>
5
6  #define NMAX 1000000000
7
8  int main( int argc, char * argv[] )
9  {
10    int N;                // quantity of numbers
11                          // in file input.txt
12
13    int rank, size;       // process rank and
14                          // total number of
```

```
15                         // processes
16
17    const int root = 0;
18
19    int i, k = 0;
20
21    int flag = 1;        // flag and t are
22    double t;            // auxiliary variables
23                         // for reading data
24                         // from the input file
25
26    double * list, * local_list;
27                         // arrays for storing data
28                         // in the main process and
29                         // each of the executing
30                         // processes
31
32    int local_length;    // size of array
33                         // local_list
34
35    int residual;        // remainder of division
36                         // of N by the number
37                         // of processes
38
39    int * counts_array;  // auxiliary arrays
40    int * displs;        // for function
41                         // MPI_Scatterv()
42
43    FILE * fp;
44
45    // initialization of the execution environment
46    MPI_Init(&argc, &argv);
47
48    // determining the process rank and
49    // the total number of processes in progress
50    MPI_Comm_rank(MPI_COMM_WORLD, &rank);
51    MPI_Comm_size(MPI_COMM_WORLD, &size);
52
53    if ( rank == root )
54       {
55          if ((list = (double *) \
56              malloc(NMAX*sizeof(double))) == NULL)
57             {
58                perror("\nError allocating memory " \
```

```
59                                  "to array list[]");
60                     MPI_Abort(MPI_COMM_WORLD,    \
61                               MPI_ERR_OTHER);
62                 }
63
64        if ((fp = fopen("input.txt","r")) == NULL)
65            {
66                 perror("\nError opening "    \
67                        "initial file "       \
68                        "\"input.txt\"");
69                 fclose(fp);
70                 MPI_Abort(MPI_COMM_WORLD,     \
71                           MPI_ERR_OTHER);
72            }
73
74        while( flag != EOF )
75            {
76                 flag = fscanf(fp, "%lf", &t);
77                 list[k] = t;
78                 k++;
79            }
80
81        N = k - 1;              // storing the size
82                               // of the input data
83        fclose(fp);
84
85        if ((list = (double *) \
86            realloc(list,N*sizeof(double)))==NULL)
87            {
88                 perror("\nError changing " \
89                        " the size of array list[]");
90                 MPI_Abort(MPI_COMM_WORLD, \
91                           MPI_ERR_OTHER);
92            }
93      }
94
95   // communicating to all available processes
96   // the quantity of numbers being analyzed
97   MPI_Bcast((void *)&N, 1, MPI_INT, root, \
98           MPI_COMM_WORLD);
99
100  residual = N%size;
101  i = 0;
102
```

```
103   counts_array = (int *)malloc(size*sizeof(int));
104   displs = (int *)malloc(size*sizeof(int));
105
106   for(k=0; k<size; k++)
107     {
108       if( k<residual )
109         counts_array[k] = N/size + 1;
110       else
111         counts_array[k] = N/size;
112
113       displs[k] = i;
114       i = i + counts_array[k];
115     }
116
117   local_length = counts_array[rank];
118
119   if ((local_list = (double *) \
120     malloc(local_length*sizeof(double)))==NULL)
121     {
122       perror("\nError allocating memory " \
123               "to array local_list[]");
124       MPI_Abort(MPI_COMM_WORLD, MPI_ERR_OTHER);
125     }
126
127   MPI_Scatterv((void *)list, counts_array,     \
128               displs, MPI_DOUBLE,              \
129               (void *)local_list,             \
130               local_length, MPI_DOUBLE,       \
131               root, MPI_COMM_WORLD);
132
133   if ( rank == root )
134     free(list);
135
136   struct
137     {                      // auxiliary structure
138       double data;   // for saving the results
139       int index;     // of the reduction
140     }                      // operation
141       in, out;
142
143   in.data = local_list[0];
144   in.index = 0;
145
146   // computing the local maxima
```

```
147    for (k=1; k<local_length; k++)
148      if (in.data < local_list[k])
149        {
150            in.data = local_list[k];
151            in.index = k;
152        }
153
154    // converting the relative index
155    //`into the absolute value
156    in.index = displs[rank] + in.index;
157
158    MPI_Reduce((void *)&in, (void *)&out, 1,         \
159              MPI_DOUBLE_INT, MPI_MAXLOC, root, \
160              MPI_COMM_WORLD);
161
162    free(counts_array);
163    free(displs);
164    free(local_list);
165
166    if ( rank == root )
167      {
168          if ((fp = fopen("output.txt","w"))==NULL)
169            {
170                perror("\nError opening file " \
171                        "\"output.txt\"");
172                fclose(fp);
173                MPI_Abort(MPI_COMM_WORLD, \
174                          MPI_ERR_OTHER);
175            }
176
177          fprintf(fp, "Maximum value = "    \
178                      "%lf\nIndex = %d",     \
179                       out.data, out.index+1);
180          printf("The result is written to file " \
181              "\"output.txt\"\n");
182
183          fclose(fp);
184      }
185
186    MPI_Finalize();
187    return 0;
188 }
```

4.7   Test Questions

1. How is the abbreviation MPI expanded?
2. Name the known implementations of the MPI standard.
3. What minimal set of six functions of the MPI environment allows one to create a parallel program with data exchange between processes?
4. Is it possible to call any of the functions of the MPI environment outside the parallel region of a program? If yes, what are these functions? If no, why not?
5. Is there a way to know the version of the MPI standard being used from within a parallel program?
6. Is it possible to know the version of the MPI library being used from within a parallel program?
7. Give a definition of the term "communicator."
8. Is it true that all MPI functions return an integer value int? If it is true, substantiate the existence of such a rule. If it is not true, what exceptions are known?
9. What functions are used for pairwise message exchange?
10. What does the MPI standard provide group names for?
11. How can the run time of the computational part of a program be measured by means of MPI?
12. List the pairwise message exchange methods provided by the MPI standard.
13. In what cases is it appropriate to use nonblocking operations for communication between processes?
14. With the help of what function is the process synchronization operation performed?
15. Describe the action of the broadcast, gather, scatter, allgather, and alltoall functions.
16. In what cases are the "vector" options of collective operations used?
17. Describe how to organize a reduction operation in the MPI environment.

4.8   Problems

4.1. In an examination on parallel programming, a student claims that within a communicator any process using the MPI_Send() function may send a message to any process, including itself. Is the student right?
4.2. Let a pairwise message exchange within the MPI_COMM_WORLD communicator be organized, and the number of processes in the parallel program be equal to N. Write down:

   (a) a set of ranks available for use as recipient process ranks in MPI_Send();
   (b) a set of ranks available for use as sender process ranks in MPI_Recv().

Fig. 4.4 A computer
network consisting of `size`
processors

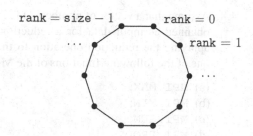

4.3. This chapter describes how to measure the running time of a portion of program code (see Sect. 4.4). Suggest a method for performing such a measurement using only one variable of type `double`.

4.4. Write a program in which the sending of a message of a size not exceeding NMAX characters from a process of rank `size` − 1 to a process of the rank 0 is executed, where `size` is the number of available computational nodes.

4.5. In an examination on parallel programming a student is asked to write a program for message exchange in a computer network organized as a ring (Fig. 4.4). The process `rank` (0 ⩽ `rank` ⩽ `size` − 1) must pass a string of N symbols to the next process clockwise. A portion of the program code written by the student is given below:

```
int rank, size, prev, next;
int tag = 1;
MPI_Status status;
char buf[N];

... // determination of the values
... // rank, size, prev, next;

MPI_Send(buf, N, MPI_CHAR, next, tag, MPI_COMM_WORLD);
MPI_Recv(buf, N, MPI_CHAR, prev, tag, MPI_COMM_WORLD, \
        &status);
```

Explain why the execution of this program may lead to a deadlock situation and offer a correct solution to this problem.

4.6. In the operation of `MPI_Bcast()`, broadcasting the process of rank `root` sends a message to all other processes within the communicator. Suggest your version of an `MPI_Bcast()` implementation which uses only pairwise data exchanges (namely, the functions `MPI_Send()` and `MPI_Recv()`).

*4.7. As is well known, a prime number is an integer $p > 1$ that has only two divisors: unity and the number p itself. In a text file `input.txt`, two natural numbers N_{min}, N_{max} are written with a space between, and $N_{max} > N_{min}$. Using the MPI technology, calculate and write into a file `output.txt` all prime numbers in the closed interval $[N_{min}, N_{max}]$ in ascending order.

4.8. Assume that a vector of numbers $(11, 21, 31, 41, 51)$, of type `int`, has been obtained as input data for a reduction operation. Determine the result of applying the reduction operation to the components of this vector if each one of the following functions of the MPI environment is used:

(a) `MPI_MAX`;
(b) `MPI_MIN`;
(c) `MPI_SUM`;
(d) `MPI_PROD`;
(e) `MPI_LAND`;
(f) `MPI_BAND`;
(g) `MPI_LOR`;
(h) `MPI_BOR`;
(i) `MPI_LXOR`;
(j) `MPI_BXOR`.

4.9. Find how the answer to the previous problem changes if the components of the input data vector belong to the type `short int`.

4.10. Example 4.1 is about computing the maximum of some real numbers written into a file. If among these numbers there are numbers that are equal to each other, then several variables with different ordinal numbers may satisfy the condition of maximality. Investigate what ordinal number will be output by the program presented in Example 4.1.

4.11. Using the MPI technology, write a parallel program that computes the mean value $E(\mathbf{x})$ and the standard deviation $D(\mathbf{x})$ of a sample $\mathbf{x} = (x_1, x_2, \ldots, x_N)$ according to the formulas

$$E(\mathbf{x}) = \frac{1}{N} \sum_{i=1}^{N} x_i,$$

$$D(\mathbf{x}) = \frac{1}{N-1} \sum_{i=1}^{N} (x_i - E(\mathbf{x}))^2.$$

The components of the vector $\mathbf{x}$ are integers written, separated by spaces, in a text file `input.txt`. Output the values of $E(\mathbf{x})$ and $D(\mathbf{x})$ obtained into a text file `output.txt`.

*4.12. Prime twins are pairs of prime numbers whose difference is equal to 2. For example, among the first 20 natural numbers there are four prime twins: $(3, 5)$, $(5, 7)$, $(11, 13)$, and $(17, 19)$. Using the MPI technology, determine the number of prime twins $(p, p+2)$, where p is a prime number satisfying the condition $p + 2 \leqslant N$. The natural number $N \geqslant 5$ is in a text file `input.txt`; write the answer into a file `output.txt`.

Chapter 5
The OpenMP Technology

This chapter provides a description of the computational model used in the OpenMP technology, as well as a brief description of the basic structures of this environment [50].

OpenMP is the standard application programming interface for parallel systems with shared memory. This standard has been implemented for Fortran and C/C++ and consists of a set of directives for compilers, function libraries, and a set of environment variables.

Fortran is widely used for solving resource-intensive scientific and technical problems arising in both academic research and applied fields [57, 63]. The first versions of Fortran date back to the 1950s, and the newer editions of the language standard take into account the features of modern computer systems and programming technologies. One of the main reasons for the popularity of Fortran is the existence of an extensive database of applied programs and libraries created during the years of its intensive application.

The C programming language was designed for use in system programming [32]. Universality of the language is achieved because of its great generality and the absence of strict limitations on working with memory. C and C++, which is based on it, are also widely used in high-performance computing.

From now on in this book, unless otherwise specified, the C language is used in accordance with the C99 standard [14]. In some places, explanations are given on the use of Fortran.

5.1 The Parallel Program Model

In the OpenMP environment, a program has sequential and parallel regions, or *sections*. Immediately after launch, the program is a single *thread*, or, as it is called, a *master thread*. The master thread is executed in a sequential manner until, in the

© Springer Nature Switzerland AG 2019
S. Kurgalin, S. Borzunov, *A Practical Approach to High-Performance Computing*,
https://doi.org/10.1007/978-3-030-27558-7_5

program code, the compiler meets a specific type of instruction describing a parallel region, a *directive* of the OpenMP environment. As a result of the execution of that directive, a *team of threads* is generated. The team threads are numbered with sequential nonnegative integers, and the master thread is assigned the number 0.

After a parallel region has been completed, the main thread continues the execution in a sequential manner. Note that there can be several parallel regions in a program.

The regions of parallel execution can be nested inside each other. Each team thread in this case creates its own team, in which it plays the role of the master thread.

A schematic description of the program structure is shown in Fig. 5.1.

We need to pay attention to the difference between the concepts of "process" and "thread." Each process has its own address space assigned to it. Threads are created within the address space of an existing process. Accordingly, in the address space of some process, several threads can be executed in parallel.

Threads, in comparison with processes, have the following specific features:

- creating a thread or completing its work requires less time than similar operations with a process;
- switching between threads of one process is faster than between processes;

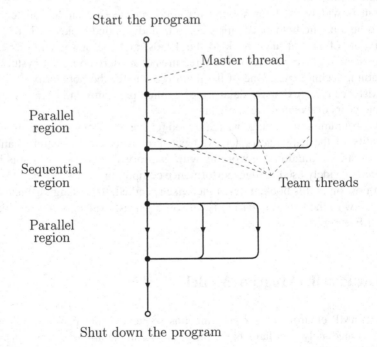

Fig. 5.1 The program model in the OpenMP environment

- the threads running in a process have access to the memory space and resources of that process, whereas processes do not have a shared (that is, available to several processes at once) address space.

Note Threads are often referred to as *lightweight processes.*

5.2 OpenMP Directives

Directives in the OpenMP environment are written using the following prefixes:

- for C and C++, `#pragma omp`;
- for Fortran (for code in the so-called free format), `!$OMP`.

The prefix is followed by a space followed by the name of the directive and, if necessary, a list of the parameters related to it.

The procedure for compiling a program will be considered using the example of the GCC compiler [78].

Compiling and running a sequential program, the code of which is in a file `task.c` in the current directory, is done with the help of the commands

```
>gcc -g -Wall -std=c99 task.c -o task.out
>./task.out
```

Here, > denotes the command line prompt.

The parameter `-g` includes the recording of additional information in the executable file for a debugging procedure, the parameter `-Wall` includes the use of an extended set of warnings, and the parameter `-std=c99` indicates compilation according to the C99 standard. The name of the executable file to be created is indicated after `-o`.

Support for the OpenMP environment is enabled using the key `-fopenmp`:

```
>gcc -g -Wall -std=c99 -fopenmp task.c -o task.out
>./task.out
```

After the above command has been executed from the file `task.c` in the current directory with a parallel program in the C99 standard, an executable file `task.out` is created in the same directory, and this file is transferred for execution. As can be seen, the start operation for the file `task.out` is the same as for the start of a sequential program.

Brief information about working with the command line, as well as information about the file system and user processes, is given in Appendix B.

The most important feature of a programming environment for multiprocessors is the organization of access to a single address space by different threads.

The variables used in parallel constructions are divided into *private* and *shared* variables. The difference between the nonintersecting private and shared classes is that the shared variables are available from any thread, whereas, for each private variable, copies of it are created in all threads.

Consider one of the basic operations of the OpenMP environment, the generation of a parallel region. For this purpose, the directive `parallel` needs to be specified in the program, followed by the operators creating the parallel section:

```
#pragma omp parallel
{
    ... // parallel block operators
}
```

After the keyword `parallel`, the following parameters, or *clauses*, can be used:

shared (*list*)
private (*list*)
default (private | shared | none)
firstprivate (*list*)
lastprivate (*list*)
reduction (*operation* : *list*)
if (*boolean condition*)
copyin

(A record of the form (a | b) means that, in the parentheses, exactly one of the given parameters i.e., either (a) or (b), must be specified.)

Let us set out the features of these parameters and commands.

shared (*list*)
The variables specified in this list are declared as shared.

private (*list*)
The variables specified in this list are declared as private. Note that the initial values of the copies of the variables available from the threads are not defined.

default (private | shared | none)
This command defines the class to which the variables belong that are not included in the lists of the above two parameters. The presence of the keyword none requires that all variables must be present either in the private (...) list or in the shared (...) list.

firstprivate (*list*)
The private variables in this list get the initial values of the original variables that existed before the parallel block was entered.

lastprivate (*list*)
At the end of the parallel region, the local variables in this list update the values of the original variables.

reduction (*operation* : *list*)
The reduction, which is important for the development of high-performance programs, runs as follows. Upon exiting from a parallel loop, the operation specified as a parameter of this command is performed on the copies of the variable in all threads, after which the result is assigned to the original variable. After the colon

in the parentheses, the variables to which the reduction operation should be applied are listed. In other words, this reduction directive defines the method for the output processing of a team of private variables.

if (*boolean condition*)
The block following this command is executed in parallel by all threads of the team if the value of the argument of the if (...) command is different from zero (or equal to .TRUE. in Fortran). The directive parallel if(...) is ignored if the value of the argument of the if command is zero (or equal to .FALSE. in Fortran).

copyin
Upon entering the parallel region, private copies of the variables declared as threadprivate from the list of this command get initial values in accordance with their values in the master thread. The threadprivate directive prescribes that all variables in its list should be replicated, i.e., each thread should receive its own private copy of each variable in the list.

5.3 Auxiliary Functions and Environment Variables

For work with parameters such as the number of threads and the thread number in a team, the following major functions are used.

void omp_set_num_threads(int num);
After the function omp_set_num_threads(num) is called, the number of the threads executing the parallel region is set to num.

int omp_get_num_threads(void);
This function returns the number of threads in the parallel region.

int omp_get_thread_num(void);
This function returns the number of the current thread in the team, i.e., the thread from which the function was called.

int omp_get_dynamic(void);
This function, omp_get_dynamic(), checks if it is possible to dynamically change the number of threads used by the implementation of the environment to execute the parallel region. The system may offer the possibility of changing the team size, in particular for optimizing the use of computing resources. If this is possible, then the function returns the value 1, otherwise 0.

void omp_set_dynamic(int dynamic_threads);
This function sets the possibility of dynamically changing the number of threads (if dynamic_threads=1) or disables this possibility (if dynamic_threads=0).

To measure time intervals using the system timer, the following functions are used:

```
double omp_get_wtime(void);
double omp_get_wtick(void);
```

The function `omp_get_wtime()` returns the astronomical time in seconds, counted from some point in the past. It is guaranteed that the time reference point will not change during the working time of the thread from which this function is called. The function `omp_get_wtick()` is used to calculate the timer resolution in seconds.

To use the functions of the OpenMP environment, it is necessary to connect to the program the header file `omp.h` (for programs in Fortran, the file `omp_lib.h` or module `omp_lib`). Conversely, all OpenMP directives can be used without connecting this header file.

It is possible to use a set of *environment variables* to manage some of the settings of the OpenMP environment from the operating system. Recall that environment variables are text variables of the operating system used for storing system settings and other service data. We list the most important of such variables below.

`OMP_NUM_THREADS`
This environment variable sets the number of threads created in the parallel regions. The value of this variable must be a list of positive integers. The values in the list define the team sizes in the parallel regions, taking nesting into account. For example, the value of `OMP_NUM_THREADS` can be set like this:

```
>export OMP_NUM_THREADS=8,4
```

(as before, > denotes the command line prompt). After this command is executed, the number of threads in the parallel region is equal to 8, and that in the nested parallel region is equal to 4. Note that in the case, when at least one of the values in the list exceeds the maximum possible size of the thread team in the computer system, the result will depend on the implementation of OpenMP.

`OMP_SCHEDULE`
This environment variable sets the distribution rule for the computational load in parallel loops using the directive `schedule(runtime)` (see the `for` parameter of the directive `parallel` on Sect. 5.4.1). The variable `OMP_SCHEDULE` contains a string that corresponds to the parameter of the `schedule` directive used, for example,

```
>export OMP_SCHEDULE="static, 4"
```

`OMP_DYNAMIC`
This variable controls the ability to dynamically change the number of threads in parallel regions of the program. It takes two possible values: `true` or `false`. An example of working with the variable `OMP_DYNAMIC` is

```
>export OMP_DYNAMIC=true
```

`OMP_NESTED`

This environment variable manages the implementation of nested parallelism. Similarly to the previous variable, only two values are admissible for it: `true` or `false`. For example, the command

```
>export OMP_NESTED=true
```

enables the creation of a new nested parallel region from a parallel region of the program.

Note that the environment variables have lower priority than the OpenMP directives and functions.

5.4 Basic Methods for Parallelization: Parallel Loops and Parallel Sections

There are two main methods for using the resources of parallelism in a program: parallel loops and parallel sections.

5.4.1 Parallel Loops

The most commonly used method for parallelizing programs is the distribution of resource-intensive loop iterations across various team threads. For this purpose, the keyword `for` is used. This indicates that the loop following a directive should be parallelized:

```
#pragma omp parallel
   {
     ... // parallel block operators
     #pragma omp for
       for (i=0; i<N; i++)
         {
           ... // the loop body
         }
     ... // parallel block operators
   }
```

In this section of the code, the loop iterations with respect to the variable i will be distributed across several team threads. The loop variable is considered private, and it may be not specified in the list of a `private` directive.

The general requirement on the form of a loop to be parallelized is that there is a possibility of preliminary calculation of all the values of the loop variable before the loop body is entered. As a consequence, the directive `for` can be applied only to unconditional loops that do not provide the possibility of an early exit beyond the loop body.

As parameters for the directive `parallel for`, the following keywords can be used:

```
schedule(static | dynamic | guided | auto | runtime)
private(list)
firstprivate(list)
lastprivate(list)
reduction(operation : list)
ordered
nowait
```

The distribution of loop iterations across the threads is managed by the parameter of the directive `schedule`. The use of the keyword `static` gives the compiler an instruction to divide the loop into blocks (called *chunks*) of equal (or approximately equal) size, and each thread executes exactly one block. Such a method for distributing the computational load is called a *static* method.

Let there be a loop to be parallelized consisting of N iterations. In the general case, a thread with number $k = 0, 1, \ldots, p - 1$ from a team of size p gets iterations from an interval $[i_{min}, i_{max}]$, where

$$\begin{cases} i_{min} = k \left\lceil \dfrac{N}{p} \right\rceil + 1, \\ i_{max} = \min\left((k + 1)\left\lceil \dfrac{N}{p} \right\rceil, N\right). \end{cases}$$

Here $\lceil x \rceil$ is the ceiling, i.e. the smallest integer which is greater than or equal to x: $\lceil x \rceil = \min(n \in \mathbb{Z}, \ n \geqslant x)$.

The chunk size can be specified by writing it as an optional parameter in parentheses. For example, the directive

```
#pragma omp for schedule(static, m)
```

will create equal-sized blocks of m iterations, except possibly for the last block when the number of loop iterations is not a multiple of m.

The second method of distributing the computational load in parallel loops is called *dynamic* and is specified by the keyword `dynamic`. In this case, a thread that has completed a block of calculations receives the next block of iterations.

The third method of distributing the load is indicated by the keyword `guided`. In this case, the threads receive new blocks dynamically, but the block size at each stage of the loop iteration is proportional to the ratio of the remaining number of iterations to the team size. The minimum value of the block size is equal to 1 by default, and, if necessary, this value can be adjusted as follows:

```
#pragma omp for schedule(guided, m)
```

Here, m is the minimum block size.

It should be noted that the use of the `dynamic` and `guided` methods, in contrast to the `static` method, makes it possible to balance the computational load of the threads better, but leads to a loss of determinism in the parallel program. This is due to the fact that it is not known in advance precisely which thread will perform a given loop iteration.

If the parameter `auto` is specified in the command `schedule`, the programmer gives the right to choose the method of distributing iterations across the threads to the compiler and/or the execution system.

Finally, if the keyword `runtime` is indicated in this command, the method of distributing iterations is chosen in the course of program execution in accordance with the value of the variable `OMP_SCHEDULE` (see the description on Sect. 5.3).

After completion of a parallel loop, an implicit synchronization of all working threads (see Sect. 5.5) is envisioned. Using the `nowait` parameter eliminates this synchronization if there is no need for it.

As a simple example of the use of parallel loops and a reduction operation in the OpenMP environment, we provide a program for the computation of harmonic numbers.

Example 5.1 Write a parallel program to computate the harmonic numbers H_N from the formula $H_N = \sum_{i=0}^{N} 1/i$, where $N \geqslant 1$.

Solution A sum of the form $\sum_{i=0}^{N} 1/i$ can easily be computed using a distribution of iterations over the threads of a parallel team. The partial sums obtained in each thread can be combined conveniently into a final answer via applying a reduction operation to them. The section of program code that realizes this computation method has a very simple form:

```
#pragma omp parallel for reduction(+:sum)
  for (i=1; i<=N; i++)
    sum += 1.0/i;
```

The value of H_N is accumulated in the variable sum.

We now analyze the computational accuracy. As is well known, the bounded word size of a computing system, in the general case, leads to an approximate representation of real numbers in memory. Because of this, when loop iterations are performed, computational errors accumulate.

Note that the error becomes especially large in the case of the addition of numbers whose orders of magnitude differ considerably. In the code section considered, such additions are performed many times. Let us denote the absolute value of the computational error in H_N by Δ.

The value of Δ can be reduced somewhat with the help of the following trick, in which we reverse the order of the loop iterations. The passing of the iterations from the maximum value $i = N$ to the minimum value $i = 1$ will lead to the computation of sums where the summands differ by only a small amount. Hence, the option of the summation $\sum_{i=N}^{1} 1/i$ is preferable in this case from the point of view of reducing computational errors. It should be noted, however that this increase in accuracy in the computation of H_N will only be achieved for sufficiently large values of the parameter N, namely when N is of the order of the maximum value represented by the standard type `long int`.

Taking into account the code correction described above, we obtain a parallel program whose code is shown in Listing 5.1.

Listing 5.1

```
1  #include <stdio.h>
2
3  #define N 1000000000
4
5  int main ( void )
6  {
7    long int i;
8    double sum = 0;
9
10   #pragma omp parallel for reduction(+:sum)
11   for (i=N; i>=1; i--)
12     sum += 1.0/i;
13
14   printf("H_%d = %.15lf\n", N, sum);
15   return 0;
16 }
```

It is not difficult to estimate the value of the error Δ if we remember the asymptotic formula for harmonic numbers [24] known from mathematical analysis. For sufficiently large N, the following asymptotic equality is valid:

$$H_N = \ln N + \gamma + \frac{1}{2N} - \sum_{k=1}^{k_{max}} \frac{B_{2k}}{2kN^{2k}} + O\left(\frac{1}{N^{k_{max}+2}}\right),$$

where $\gamma = 0.5772156649015\ldots$ is *Euler's*[1] *constant*, and B_{2k} are the *Bernoulli*[2] *numbers* $B_0 = 1$, $B_2 = 1/6$, $B_4 = -1/30$, ...

In order to estimate the absolute error in the computation of H_N for all values of the parameter N in the range $10^4 \leqslant N \leqslant 10^9$, it is sufficient to retain just a small number of terms of the expansion:

$$H_N = \ln N + \gamma + \frac{1}{2N} - \frac{1}{12N^2} + \frac{1}{120N^4} + O(N^{-6}).$$

The results of computation of the numbers H_N are presented in Table 5.1. Here, the first column contains the ordinal number of the harmonic number, the second column contains the results of the numerical computation with the help of the program shown in Listing 5.1, and the third column contains the exact values

---

[1] Leonhard Euler (1707–1783), Swiss mathematician.

[2] Jacob Bernoulli (1654–1705), Swiss mathematician.

Table 5.1   The harmonic numbers H_N and the errors in their computation ε for $N = 10^k$, where $k = 4, 5, \ldots, 9$

N	H_N (numerical computation)	H_N (exact value)	ε
10^4	9.787606036044383	9.787606036044382	1.0×10^{-16}
10^5	12.090146129863423	12.090146129863427	3.3×10^{-16}
10^6	14.392726722865761	14.392726722865723	2.6×10^{-15}
10^7	16.695311365859847	16.695311365859851	2.4×10^{-16}
10^8	18.997896413853890	18.997896413853898	4.2×10^{-16}
10^9	21.300481502348279	21.300481502347944	1.6×10^{-14}

The differing decimal places are underlined for visual clarity

obtained from the asymptotic formula. Finally, the last column shows the relative error in the computation, $\varepsilon = \Delta/H_N$. It cad be seen from the table that the computational errors in all cases have values $\lesssim 10^{-14}$.

Note that the program does not use the functions of the OpenMP environment `omp_get_num_threads()`, `omp_get_thread_num()`, and similar. This results in the absence of a necessity to connect the header file `omp.h`. As a result, the application of the reduction operation allows a minimal number of variables to be used in the program and particular simplicity and clarity of the program code to be achieved.   □

5.4.2   Parallel Sections

In OpenMP, the possibility of specifying a sequence of operators to be executed in each of the team threads independently is provided:

```
#pragma omp sections
{
  #pragma omp section
    {
       ... // the first section operators
    }
  #pragma omp section
    {
       ... // the second section operators
    }
}
```

As parameters for the directive `sections`, the following can be used:
   `private` (*list*)
   `firstprivate` (*list*)
   `lastprivate` (*list*)
   `reduction` (*operation* : *list*)

Note that sometimes within a parallel region it is required to execute several operators in a single thread. To perform this task, the directive `single` is provided. The section following it will be executed by a single thread, namely the first one to reach this directive:

```
#pragma omp single
  {
    ... // sequential part operators
  }
```

After the keyword `single`, the following parameters can be used:

    `private`(*list*)
    `firstprivate`(*list*)
    `nowait`
    `copyprivate`(*list*)

The keyword `copyprivate` means that after execution of a `single` section by a single thread the updated values of the variables in the list will be copied into the corresponding variables of other threads, if these variables are described as `private` or `firstprivate`.

The directive `master` restricts a code section to be executed only by the master thread:

```
#pragma omp parallel
{
  #pragma omp master
    {
      ... // code section will be executed
      ... // only by the master thread
    }
}
```

The remaining team threads will skip all the operators in the section subject to the directive `master`.

5.5 Synchronization

Synchronization in OpenMP can be realized explicitly, via specifying the directives described in this sections; however, the realization can also use implicit synchronization (usually after the completion of parallel loops, etc.).

The most common synchronization method is one that uses a *barrier* placement. This is done with the help of the directive

```
#pragma omp barrier
```

The threads that are executing the current parallel region, upon reaching this directive, stop and wait until all the threads have reached this point in the program. When all the team threads have reached the barrier, the program continues to run.

For the directive `master`, no implicit synchronization is envisioned either before entering the action block or after exiting the block.

When working with shared variables, to avoid access conflicts, the mechanism of critical sections is used. For their description, the directive `critical` is used; the main property of such sections is that at each moment in time no more than one thread can be present in a critical section. In other words, the directive `critical` singles out, inside a parallel region of a program, a set of operators that will be executed alternately by the processes:

```
#pragma omp critical(name)

{
    ... // critical section operators
}
```

The optional parameter *name* is used for identification of a given section when several critical sections are present in the program.

An alternative method of working with shared variables consists in the use of the directive `atomic`. This directive declares the assignment statement following immediately after it to be *atomic*, which guarantees correct working with the shared variable on the left of that statement. Access to an atomic variable is blocked for all threads except the one that is executing this operation. In other words, the directive `atomic` arranges the order of rewriting of the value of the variable into memory. For example, when it is necessary to increase the value of a shared variable x by the value of a obtained from various threads, the code section

```
#pragma omp atomic
    x = x + a;
```

will require that the update x should be executed sequentially, and hence correctly.

It is often required to ensure consistency of the random access memory for different threads, at least for several variables used in the program.

The directive

```
#pragma omp flush (list)
```

transfers to the random access memory the values of the variables enumerated in the list, which are temporarily stored in the registers and cache memory of the processes. Implicitly, this directive is called without parameters at the entry and exit of the region of operation of the directives `parallel`, `critical`, and `ordered`, after executing synchronization with the help of the buffer, and in many other cases [12].

Finally, there is the directive `ordered`, which prescribes the execution of the loop body iterations in exactly the order in which the iterations would be executed in a sequential loop. In practice, the application of this method is convenient, for example, for ordering the output operations of parallel threads.

5.6   The Lock Mechanism

As one more synchronization mechanism, let us consider the mechanism of *locks*. In OpenMP, a lock means a shared integer variable used exclusively for the synchronization of threads.

An arbitrary lock can be in one of three states:

1. Uninitialized.
2. Unlocked.
3. Locked.

Any thread can bring an unlocked lock into a locked state, i.e., *acquire* it. A lock can be unlocked only by the thread that acquired it. Any other thread attempting to access an already acquired lock will be blocked until the lock returns to the unlocked state.

Two lock types are provided for, differing in the possibility of being reacquired by the same thread: *simple locks* and *nestable locks*.

A nested lock can be reacquired several times by one thread; a simple lock, on the contrary, can only be reacquired once by each thread. For a nested lock, there exists an acquisition coefficient (or nesting count). At each successive acquisition this increases by one, and at each release it decreases by one. A nested lock is deemed to be unlocked if its nesting count is equal to zero.

We now show a list of functions intended for working with locks, with a brief description of the operation of these functions.

```
void omp_init_lock(omp_lock_t *lock);
void omp_init_nest_lock(omp_nest_lock_t *lock);
```
These functions are used for initialization of a simple or a nested lock, respectively.

```
void omp_destroy_lock(omp_lock_t *lock);
void omp_destroy_nest_lock(omp_nest_lock_t *lock);
```
These functions bring a lock (simple or nested, respectively) into the uninitialized state.

```
void omp_set_lock(omp_lock_t *lock);
void omp_set_nest_lock(omp_nest_lock_t *lock);
```
These functions perform acquisition of a lock.

In order to arrange for a nonblocking attempt at lock acquisition, the following functions are used
```
int omp_test_lock(omp_lock_t *lock);
int omp_test_nest_lock(omp_lock_t *lock);
```
These return 1 (for a simple lock) or an acquisition coefficient (for a nested lock) if it is successful, and 0 otherwise.

Finally, with the help of another two functions,
```
void omp_unset_lock(omp_lock_t *lock);
void omp_unset_nest_lock(omp_lock_t *lock);
```

the release of a lock is organized. In the case of a nested lock, the nesting count is decremented. When this count is equal to zero, the lock is released, following which it can be acquired by one of the threads awaiting it.

Example 5.2 Construct a table of values of the Bessel[3] function $J_0(x)$ of order zero on an interval $[a, b]$ with a step size δ.

Solution The Bessel function of the first kind $J_\nu(x)$ of order ν, like any other cylinder function, satisfies the differential equation

$$x^2 \frac{d^2 y}{dx^2} + x \frac{dy}{dx} + (x^2 - \nu^2)y = 0.$$

We use the known series expansion [49], which is convergent for $x \geqslant 0$:

$$J_\nu(x) = \left(\frac{x}{2}\right)^\nu \sum_{k=0}^{\infty} (-1)^k \frac{x^{2k}}{4^k k! \Gamma(\nu + k + 1)},$$

where $\Gamma(x)$ is the gamma function (recall that $\Gamma(n) = (n-1)!$ for natural-number values of the argument). For the zero-order Bessel function, this series is the Taylor[4] series about the point $x = 0$ and has the simple form

$$J_0(x) = \sum_{k=0}^{\infty} a_k x^{2k} = \sum_{k=0}^{\infty} \frac{(-1)^k}{4^k (k!)^2} x^{2k}.$$

The relation obtained allows the values of $J_0(x)$ to be computed. Naturally, the program used for the computation can only sum a finite number of summands in the expression:

$$\sum_{k=0}^{\infty} a_k x^{2k} = (a_0 + a_1 x^2 + \ldots + a_{k_{\max}} x^{2k_{\max}}) + \sum_{k=k_{\max}+1}^{\infty} a_k x^{2k}.$$

Note that the error in the computation of the alternating series can easily be estimated—it does not exceed $a_{k_{\max}}$ in absolute magnitude, i.e., the last summand considered. This is a consequence of Leibniz's[5] alternating series test.

It should be noted that although the Taylor series $\sum_{k=0}^{\infty} a_k x^{2k}$ for the function $J_0(x)$ converges for all $x \in \mathbb{R}$, the terms of this series increase with the index k for values of k up to $\sim |x|$. This insufficiently rapid convergence results in the necessity to take into account no fewer than $k_{\max} \gg |x|$ summands of the power series to

---

[3] Friedrich Wilhelm Bessel (1784–1846), German astronomer and mathematician.

[4] Brook Taylor (1685–1731), English mathematician.

[5] Gottfried Wilhelm Leibniz (1646–1716), German philosopher, mathematician, and mechanician.

compute the Bessel function $J_0(x)$. In practice, the following convenient criterion for achieving the required accuracy is used: the expansion is continued until the current term of the alternating power series becomes less in absolute magnitude than a preset constant, namely the computational accuracy.

The program for tabulation of the function $J_0(x)$ is organized as follows. The computational accuracy for the values of the function is denoted by the symbolic constant EPSILON and is taken equal to 10^{-14}. The left and right bounds of the interval, a, b, and the computational step size δ are set in the source file input.txt, located in the current directory. The number of points at which the value of the function needs to be computed is greater by one than the ratio of the length of the interval $(b - a)$ to the step size δ.

The function BesselJ0(), with the help of the Taylor series, computes $J_0(x)$ at a certain point x. The coefficients $a_k = (-1)^k/4^k(k!)^2$ in the sum for $J_0(x)$ satisfy, as is easy to see, the recurrence relation

$$\begin{cases} a_k = -\dfrac{1}{4k^2}a_{k-1}, & k \geqslant 1, \\ a_0 = 1. \end{cases}$$

The main computation loop searches the points of the interval $[a, b]$ and fills the array res with the values $J_0(x)$. Since the loop iterations are independent, the application of the directive

#pragma omp parallel for schedule(guided)

distributes the iterations over the available threads of the team. Finally, a table of values of the zero-order Bessel function, written in the array res, is output to the file output.txt. The program code is shown in Listing 5.2.

Listing 5.2

```
1  #include <stdio.h>
2  #include <stdlib.h>
3  #include <math.h>
4  #include <omp.h>
5
6  #define EPSILON 1.0e-14      // function value
7                               // computing accuracy
8  double BesselJ0(double);
9
10 int main()
11 {
12    double a, b, delta;
13    double * res;             // declaration of
14                              // the function
15                              // values array
16    int N;
17
```

```
18    FILE * fp;
19
20    if ((fp = fopen("input.txt","r")) == NULL)
21      {
22          perror("\nError opening file "
23                  "\"input.txt\"");
24          exit(EXIT_FAILURE);
25      }
26    fscanf(fp, "%lf %lf %lf", &a, &b, &delta);
27    fclose(fp);
28
29    if ((delta < 0.0) || (a >= b))
30      {
31          printf("\nIncorrect input data\n");
32          exit(EXIT_FAILURE);
33      }
34
35    N = (b - a) / delta + 1;
36    res = (double *)malloc(N*sizeof(double));
37    if ( res == NULL )
38      {
39          perror("\nError allocating memory "
40                  "for array res");
41          exit(EXIT_FAILURE);
42      }
43
44    double t1 = omp_get_wtime();
45
46    #pragma omp parallel for schedule(guided)
47    for(int i = 0; i < N; i++)
48      res[i] = BesselJ0(a + i * delta);
49
50    double t2 = omp_get_wtime();
51
52    printf("Time spent on the computation cycle "
53            "is equal to %.3lf sec.\n", t2 - t1);
54
55    fp = fopen("output.txt", "w");
56    for(int i = 0; i < N; i++)
57      fprintf(fp, "% .14e\t % .14e\n",
58              a + i * delta, res[i]);
59
60    fclose(fp);
61    free(res);
```

```
62
63      return 0;
64 }
65
66 double BesselJ0(double x)
67 {
68      int k=0;
69      double a=1.0;              // current coefficient
70                                 // of Taylor series
71      double f=1.0;              // partial sum
72                                 // of Taylor series
73      while ( fabs(a) >= EPSILON )
74        {
75            k++;
76            a = -a*x*x/(4.0*k*k);
77            f += a;
78        }
79      return f;
80 }
```

Speedup values S_p of the computational part of the program code, obtained using the supercomputer at Voronezh State University, are shown in Fig. 5.2. This figure demonstrates a monotonic increase of S_p with the size of the team p, close to the theoretical limit defined within the PRAM model by the relation $\left(S_p\right)_{\max} = p$. □

Example 5.3 Compute the double integral

$$\mathcal{I} = \iint_{\mathcal{D}} e^{-(x^2+y^2)}\, dx\, dy$$

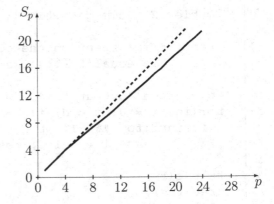

Fig. 5.2 Speedup S_p of the computational part of the program code in Example 5.2 (*solid line*) and theoretical limit $\left(S_p\right)_{\max}$ (*dashed line*) as a function of the number of threads p. The calculation of the Bessel function $J_0(x)$ was performed over the interval [0, 1] with a step size $\delta = 10^{-9}$

over the rectangle $\mathcal{D} = \{(x, y): 0 \leqslant x \leqslant 2, 0 \leqslant y \leqslant 3\}$ with an absolute error μ not exceeding 10^{-8}.

Solution The computation of multiple and, in particular, double integrals usually presents considerable difficulty in comparison with the one-dimensional case [57]. Firstly, to maintain the required accuracy, it is required to compute the values of the integrand at a large number of points. Secondly, the domain of integration in the general case may have a rather complex form.

In the simplest cases, to estimate the values of multidimensional integrals, it is possible to use a numerical integration (quadrature) method based on one-dimensional quadrature formulas.

The essence of this method is the following. Consider the double integral

$$I = \iint_S f(x, y)\, dx\, dy,$$

where the domain of integration S is a rectangle $S = \{(x, y): a_1 \leqslant x \leqslant b_1, a_2 \leqslant y \leqslant b_2\}$, and the function $f(x, y)$ is continuous in S and twice differentiable in this domain.

We rewrite the multiple integral in the form of an iterated integral;

$$I = \iint_S f(x, y)\, dx\, dy = \int_{a_2}^{b_2} dy \int_{a_1}^{b_1} f(x, y)\, dx$$

and apply to the inner integral the *midpoint quadrature formula*, known from any course in numerical methods. For this purpose, we split the interval $[a_1, b_1]$ into $N_1 = (b_1 - a_1)/\delta_1$ intervals, and the value of the function in each interval is chosen at the points $x_i = a_1 + (i - 1/2)/\delta_1, i = 1, 2, \ldots, N_1$. Then, we apply the midpoint quadrature formula to the outer integral over the variable y, which takes $N_2 = (b_2 - a_2)/\delta_2$ values $y_j = a_2 + (j - 1/2)/\delta_2, j = 1, 2, \ldots, N_2$, in the interval $[a_2, b_2]$. Here, δ_1, δ_2 are the lengths of the subintervals on the X and Y axes, respectively.

As a result, we obtain the following formula for numerical integration over a two-dimensional domain, based on the one-dimensional quadrature formulas:

$$I = \iint_S f(x, y)\, dx\, dy = \delta_1 \delta_2 \sum_{i=1}^{N_1} \sum_{j=1}^{N_2} f(x_i, y_j) + R,$$

where R is the error of the quadrature formula. The following estimate of the variable R is well known:

$$R \leqslant \frac{(b_1 - a_1)(b_2 - a_2)}{24} \left(\delta_1^2 M_{2x} + \delta_2^2 M_{2y} \right),$$

where M_{2x} and M_{2y} denote the maximum absolute values of second partial derivatives:

$$M_{2x} = \max_{(x,y)\in S}\left|\frac{\partial^2 f(x,y)}{\partial x^2}\right|, \quad M_{2y} = \max_{(x,y)\in S}\left|\frac{\partial^2 f(x,y)}{\partial y^2}\right|.$$

So, having determined the values of the integrand at $N_1 \times N_2$ points and having used the quadrature method described above, we will obtain the value of the double integral I over the rectangular area S with an absolute error not exceeding R.

Consider the function $f(x,y) = e^{-(x^2+y^2)}$ over the rectangle $\mathcal{D} = \{(x,y)\colon 0 \leqslant x \leqslant 2,\ 0 \leqslant y \leqslant 3\}$. Having computed the partial derivatives

$$\frac{\partial^2 f(x,y)}{\partial x^2} = -2(1-2x^2)e^{-(x^2+y^2)} \quad \text{and} \quad \frac{\partial^2 f(x,y)}{\partial y^2} = -2(1-2y^2)e^{-(x^2+y^2)},$$

it is easy to show that for this function the variable R takes values

$$R \leqslant \frac{1}{2}(\delta_1^2 + \delta_2^2).$$

Hence, to obtaining an accuracy such that the absolute error does not exceed $\mu = 10^{-8}$, it is sufficient to take $\delta_1 = \delta_2 = 10^{-4}$.

The code of a program that realizes the algorithm described above for approximate computation of a double integral is shown in Listing 5.3. It is convenient to parallelize the computation loop with the help of a reduction operation, which is achieved by adding before the inner loop over the variable i the directive

```
#pragma omp parallel for private (x, y, j) reduction(+:
sum)
```

The limits of the intervals of integration over the variables x and y, and the parameters of the partitioning of these intervals, δ_1 and δ_2, are read from a file input.txt. Into the output file output.txt is written the result, limited to eight decimals, $\mathcal{I} = 0.78170701$.

Listing 5.3

```
1  #include <stdio.h>
2  #include <stdlib.h>
3  #include <math.h>
4  #include <omp.h>
5
6  void integral(const double a1, const double b1,
7     const double a2, const double b2,
8     const double delta1, const double delta2,
9     double *res)
10 {
```

```
11      int i, j;
12      int N1, N2;    // sizes of the integration grid
13                     // over x and y axes
14      double x, y; // coordinates
15                   // of the grid point
16      double sum = 0.0;// the variable sum
17                       // accumulates the values of the
18                       // function at grid points
19
20      // computing the integration grid sizes
21      N1 = (int)((b1 - a1) / delta1);
22      N2 = (int)((b2 - a2) / delta2);
23
24      #pragma omp parallel for private (x, y, j) \
25                             reduction(+: sum)
26      for(i = 1; i <= N1; i++)
27         {
28            for(j = 1; j <= N2; j++)
29               {
30                  x = a1 + i * delta1 - delta1 / 2.0;
31                  y = a2 + j * delta2 - delta2 / 2.0;
32                  sum += delta1*delta2*exp(-(x*x+y*y));
33               }
34         }
35      *res = sum;
36 }
37
38 int main()
39 {
40    double a1, b1;      // left and right bounds
41                        // of integration over x
42    double a2, b2;      // left and right bounds
43                        // of integration over y
44    double delta1, delta2; // integration steps
45                        // over coordinates x and y
46                        // respectively
47    double res;
48
49    FILE * fp;
50
51    if ((fp = fopen("input.txt","r")) == NULL)
52       {
53          perror("\nError opening file "
54                 "\"input.txt\"");
```

```
55        exit(EXIT_FAILURE);
56      }
57    fscanf(fp, "%lf %lf %lf %lf %lf %lf", \
58            &a1, &b1, &a2, &b2, &delta1, &delta2);
59    fclose(fp);
60
61    if ((delta1 < 0.0) || (delta2 < 0.0) || \
62        (a1 >= b1) || (a2 >= b2))
63      {
64        printf("\nIncorrect input data\n");
65        exit(EXIT_FAILURE);
66      }
67
68    double t1 = omp_get_wtime();
69    // call of the integration function
70    integral(a1, b1, a2, b2, delta1, delta2, &res);
71    double t2 = omp_get_wtime();
72
73    printf("Time spent on the computation cycle "
74            "is equal to %.3lf sec.\n", t2 - t1);
75
76    if ((fp = fopen("output.txt","w")) == NULL)
77      {
78        perror("\nError opening file "
79                "\"output.txt\"");
80        exit(EXIT_FAILURE);
81      }
82    fprintf(fp, "%.8lf", res);
83    fclose(fp);
84
85    return 0;
86  }
```

Figure 5.3 shows the values of the speedup S_p of the computational part of the program code as a function of the number of threads p. The monotonic increase of S_p is explained by the relatively good scalability of the computation loop over the variable i.   □

Note Analytically, the value of the integral $\mathcal{I}$ can be expressed by use of the *error function*, $\mathrm{erf}(z) = (2/\sqrt{\pi}) \int_0^z e^{-t^2} dt$ [49]:

$$\mathcal{I} = \iint_{\mathcal{D}} e^{-(x^2+y^2)} \, dx \, dy = \frac{\pi}{4} \, \mathrm{erf}(2) \, \mathrm{erf}(3).$$

Fig. 5.3 Speedup S_p of the computational part of the program code in Example 5.3 (*solid line*) and theoretical limit $(S_p)_{max}$ (*dashed line*) as a function of the number of threads p. The values of the parameters were $a_1 = 0$, $b_1 = 2$, $a_2 = 0$, $b_2 = 3$, and $\delta_1 = \delta_2 = 10^{-4}$

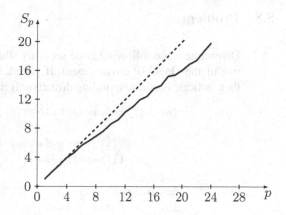

This makes it possible to debug programs for the above computation by checking the values of the error function obtained, via comparing them with data in tables or with the results of computation using mathematical libraries (see the links in [49]).

Examples of the implementation of algorithms in OpenMP are shown in the next chapter.

5.7 Test Questions

1. Describe the model of a parallel program in the OpenMP environment.
2. How are the OpenMP directives formed?
3. Describe the process of compiling and starting a program that uses the OpenMP parallelizing technology.
4. What is the criterion for separation of variables in a parallel program into private and shared ones?
5. What are environment variables used for?
6. What values can the environment variables OMP_NUM_THREADS, OMP_SCHEDULE, OMP_DYNAMIC, and OMP_NESTED take?
7. Enumerate the basic functions of the OpenMP environment.
8. What two main parallelizing methods are provided for in OpenMP?
9. Describe the parameters used when working with the directive schedule.
10. Explain the meaning of the keywords shared, private, default, firstprivate, lastprivate, if, reduction, and copyin.
11. What synchronization methods are provided for in the OpenMP environment?
12. What can atomic operations be useful for?
13. Describe the lock mechanism in the OpenMP environment.

5.8 Problems

5.1. Determine if the following code sections allow parallelization using a directive of the OpenMP environment. If parallelization in this way is possible, then indicate the corresponding directive; if it is not possible, explain why.

(a)
```
for(int i=0;i<(int)log2(N);i++)
{
    list[i] = 2.0*i*log2(i+1);
    if ((i>=IMIN) && (i<=IMAX)) temp[i] = list[i];
}
```

(b)
```
double res = 0.0;
for(int i=0;i<N;i++)
    res += list[i]*list[i];
```

(c)
```
for(int i=0;i<N;i++)
{
    list[i] = 1.5*exp(i);
    if ( list[i] <= LMAX )
        break;
}
```

(d)
```
for(int i=2*IMIN;i<N;i++)
    list[i] = LMAX*list[i-2*IMIN];
```

5.2. Find the errors in the following code sections:

(a)
```
// message output only by a single
// thread of the team
#pragma omp parallel
{
    #pragma single
        printf("Single message\n");
}
```

(b)
```
// distribution of the loop iterations
// across all threads of the team
#pragma omp parallel
    for(int i=0;i<N;i++)
        res[i]=func(1.0/(i+1));
```

(c)
```
// filling the array res[] in the order in which
// iterations follow in a sequential loop
#pragma omp parallel ordered
    for(int i=0;i<ceil(log2(N));i++)
        res[i]=func(1.0/(i+1));
```

(d)
```
// writing the values of func() into a file,
// the order of the lines does not matter
#pragma omp parallel private(k,y)
{
```

```
k = omp_get_thread_num();
y = func(k);
fprintf(fp, "%d\t %lf\n", k, y);
}
```

5.3. Suppose that the size m of the blocks for parallelizing a loop of N iterations in a static way is given. What is the number k of the thread that will implement the i-th loop iteration if the number of threads in the team is equal to p?

5.4. A student in an examination needs to solve the following problem in combinatorics: "How many ways are there to distribute 62 students to perform practical work at various enterprises, if an employment contract is concluded with six of them? There are no restrictions on the number of students working at any one enterprise." Write a parallel program that allows you to check an answer obtained analytically by an exhaustive search.

5.5. A student in an examination needs to solve the following problem in combinatorics: "A computer company employs 11 engineers, 15 programmers, and 9 software testing specialists. In order to agree who will be awarded New Year's bonus payments, it is decided to form a committee of 8 people. How many ways are there to do this if it is necessary to ensure the participation of representatives of each of these three groups in the committee?" Write a parallel program that allows you to check an analytical answer by an exhaustive search.

5.6. Create a table of values on an interval $[a, b]$ with a step size δ for the following functions:

(a) the Bessel function of the first kind $J_1(x)$;
(b) the Bessel function of the first kind $J_2(x)$;
(c) the Bessel function of the second kind (Neumann[6] function) $Y_1(x)$;
(d) the bessel function of the second kind (Neumann function) $Y_2(x)$.

5.7. Create a table of values on an interval $[a, b]$ with a step size δ for the following functions:

(a) the modified Bessel function of the first kind $I_1(x)$;
(b) the modified Bessel function of the first kind $I_2(x)$;
(c) the modified Bessel function of the second kind (Macdonald[7] function) $K_1(x)$;
(d) the modified Bessel function of the second kind (Macdonald function) $K_2(x)$.

---

[6] Carl Gottfried Neumann (1832–1925), German mathematician.
[7] Hector Munro Macdonald (1865–1935), Scottish mathematician.

5.8. Using the midpoint quadrature formula, calculate the double integral

$$\mathcal{I} = \iint\limits_{\mathcal{D}} e^{-(x^2+y^2)} \, dx \, dy$$

over the rectangle $\mathcal{D} = \{(x, y) \colon a_1 \leqslant x \leqslant b_1,\ a_2 \leqslant y \leqslant b_2\}$ with an absolute error not exceeding $\mu = 10^{-10}$. Consider the following cases:

(a) $a_1 = 0, b_1 = 3/2, a_2 = 0, b_2 = 5/3$;
(b) $a_1 = 0, b_1 = 3/2, a_2 = 0, b_2 = 1$;
(c) $a_1 = -3/2, b_1 = 5/2, a_2 = -1, b_2 = 1$;
(d) $a_1 = -4, b_1 = 4, a_2 = -4, b_2 = 4$.

5.9. Using the midpoint quadrature formula, calculate the double integral

$$\mathcal{I} = \iint\limits_{\mathcal{D}} \ln(x^2 + y^2 + 1) \, dx \, dy$$

over the rectangle $\mathcal{D} = \{(x, y) \colon a_1 \leqslant x \leqslant b_1,\ a_2 \leqslant y \leqslant b_2\}$ with an absolute error not exceeding $\mu = 10^{-10}$. Consider the following cases:

(a) $a_1 = -1, b_1 = 1, a_2 = -1, b_2 = 1$;
(b) $a_1 = 1, b_1 = 3/2, a_2 = 1, b_2 = 5/3$;
(c) $a_1 = -3/2, b_1 = 5/2, a_2 = 3/2, b_2 = 5/2$;
(d) $a_1 = -2, b_1 = 2, a_2 = -2, b_2 = 2$.

5.10. When complex program suites are being developed, the *forward compatibility* of program code is of great importance [15, 55]. In parallel programming, this term means the possibility of compiling the parallel version of the code in a sequential mode, i.e., when using the OpenMP environment, without specifying the key -fopenmp in the parameter list transferred to the compiler. Suggest a method of achieving forward compatibility of parallel programs written using OpenMP.

Chapter 6
Implementation of Parallel Algorithms

In many cases, the development of an efficient parallel algorithm for the solution of some problem requires new ideas and methods in comparison with the creation of a sequential version of the algorithm. Examples are the practically important problems of searching for a target element in a data structure and of computation of the value of an algebraic expression. The present chapter discusses algorithms for array element summation and data sorting. These parallel algorithms and the peculiarities of their implementation are discussed in [1, 11, 38, 53, 77].

6.1 The Array Element Sum Problem

Let us compute the sum of the elements of an array $list[1..N]$, where $N = 2^m$, for some positive integer m.

The simplest sequential variant for solution of the problem, of the form

```
double Sum(double * list)
{
    double sum = 0;
    for (long int i = 0; i < N; i++)
        sum += list[i];
    return sum;
}
```

cannot be parallelized. However, a parallel version of an algorithm for solving this problem can be obtained by the following reasoning.

We construct a complete binary tree whose leaves correspond to the elements of $list[1..N]$, $1 \leqslant i \leqslant N$. In each of the internal vertices we place the sum of the values in the two vertices, above that vertex. Then, at the lowest level we obtain the required value, $\sum_{i=1}^{N} list[i]$. A peculiarity of this summing algorithm is the independence of

© Springer Nature Switzerland AG 2019

S. Kurgalin, S. Borzunov, *A Practical Approach to High-Performance Computing*,
https://doi.org/10.1007/978-3-030-27558-7_6

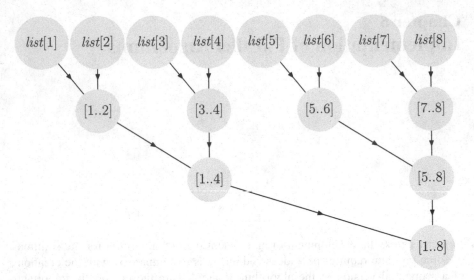

Fig. 6.1 Parallel summation of elements for $N = 8$

each addition operation at the i-th level of the tree from the remaining operations at that level [45, 81].

An example of the calculation of the sum for $N = 8$ is shown in Fig. 6.1. The notation $[i..j]$ in an internal vertex in the figure indicates that the cell contains the sum $\sum_{k=i}^{j} list[k]$.

Listing 6.1 shows the code of a program for parallel summation of the elements of an array *list* of length $N = 2^m$ for some positive integer m. Let us estimate the running time of this program.

Listing 6.1

```
 1  #include <stdio.h>
 2  #include <stdlib.h>
 3  #include <math.h>
 4  #include <omp.h>
 5
 6  #define N 256*1024*1024
 7  #define CHUNK 1024
 8
 9  double parSum(double * list)
10  {
11      long int i=0,j=0,k=2;
12      for (i=0;i<log2(N);i++)
13          {
14  #pragma omp parallel for shared(k) private(j) \
```

```
15                               schedule(static,CHUNK)
16          for (j=N/k;j>0;j--)
17             list[k*j-1]=list[k*j-k/2-1]+list[k*j-1];
18          k *= 2;
19       }
20    return(list[N-1]);
21  }
22
23  int main()
24  {
25    long int j;
26    double * a;
27    a=(double *)malloc(N*sizeof(double));
28
29    if ( a == NULL )
30       {
31          perror("\nError allocating memory "
32                  "for array a");
33          exit(EXIT_FAILURE);
34       }
35    for (j=0; j<N; j++) a[j]=j;
36    printf("\nResult: %lf\n", parSum(a));
37    printf("\nResult verification: %ld\n", \
38          j*(j-1)/2);
39
40    free(a);
41    return 0;
42  }
```

The sequential variant will need

$$\frac{N}{2} + \frac{N}{4} + \ldots + 1 = N - 1$$

addition operations. With the availability of a multiprocessor computation system with $p = N/2$, the complexity of the algorithm for finding the sum will become proportional to the height of the "operations–operands" digraph, $T_p(N) = \Theta(\log_2 N)$.

The speedup value S_p of the computational part of the program code as a function of the number of threads p is presented in Fig. 6.2. As one can see, the speedup does not have a linear dependence on the value of the argument, which is explained by the finite rate of access to the random access memory. This effect is disregarded in the PRAM model.

Fig. 6.2 Speedup S_p of the computational part of the element summation program code as a function of the number of threads p

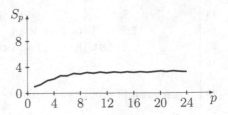

6.2 Sorting Algorithms

Consider the problem of sorting a sequence $list[i]$, where $1 \leqslant i \leqslant N$, on a PRAM with N processors. The simplest possible approach is a generalization of bubble sort. In the standard bubble sort method, pairs of values in the array are compared strictly sequentially. We can change the algorithm so that the comparisons in each iteration are independent and can be performed by different processors. It is possible to do this if we divide the elements into two classes depending on the parity of the index, and compare the values of $list[i]$ with their neighboring elements to the right. Such a modification of bubble sort is called *odd–even sort*.

The actions of this algorithms are divided into two steps: during the "even" step, each element $list[i]$, where $i = 1, 3, 5, \ldots$, is compared with the previous element ($list[i - 1]$), and, when necessary, an exchange of the values of these elements takes place. During the "odd" step, each element $list[i]$, where $i = 2, 4, 6, \ldots$, is compared with the next element ($list[i + 1]$), and, when necessary, a permutation of them takes place.

After these steps have been repeated N times, the array becomes ordered [1, 53].

Listing 6.2

```
1   #include <stdio.h>
2   #include <stdlib.h>
3   #include <omp.h>
4   #define N 100000
5
6   void Oddevensort(int * list)
7   {
8       int step, i, temp;
9       #pragma omp parallel shared(list) \
10                            private(i, temp, step)
11      for (step = 0; step < N; step++)
12        if (step % 2 == 0)
13          {
14              #pragma omp for
15              for (i = 1; i < N; i += 2)
16                if (list[i-1] > list[i])
17                  {
```

```
18              temp = list[i];
19              list[i] = list[i-1];
20              list[i-1] = temp;
21            }
22        }
23    else
24      {
25        #pragma omp for
26        for (i = 1; i < N-1; i += 2)
27          if (list[i] > list[i+1])
28            {
29              temp = list[i];
30              list[i] = list[i+1];
31              list[i+1] = temp;
32            }
33      }
34 }
35
36 int main(void)
37 {
38    int * a;
39    double t1, t2;
40    a = (int *)malloc(N*sizeof(int));
41
42    for (int i = 0; i < N; i++)
43      a[i] = N - i;
44
45    t1 = omp_get_wtime();
46    Oddevensort(a);
47    t2 = omp_get_wtime();
48
49    printf("\nExecution time: %lf\n sec.", \
50           t2 - t1);
51    free(a);
52    return 0;
53 }
```

Listing 6.2 shows the program code of an implementation of this algorithm. The running time of the algorithm Oddevensort is $O(N)$, and its cost is $C_p = O(N^2)$. The algorithm is not cost-optimal. Apart from this, the small speedup $S_p = O(\log_2 N)$ and the considerable number of processes used, $p = O(N)$, complement the list of the algorithm's drawbacks.

Figure 6.3 presents the speedup values of the computational part of the program code of this algorithm as a function of p. As can be seen, the value S_p does not have a linear dependence on the value of the argument, which is explained by the finite

Fig. 6.3 Speedup S_p of the
computational part of the
odd–even sort program code
as a function of the number of
threads p

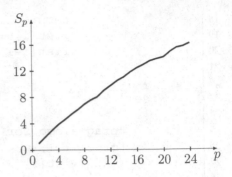

rate of access to the random access memory, which is disregarded in the PRAM model.

Shellsort is also used to sort data using multiprocessor computing systems. As is well known, this method is an improvement of insertion sort. Shell[1] foresaw the possibility of permutation of elements located at a fixed distance from each other [68].

An h-ordered array is defined as follows: an array *list* is *h-ordered* if a collection of the elements positioned at a distance h from each other forms a sorted array [66]. The Shellsort algorithm carries out h-ordering of an array for several decreasing values of h, called *increments*, the last of which is equal to 1. The entire array, of length N, is viewed as a collection of interleaved subarrays, and the sorting reduces to multiple application of insertion sort.

The analysis of Shellsort is rather complex and is based on the concept of *inversion* [34, 42]. An inversion is a pair of elements arranged in incorrect order, i.e., a pair (a_i, a_j) for which $a_i > a_j$, where $1 \leqslant i < j \leqslant N$. For example, in an array of size N whose elements are written in reverse order, the number of inversions is $N(N-1)/2$. Each comparison in insertion sort results in deleting no more than one inversion, but in Shellsort an exchange of elements can remove several inversions at once.

Obtaining an estimate of the complexity of the algorithm for a defined sequence of increments is a serious mathematical problem. Some results of analysis of the Shellsort algorithm that have been obtained are presented below [66].

Theorem of h- and k-ordering *The result of h-sorting of a k-ordered array generates an h- and k-ordered array.*

For a proof of the theorem of h- and k-ordering, see [38, 66].

There are known estimates of the complexity for some sequences of increments; for example, for the sequence of increments 1, 3, 7, 15, 31, 63, ..., the worst-case asymptotic complexity is $O(N^{3/2})$.

---

[1] Donald Lewis Shell (1924–2015), American researcher in the field of computer science.

Pratt[2] suggested a sequence of values of h leading to an algorithm of complexity $W(N) = \Theta(N(\log_2 N)^2)$. It should be noted that the advantage of using this sequence becomes apparent only for sufficiently large sizes N of the array.

Listing 6.3 shows the code of a Shellsort program for a sequence of increments suggested by Hibbard[3] [30, 34].

Listing 6.3

```
1  #include <stdio.h>
2  #include <stdlib.h>
3  #include <math.h>
4  #include <omp.h>
5  #define N 10000000
6
7  void hfill(int * h, int L)
8  {
9    // forming the increment array h[]
10   h[0]=1;
11   for(int s=1; s<L; s++)
12     h[s] = 2*h[s-1] + 1;
13 }
14
15 void Shellsort(int * list, int * h, int L)
16 {
17   for(int s = L - 1; s > 0; s--)
18     {
19         long H = h[s];      // current increment
20         #pragma omp parallel for
21         for (int k = 0; k < H; k++)
22           {
23               int i, j, temp;
24               for (i = k + H; i < N; i += H)
25                 {
26                     temp = list[i];
27                     j = i;
28                     while (list[j - H] > temp)
29                       {
30                           list[j] = list[j - H];
31                           j -= H;
32                           if (j <= H) break;
33                       }
```

---

[2] Vaughan Ronald Pratt (b. 1944), American researcher, specializing in the fields of informatics and computing.

[3] Thomas Nathaniel Hibbard (1929–2016), American researcher in the field of computer science.

```
34              list[j] = temp;
35           }
36        }
37     }
38     // final run with the increment equal to 1
39     for(int i = 1; i < N; i++)
40        {
41           int temp = list[i];
42           int j = i - 1;
43           while ((j >= 0) && (list[j] > temp))
44              {
45                 list[j + 1] = list[j];
46                 list[j] = temp;
47                 j--;
48              }
49        }
50 }
51
52 int main(void)
53 {
54    int * a;
55
56    a = (int *)malloc(N*sizeof(int));
57    if ( a == NULL )
58       {
59          perror("\nError allocating memory  " \
60                 "for array a");
61          exit(EXIT_FAILURE);
62       }
63    for(int i = 0; i < N; i++)
64       a[i] = N - i;
65
66    // L - size of increment array h[]
67    int L = (int)floor(log2(N));
68    int * h = (int *)malloc(L*sizeof(int));
69
70    hfill(h,L);
71
72    double t1 = omp_get_wtime();
73    Shellsort(a,h,L);
74    double t2 = omp_get_wtime();
75    free(a); free(h);
76    printf("\nAlgorithm execution time: " \
77           "%lf sec.\n", t2 - t1);
```

```
78 |    return 0;
79 | }
```

The loop iterations over the variable k are distributed over various computing nodes [10]. The procedure hfill (h, L) fills the integer array h [], of size L, with the increment values suggested by Hibbard [30, 34]: 1, 3, 7, 15, 31, 63, ... Each element in this sequence is equal to the sum of twice the previous element and one. It is known that the running time of the sequential algorithm is $O(N^{3/2})$ in the worst case [34].

The procedure Shellsort (a, h, L) performs ordering of the array a, based on the increments stored in the array h. The parallel version of the algorithm is realized by distribution of the outer loop iterations over the variable s among the available threads.

The asymptotic complexity of the parallel version of Shellsort was investigated in [38]. The speedup values are shown as a function of p in Fig. 6.4. The dependence of S_p on p, as can be seen from this figure, is a monotonic but nonlinear function. With increasing p, the growth rate of the speedup decreases; this is due to the limitations on access to the cells of the random access memory in the computing system.

To conclude this section on data-ordering algorithms, let us consider *merge sort*.

The merge sort algorithm runs as follows: it partitions an array into two parts of equal size (to an accuracy of one element), sorts each part, and then unites them into a single array. The operation of merging of the sorted parts is based on the following operations. A one-element array is sorted, by definition, so in this case the sort function performs no actions. An array consisting of two or more elements is partitioned at each step into two parts of equal size (to an accuracy of one element), and then each part is recursively sorted, following which the two parts are united into one sorted array.

Recursive calls of the function mergesort_par (see Listing 6.4) can be performed in different threads, since the actions performed by them are independent. For parallelization, we place these functions in parallel sections with the help of the directive #pragma omp section.

Fig. 6.4 Speedup of the computational part of the Shellsort program code as a function of the number of threads p

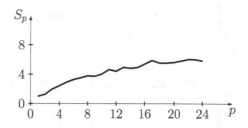

Listing 6.4

```
1  #include <stdio.h>
2  #include <stdlib.h>
3  #include <string.h>
4  #include <omp.h>
5
6  #define N 128*1024*1024
7
8  void merge(int * list, int size, int * temp)
9  {
10   int i = 0, j = size / 2, k = 0;
11   while(i < size/2 && j < size)
12     {
13        if (list[i] <= list[j])
14          {
15             temp[k] = list[i];
16             i++;
17          }
18        else
19          {
20             temp[k] = list[j];
21             j++;
22          }
23        k++;
24     }
25   while (i < size/2)
26     {
27        temp[k] = list[i];
28        i++;
29        k++;
30     }
31   while (j < size)
32     {
33        temp[k] = list[j];
34        j++;
35        k++;
36     }
37   memcpy(list, temp, size*sizeof(int));
38 }
39
40 void mergesort_seq(int * list, int size, \
41                    int * temp)
42 {
43   if (size == 2)
```

```
44        {
45          if (list[0] <= list[1])
46            return;
47          else
48            {  // exchanging values a[0] and a[1]
49              int t = list[0];
50              list[0] = list[1];
51              list[1] = t;
52              return;
53            }
54        }
55    mergesort_seq(list, size/2, temp);
56    mergesort_seq(list+size/2,size-size/2,temp);
57    merge(list, size, temp);
58 }
59
60 void mergesort_par(int *list, int size, \
61                    int *temp, int threads)
62 {
63    if ( threads == 1 )
64      mergesort_seq(list, size, temp);
65    else
66      if ( threads > 1 )
67        {
68            #pragma omp parallel sections
69            {
70                #pragma omp section
71                mergesort_par(list, size/2,    \
72                              temp, threads/2);
73                #pragma omp section
74                mergesort_par(list + size/2, \
75                  size-size/2, temp + size/2, \
76                  threads-threads/2);
77            }
78          merge(list, size, temp);
79        }
80 }
81
82 int main()
83 {
84    int * a, * temp, i, num_threads;
85
86    a = (int *)malloc(N*sizeof(int));
87    if ( a == NULL )
```

```
88    {
89        perror("\nError allocating memory "
90                " for array a");
91        exit(EXIT_FAILURE);
92    }
93    temp = (int *)malloc(N*sizeof(int));
94    if ( temp == NULL )
95    {
96        perror("\nError allocating memory "
97                "for array temp");
98        exit(EXIT_FAILURE);
99    }
100
101   // array initialization with natural numbers
102   // in reverse order
103   for (i=0; i<N; i++)
104     a[i] = N-i;
105
106   #pragma omp parallel
107   {
108       #pragma omp single
109         num_threads = omp_get_num_threads();
110   }
111
112   double t1 = omp_get_wtime();
113   mergesort_par(a, N, temp, num_threads);
114   double t2 = omp_get_wtime();
115
116   printf("Run time of parallel merge sort "
117           "is equal to %lf sec.\n", t2-t1);
118   free(a); free(temp);
119   return 0;
120 }
```

The speedup values S_p for merge sort are shown as a function of p in Fig. 6.5. For $p \geqslant 2$, the speedup is almost independent of the number of threads, which is due to a peculiarity of the parallelization of this sort algorithm, namely the availability of two parallel sections only.

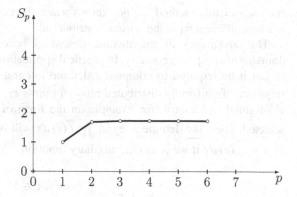

Fig. 6.5 Speedup S_p of the computational part of the merge sort program code as a function of the number of threads p

6.3 Parallel Implementation of the Monte Carlo Method

The Monte Carlo method of solution of computational problems is based on the use of statistical sampling. This method is most widely used in problems of numerical integration over multidimensional domains, solving partial differential equations, and mathematical modeling of physical, biological, economic, and other processes [57, 58].

Consider N points belonging to some subset $\mathcal{V}$ of a space $\mathbb{R}^k$, where $k \geqslant 1$, $\mathbf{r}_1, \mathbf{r}_2, \ldots, \mathbf{r}_N$. The volume of $\mathcal{V}$ is equal to V. For a function $f(\mathbf{r})$, defined and integrable on $\mathcal{V}$, we introduce the mean of the function, $\langle f \rangle = (1/N) \sum_{i=1}^{N} f(\mathbf{r}_i)$, and the mean of the square of the function, $\langle f^2 \rangle = (1/N) \sum_{i=1}^{N} f^2(\mathbf{r}_i)$.

The basis of the Monte Carlo method for the computation of an integral of a multidimensional function is the relation

$$\int_{\mathcal{V}} f(\mathbf{r}) \, d\mathbf{r} = \left(V \langle f \rangle \right)_{\pm \Delta},$$

where the variable $\Delta = V\sqrt{(\langle f^2 \rangle - (\langle f \rangle)^2)/N}$ defines the confidence interval, and the notation $(A)_{\pm B}$ means that with a probability corresponding to one standard deviation, the following membership relation is fulfilled:

$$\int_{\mathcal{V}} f(\mathbf{r}) \, d\mathbf{r} \in \left(V \langle f \rangle - \Delta, \, V \langle f \rangle + \Delta \right).$$

The above estimate for the integral can be deduced if we assume that the error distribution follows a Gaussian[4] law [57]. Unfortunately, strict estimates of the

---

[4] Johann Carl Friedrich Gauss (1777–1855), a prominent German mathematician and astronomer.

accuracy of this method are not known when the errors are distributed according to a law different from the normal distribution.

The advantages of the method described become apparent for integration domains of complex geometry. In practical applications, we proceed as follows.

Let it be required to compute a definite integral $I = \int_V f(\mathbf{r}) \, d\mathbf{r}$. For this, a sequence of uniformly distributed random points $\mathbf{r}_1, \mathbf{r}_2, \ldots, \mathbf{r}_N$ in a domain $\tilde{V} \supset V$ of simple geometry (for example, in the form of a multidimensional cube) is selected. Then, the definite integral $\int_{\tilde{V}} \tilde{f}(\mathbf{r}) \, d\mathbf{r}$ will be equal to the sought value of $I = \int_V f(\mathbf{r}) \, d\mathbf{r}$ if we select the auxiliary function

$$
\tilde{f}(\mathbf{r}) = \begin{cases} f(\mathbf{r}) & \text{if } \mathbf{r} \in V, \\ 0 & \text{if } \mathbf{r} \notin V. \end{cases}
$$

This assertion follows from the property of additivity of definite integrals:

$$
\int_{\tilde{V}} \tilde{f}(\mathbf{r}) \, d\mathbf{r} = \int_{V \cup (\tilde{V} \setminus V)} \tilde{f}(\mathbf{r}) \, d\mathbf{r} = \int_V \tilde{f}(\mathbf{r}) \, d\mathbf{r} + \int_{\tilde{V} \setminus V} \tilde{f}(\mathbf{r}) \, d\mathbf{r}.
$$

Taking into account the definition of the function $\tilde{f}(\mathbf{r})$, we obtain $\int_{\tilde{V}} \tilde{f}(\mathbf{r}) \, d\mathbf{r} = \int_V f(\mathbf{r}) \, d\mathbf{r} = I$.

Algorithms based on the Monte Carlo method usually contain computation loops with a small number of dependencies between the operators and can easily be parallelized with the help of OpenMP directives.

Example 6.1 Show that an arbitrary point of the Cartesian plane $M \in [0, 1] \times [0, 1]$ falls within a sector of a circle with its center at the origin of coordinates, limited to the first quadrant of the plane, with a probability $p = \pi/4$. Using this fact, estimate the value of the number π by the Monte Carlo method.

Solution The value of π can be estimated as follows. It is well known that the area of the quadrant of the unit circle in the first quadrant of the Cartesian plane is equal to $\pi/4$. This is equivalent to the assertion that an arbitrary point $M \in \mathcal{D} = [0, 1] \times [0, 1]$ lies in this sector with probability $p = \pi/4$. Hence, the double integral of the function

$$
f(x, y) = \begin{cases} 1 & \text{if } x^2 + y^2 \leqslant 1, \\ 0 & \text{if } x^2 + y^2 > 1, \end{cases}
$$

taken over the domain $\mathcal{D}$, is equal to $\iint_{\mathcal{D}} f(x, y) \, dx \, dy = \pi/4$, and therefore

$$
\pi = 4 \iint_{\mathcal{D}} f(x, y) \, dx \, dy.
$$

We estimate this integral with the help of the Monte Carlo method:

$$\iint\limits_{\mathcal{D}} f(x, y)\, dx\, dy = \left(\frac{1}{N_1 N_2} \sum_{i=1}^{N_1} \sum_{j=1}^{N_2} f(x_i, y_j) \right)_{\pm \Delta}.$$

To investigate the error of the method, we note that $\langle f^2 \rangle = \pi/4$ and $(\langle f \rangle)^2 = (\pi/4)^2$. Then,

$$\Delta = \sqrt{\frac{1}{N} \left(\langle f^2 \rangle - (\langle f \rangle)^2 \right)} = \sqrt{\frac{1}{N} \left(\frac{\pi}{4} - \left(\frac{\pi}{4}\right)^2 \right)} = \frac{c}{\sqrt{N}},$$

where $c = \sqrt{(\pi/4)(1 - \pi/4)}$ is a constant. So, the computational error in the integral $\iint_{\mathcal{D}} f(x, y)\, dx\, dy$ and, hence, in the number π is $\Delta = \Theta(N^{-1/2})$.

The program code for the estimation of π by the Monte Carlo method is shown in Listing 6.5. The number of sample points is taken equal to $N = 10^{10}$, which ensures an absolute error equal to $\Delta = c/\sqrt{10^{10}} = 4.105\ldots \times 10^{-6}$.

Listing 6.5

```
1   #include <stdio.h>
2   #include <stdlib.h>
3   #include <omp.h>
4
5   const long int N = 1e10;
6
7   int main(void)
8   {
9       double x, y;
10      long int i, count = 0;
11      struct drand48_data buf;  // structure buf
12                                // is required
13                                // for operation
14                                // of the functions
15                                // srand48_r() and
16                                // drand48_r()
17      unsigned int seed;
18
19      #pragma omp parallel default(none)   \
20                   private(i,x,y,seed,buf)  \
21                   shared(count)
22      {
23          seed = omp_get_thread_num();
24          srand48_r(seed, &buf);
25          #pragma omp for reduction(+:count)
```

```
26        for (i = 0; i < N; i++)
27        {
28            drand48_r(&buf, &x);
29            drand48_r(&buf, &y);
30            if ( x*x + y*y <= 1.0 ) count++;
31        }
32    }
33
34    double pi = (double)4*count/N;
35    printf("Pi is approximately equal to %.5lf\n", \
36           pi);
37    return 0;
38 }
```

To obtain a pseudorandom number sequence, the program uses the functions
srand48_r() and drand48_r() [41]. These functions satisfy modern requirements on pseudorandom number generators for use in numerical computation
programs. In comparison with the functions srand() and rand() in the standard
library of the C language [58], which are not recommended for use in multithreaded
applications, these functions have better statistical properties. The symbols _r in the
function names indicate that they can be called from various threads (thread safety).

Note that the parameter seed used in the algorithm must have different values
for different threads; this decreases the error of the method. With different values of
seed, the pseudorandom number sequences in different threads will not coincide,
which results in independence of the sampling points in the algorithm, and hence to
a reduction in the error of this method.   □

The advantages of the Monte Carlo, or statistical test, method include [58]:

• the simplicity of the idea and implementation;
• the possibility of working with domains of complex geometry;
• the size of the error does not depend on the size of the problem, which is of great
  importance when solving multidimensional problems;
• the relatively simple parallelizing.

However, among the drawbacks, we should mention the complexity of obtaining
a guaranteed estimate of the accuracy of the result in many cases, and the
nondeterminacy of the resulting algorithms and the requirement for high quality
of the random (or pseudorandom) value generator used in the implementation of
the method. Apart from this, the error of the method decreases with growth of the
number of points used N according to the law $\Theta(N^{-1/2})$, i.e., more slowly than
with many deterministic methods.

6.4 Matrix Operations in OpenMP

Among the most commonly used operations in mathematical computing are operations with matrices. Working with matrices on high-performance computer systems has its own peculiarities, which will be considered using the examples of the matrix transposition and matrix multiplication problems.

We consider a rectangular matrix *list* of size $N_1 \times N_2$, whose elements are real numbers $(list)_{ij}$, where $i = 1, 2, \ldots, N_1$ is the row number in the matrix, and $j = 1, 2, \ldots, N_2$ is the column number.

We need to make a remark concerning the implementation of matrix algorithms in the C programming language. When using this language, there is a choice between two ways of representing a matrix in the memory of the computing system. In the first method, each row of the matrix *list* is viewed as a one-dimensional array, and for access to the elements in a program we define a pointer to an array of pointers addressing these arrays or rows. The second method consists in representing the matrix *list* in the form of a one-dimensional array of size $N_1 \times N_2$, where the rows of the matrix are written sequentially.

In parallel programming, the second method is more common, and it will be used in the program code examples in this section. In particular, the memory area for placement of the elements of a real matrix *list* can be allocated as follows, for example:

```
double * list;
list = (double *)malloc(N1*N2*sizeof(double));
```
Recall that in the C language the array element numbering starts at zero. Because of this, the variable $(list)_{ij}$ in the one-dimensional array `list` corresponds to the element `list[k]` with index $k = (i - 1)N_1 + (j - 1)$.

Let us proceed to consideration of matrix transposition and matrix multiplication algorithms.

As is well known, the problem of transposing a matrix *list* consists in finding a matrix $list^T$ such that for all $i \in \{1, 2, \ldots, N_1\}$ and $j \in \{1, 2, \ldots, N_2\}$ the equalities $(list^T)_{ij} = (list)_{ji}$ are satisfied. In the transposed matrix, each row is written in the form of a column of the initial matrix in the same order.

Of course, the transposition problem presents no difficulty as far as the realization of the program is concerned if it is possible to place in the memory of the computing system a data area in which $list^T$ is formed by simple copying of elements. In high-performance computing, however, the size of the random access memory is usually limited, and so algorithms that use additional memory of the minimum possible size are of special interest.

Let us begin with the simplest special case, which is nevertheless very important in practical applications, namely the transposition of a square matrix.

Let $N_1 = N_2 = N$ and let the size of the array `list` be equal to N^2. The elements $(list)_{ij}$ and $(list)_{ji}$ need to exchange values during transposition. As already mentioned, the variable $(list)_{ij}$ in the one-dimensional array `list` corresponds to the element with index $k = (i - 1)N + (j - 1)$, and hence the variable $(list)_{ji}$ corresponds to the element with index $l = (j - 1)N + (i - 1)$ (recall that $i = 1, 2, \ldots, N_1$ is the row number, and $j = 1, 2, \ldots, N_2$ is the column number). The operation of exchange of the data stored in the cells `list[k]` and `list[l]` forms the basis of the square-matrix transposition algorithm.

An example of a function `transpose_sq_matr()` that realizes this algorithm without using additional memory is shown below:

```
void transpose_sq_matr(double * list, const int N)
{
    int i,j;
    #pragma omp parallel for schedule(static)
        for(i = 0; i < N; i++)
            for(j = 0; j < i; j++)
                swap( &list[i*N + j], &list[j*N + i] );
}
```

Here, the auxiliary function `swap(a,b)` is used, which performs an exchange of the values stored at the addresses a and b.

Several different algorithms are known that transpose nonsquare matrices. Here, we consider one of them that is easily parallelized [18].

Let $N_2 > N_1$, i.e., the number of columns of the rectangular matrix *list* is greater than the number of rows. Let us expand the matrix to a square one via adding empty cells "•" at the end of each column, as shown in the scheme below, where we take $N_1 = 2, N_2 = 3$:

$$list = \begin{pmatrix} list_{11} & list_{12} & list_{13} \\ list_{21} & list_{22} & list_{23} \end{pmatrix} \xrightarrow[\text{empty cells}]{\text{addition}} list' = \begin{pmatrix} list_{11} & list_{12} & list_{13} \\ list_{21} & list_{22} & list_{23} \\ \bullet & \bullet & \bullet \end{pmatrix}.$$

To the matrix *list'* formed in this way, we apply the square-matrix transposition algorithm:

$$(list')^{\mathrm{T}} = \begin{pmatrix} list_{11} & list_{21} & \bullet \\ list_{12} & list_{22} & \bullet \\ list_{13} & list_{23} & \bullet \end{pmatrix}.$$

After performing this procedure, it is necessary to parallelize the data in the one-dimensional array that represents $(list')^{\mathrm{T}}$ in such a manner that all the empty cells are placed at the end of the array. Then the first $N_1 \times N_2$ elements of this array form the final answer—the standard representation of $list^{\mathrm{T}}$ in the computer memory.

The case $N_2 < N_1$ is considered similarly.

We name the realization of this algorithm `transpose_rect_matr()`. We can give a description of this function as follows (see Problem 6.8):

```
void transpose_rect_matr(double * list,
                     const int N1, const int N2);
```

The investigation of the rectangular-matrix transposition algorithm presents no difficulty. It is easy to see that the running time of the algorithm on a multiprocessor computing system satisfies the relation

$$T_p(N_1, N_2) = O\left(\frac{1}{p}(M(M-1)/2 + L(M-1))\right),$$

where the notation $M = \max(N_1, N_2)$ and $L = \min(N_1, N_2)$ has been introduced. The realization of the function `transpose_rect_matr()` requires additional memory of size $\max(N_1, N_2)^2 - N_1 N_2$.

We now consider the problem of computing the product of matrices *listA* and *listB*, where *listA* is a matrix of size $N_1 \times N_2$ and *listB* is a matrix of size $N_2 \times N_3$, so that the resulting matrix, *listC*, has a size $N_1 \times N_3$.

The formula that determines the elements $(listC)_{ij}$, $i = 1, 2, \ldots, N_1$, $j = 1, 2, \ldots, N_3$, can be presented in the form

$$(listC)_{ij} = \sum_{k=1}^{N_2} (listA)_{ik}(listB)_{kj}.$$

A direct realization of this relation will lead to a program that less than fully uses the possibilities of working with memory on modern computing systems. In the loop over the variable k, the elements of the matrix *listA* are read by row, which allows access to $(listA)_{ik}$ to be accelerated by intensive use of cache memory. However, the sampling of the elements $(listA)_{kj}$ is performed by column, and this considerably decreases the speed of the algorithm.

Instead, we can apply a transposition operation to the matrix *listB*. In this case, both the elements of the matrix *listA* and the elements of the matrix *listB* can be uploaded from the cache memory.

The program code of a function `matr_mult()` that realizes the algorithm described above is shown below:

```
void matr_mult(double * listA, double * listB, double * listC,
               const int N1, const int N2, const int N3)
{
   // transposition of matrix listB
   transpose_rect_matr(listB, N2, N3);
   #pragma omp parallel
      {
         int i,j,k;
         #pragma omp for
           for(i=0; i<N1; i++)
              {
                 for(j=0; j<N3; j++)
                    {
                       double temp = 0.0;
```

```
                    for(k=0; k<N2; k++)
                        temp += listA[i*N2+k]*listB[j*N2+k];
                    listC[i*N3+j] = temp;
                }
            }
        }
    // repeated transposition of matrix listB
    // results in its initial form
    transpose_rect_matr(listB, N2, N3);
}
```

The auxiliary variable temp in this algorithm is used for accumulation of the result to be stored in $(listC)_{ij}$.

When writing high-performance programs, one usually tries to avoid the introduction of variables not essential for the running of the program. In this case, however, for computer systems with some architectures, the introduction of an auxiliary variable is justified, since it results in more active working with memory.

We begin the analysis of the matrix multiplication algorithm with the case of square matrices, $N_1 = N_2 = N_3 = N$. The asymptotic complexity of the outer computation loop over the variable i of the algorithm matr_mult in the RAM model is $O(N^3)$. The transposition operation in the same model is characterized by a complexity $O(N^2)$. Hence, the multiplication algorithm described above, in the case of square matrices on a multiprocessor computing system, will be executed in time $T_p(N) = O(N^3/p)$.

A similar analysis of nonsquare matrices leads to the relation $T_p(N) = O(N_1 N_2 N_3/p)$.

It should be noted that the algorithm matr_mult remains correct for any sequence of computation loops over the variables i, j, and k in the program code. For this reason, $3! = 6$ options for the matrix multiplication algorithm are possible. The loop sequence in each of these options is defined by one of the following ordered sets:

1. (i, j, k).
2. (i, k, j).
3. (j, i, k).
4. (j, k, i).
5. (k, i, j).
6. (k, j, i).

On some computing systems, a method of computing listC different from the standard use of (i, j, k) considered here may have an advantage owing to working with cache memory, resulting in greater performance [52].

To summarize this chapter, let us list the advantages of the OpenMP technology:

• it offers unity of sequential and parallel program code;
• it offers relatively simple program implementation;

- there is no need to connect additional libraries;
- OpenMP can be used jointly with other parallel programming technologies.

6.5 Test Questions

1. Describe a parallel method of array element summation.
2. Enumerate the sorting algorithms that you know.
3. Describe the operation of parallel versions of odd–even sort, Shellsort, and merge sort.
4. What are the advantages and drawbacks of the Monte Carlo method?
5. How does the matrix transposition algorithm work in shared-memory systems?
6. Explain how matrix multiplication is performed using the OpenMP technology.

6.6 Problems

6.1. Demonstrate the operation of a parallel algorithm for calculating the sum of elements using the example of the array

| 20 | 12 | 18 | 16 | 24 | 10 | 22 | 14 |

6.2. Find the main features of the variation with N of the speedup S and efficiency E of an algorithm for calculating the sum of N numbers if $p = N/2$.

6.3. Sort an array of N integers in ascending order with the help of Shellsort for the following increment values:

(a) Increment values equal to h_s, where $h_{s+1} = 3h_s + 1$, $h_0 = 1$, and $0 \leqslant s < \lfloor \log_3(2N + 1) \rfloor - 1$ (the sequence $1, 4, 13, 40, 121, \ldots$, proposed by Knuth[5] [34]).

(b) Increment values equal to h_s, where

$$h_s = \begin{cases} 9 \times 2^s - 9 \times 2^{s/2} + 1 & \text{if } s \text{ is even}, \\ 8 \times 2^s - 6 \times 2^{(s+1)/2} + 1 & \text{if } s \text{ is odd}. \end{cases}$$

The final element is taken to be equal to h_{s-1} provided that $3h_s > N$. (The sequence $1, 5, 19, 41, 109, \ldots$ was proposed by Sedgewick[6] [34, 65].)

---

[5] Donald Ervin Knuth (b. 1938), an American scientist, specializing in the fields of informatics and computing.

[6] Robert Sedgewick (b. 1946), an American researcher, specializing in the fields of informatics and computer technology.

(c) The sequence of increments is made up of a set of numbers of the form $2^i 3^j$ forming a smaller array, where $i, j \in \mathbb{N} \cup \{0\}$ and $2^i 3^j < N$. Increments are used in descending order. (The sequence $1, 2, 3, 4, 6, 8, 9, \ldots$ was proposed by Pratt [34, 56].)

6.4. The sequential version of the `hfill` procedure is shown on Sect. 6.2. Describe a method for parallelizing the `hfill` procedure for the increment sequences proposed by:

(a) Hibbard;
(b) Knuth;
(c) Sedgewick;
(d) Pratt.

*6.5. Sort an array of N integers in ascending order using quicksort with the OpenMP technology. Analyze the main characteristics of the parallel algorithm used.

6.6. Using the Monte Carlo method, calculate the triple integral

$$\mathcal{J} = \iiint\limits_{V} e^{-(x_1^2 + x_2^2 + x_3^2)}\, dx_1\, dx_2\, dx_3$$

with an absolute error μ not exceeding 10^{-5}, if the domain V is defined as

(a) a cube, $-1 \leqslant x_1, x_2, x_3 \leqslant 1$;
(b) a rectangular parallelepiped, $-1 \leqslant x_1 \leqslant 1$, $1 \leqslant x_2 \leqslant 2$, $-2 \leqslant x_3 \leqslant 3$;
(c) a ball, $x_1^2 + x_2^2 + x_3^2 \leqslant 1$;
(d) an ellipsoid of revolution, $x_1^2 + x_2^2 + x_3^2/2 \leqslant 1$.

6.7. Using the Monte Carlo method, calculate the improper integral

$$\mathcal{K} = \int\limits_{1}^{\infty} \sqrt{x}\, e^{-x^2} dx$$

with an absolute error μ not exceeding 10^{-5}.

6.8. Write a function for rectangular-matrix transposition `transpose_rect_matr()` (see Sect. 6.4).

6.9. The hard disks of a file server store $N = 5 \times 10^5$ files. The size in bytes of each of these files is assumed to be a uniformly distributed random integer variable V that takes values $0 < V \leqslant V_{\max}$, where $V_{\max} = 10^{10}$ is the maximum possible value of the file size. With an absolute error no greater than $\mu = 10^{-8}$, find the probability that at least two files have the same size.

6.10. Solve the previous problem for the parameter values $N = 1.5 \times 10^8$, $V_{\max} = 10^{15}$.

6.11. The hard disks of a file server store N files. The size in bytes of each of these files is assumed to be a uniformly distributed random integer variable V that takes values $0 < V \leqslant V_{max}$, where $V_{max} = 10^9$ is the maximum possible value of the file size. Find the smallest N for which the probability that at least two files have the same size exceeds the threshold value $p^* = 0.5$.

6.12. Solve the previous problem for the parameter value $V_{max} = 10^{10}$.

6.13. Show that the analytical solution of Problem 6.11 satisfies the relation $N = \sqrt{2 \ln 2\, V_{max}} + O\left(1/\sqrt{V_{max}}\right)$.

6.14. Implement a parallel algorithm for the fast Fourier transform using the OpenMP technology.

6.15. Using the OpenMP technology, implement a parallel algorithm for computing the two-dimensional discrete Fourier transform of an array $x[0..(N_1 - 1), 0..(N_2 - 1)]$,

$$(\mathcal{F}[x])_{n_1,n_2} = \sum_{k_1=0}^{N_1-1} \sum_{k_2=0}^{N_2-1} \omega_1^{k_1 n_1} \omega_2^{k_2 n_2} x_{k_1,k_2},$$

where $\omega_1 = e^{2\pi i/N_1}$ and $\omega_2 = e^{2\pi i/N_2}$.

*6.16. The known but unsolved "$3N + 1$" hypothesis [39] can be stated as follows. The members of a recurrence sequence $\{a_n\}$, $n \in \{0\} \cup \mathbb{N}$, are defined for all $n \geqslant 1$ in accordance with the following rule: *if the previous member of the sequence a_{n-1} is divisible by 2, then $a_n = a_{n-1}/2$, otherwise $a_n = 3a_{n-1}+1$.* The "$3N+1$" conjecture says that at some step of this procedure, with number f, the value $a_f = 1$ inevitably appears. The minimum number of steps f is referred as the *path length to one*. The sequence $\{a_n\}$ formed in this way is known as the *Collatz[7] sequence.*

With the help of a parallel program, check the validity of the "$3N + 1$" conjecture for all initial values of a_0 not exceeding a specified constant L, and output to a file `output.txt` the maximum path length to one among such sequences. The constant L is written in a file `input.txt`.

---

[7] Lothar Collatz (1910–1990), German mathematician.

Appendix A
Methods for Estimation of Algorithm Efficiency

When analyzing the efficiency of an algorithm, it is essential to estimate the operating time of the computer required to solve the problem, as well as the amount of memory used. For this purpose, a special mathematical apparatus is used, which is briefly presented in this appendix.

A.1 "Big O" Notation

An estimate of the running time of a computing system is usually obtained by calculating the number of elementary operations performed during computing (such operations are referred to as *basic* operations). With the supposition that one elementary operation is performed in a strictly defined time, the function $f(n)$, defined as the number of operations during computing on input data of size n, is called the *time complexity function* [42].

We introduce the notation $\mathbb{R}^+ = (0, \infty)$ for the set of positive real numbers and consider functions $f, g \colon \mathbb{N} \to \mathbb{R}^+$.

Three classes of functions are distinguished with respect to the growth rate $g(n)$.

1. *The class of functions growing no faster than* $g(n)$ is denoted by $O(g(n))$ and is defined as

$$O(g(n)) = \{f(n) \colon \exists c \in \mathbb{R}^+, \ n_0 \in \mathbb{N} \ \text{ such that for all } \ n \geqslant n_0$$

$$f(n) \leqslant cg(n) \text{ is valid}\}.$$

It is said that a function $f(n)$ belongs to the class $O(g(n))$ (read as "big O of g") if, for all values of the argument n, starting from a threshold value $n = n_0$,

© Springer Nature Switzerland AG 2019
S. Kurgalin, S. Borzunov, *A Practical Approach to High-Performance Computing*,
https://doi.org/10.1007/978-3-030-27558-7

the inequality $f(n) \leqslant cg(n)$ is valid for some positive c. The notation $f(n) \in O(g(n))$ may be read as "the function g *majorizes* (dominates) the function f."

2. *The class of functions growing at least as fast as $g(n)$* is denoted by $\Omega(g(n))$ and is defined as

$$\Omega(g(n)) = \{f(n) \colon \exists c \in \mathbb{R}^+, \ n_0 \in \mathbb{N} \ \text{ such that for all } \ n \geqslant n_0$$

$$f(n) \geqslant cg(n) \text{ is valid}\}.$$

It is said that $f(n)$ belongs to the class $\Omega(g(n))$ (read as "big omega of g") if, for all values of the argument n, starting from a threshold value $n = n_0$, the inequality $f(n) \geqslant cg(n)$ is valid for some positive c.

3. *The class of functions growing at the same rate as $g(n)$* is denoted by $\Theta(g(n))$ and is defined as the intersection of $O(g(n))$ and $\Omega(g(n))$. It is said that $f(n)$ belongs to the class $\Theta(g(n))$ (read as "big theta of g") if

$$f(n) \in O(g(n)) \cap \Omega(g(n)).$$

These definitions are illustrated in Figs. A.1 and A.2; for the purposes of illustration, the argument n is assumed to be real.

Since $O(g(n))$ denotes a set of functions growing no faster than the function $g(n)$, then, in order to indicate that a function belongs to this set, the notation $f(n) \in O(g(n))$ is used. Another notation is rather common in the literature: $f(n) = O(g(n))$, where the equals sign is understood conventionally, namely in the sense of belonging to the set. The classes of sets listed above are referred to as the "*big O notation*."

We now state some important properties of asymptotic relations [13, 40].

Let $f_1, f_2, g_1, g_2 \colon \mathbb{N} \to \mathbb{R}^+$. If $f_1(n) = O(g_1(n))$ and $f_2(n) = O(g_2(n))$, then the following are true:

1. $f_1(n) + f_2(n) = O(\max(g_1(n), g_2(n)))$.
2. $f_1(n) f_2(n) = O(g_1(n) g_2(n))$.

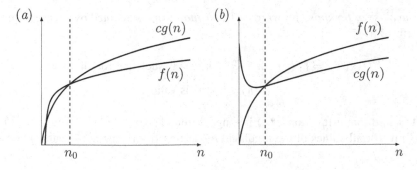

Fig. A.1 Illustration of the notation (**a**) $f(n) \in O(g(n))$ and (**b**) $f(n) \in \Omega(g(n))$

Fig. A.2 Illustration of
notation $f(n) \in \Theta(g(n))$

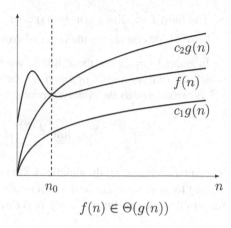

$$f(n) \in \Theta(g(n))$$

Polynomial Growth Rate Lemma *A polynomial of the form*

$$p(n) = a_d n^d + a_{d-1} n^{d-1} + \ldots + a_0,$$

where $a_d > 0$, belongs to the set $\Theta(n^d)$.

According to the above lemma, the asymptotic behavior of a polynomial function is fully determined by the degree of the polynomial.

When analyzing algorithms, the problem often arises of obtaining an approximation to the "factorial" function, and in such cases it is convenient to use *Stirling's*[1] *formula,*

$$n! = \sqrt{2\pi n} \left(\frac{n}{e}\right)^n \left(1 + \Theta\left(\frac{1}{n}\right)\right),$$

where $e = 2.718281828\ldots$ is the base of natural logarithms.

When comparing the growth rates of two functions, it is convenient to use not determinations of whether the functions belong to the set O, Ω, or Θ, but the consequences of such determinations, based on calculation of the limits of the functions under consideration for infinitely great large of their argument [40].

Assume that we need to compare the asymptotic growth rates of two functions f and g, $f, g \colon \mathbb{N} \to \mathbb{R}^+$. For this purpose, we calculate the limit $L = \lim\limits_{n \to \infty} (f(n)/g(n))$.

Four cases are possible:

1. $L = 0$. Then $f(n) = O(g(n))$ and $f(n) \neq \Theta(g(n))$.
2. $L = c$ for some $c \in \mathbb{R}^+$. Then $f(n) = \Theta(g(n))$.
3. $L = \infty$. Then $f(n) = \Omega(g(n))$ and $f(n) \neq \Theta(g(n))$.

---

[1] James Stirling (1692–1770), Scottish mathematician.

4. The limit $L = \lim\limits_{n\to\infty} (f(n)/g(n))$ does not exist. In this case, this method cannot be used for comparing the order of growth of the functions $f(n)$ and $g(n)$.

In order to calculate these limits, we may use *L'Hôpital's*[2] *rule,* according to which *the limit of a ratio of functions that are infinitely small as* $n \to \infty$ *(if the set* $\mathbb{R}^+$ *is considered as the domain) reduces to the limit of the ratio of their derivatives:*

$$\lim_{n\to\infty} \frac{f(n)}{g(n)} = \lim_{n\to\infty} \frac{f'(n)}{g'(n)}.$$

This relation is valid if the functions $f(n)$ and $g(n)$ are differentiable on the interval (c, ∞) for some c, $g'(x) \neq 0$ for all points $x \in (c, \infty)$ and there exists a limit of the ratio of derivatives $\lim\limits_{n\to\infty} (f'(n)/g'(n))$ (finite or infinite).

Example A.1 Arrange the following functions in order of increasing growth rate:

$$n^2 + \log_2 n, \quad 2^{n-2}, \quad n \log_2 n, \quad n!, \quad e^{n/2}.$$

Solution We introduce the notation $f_1(n) = n^2 + \log_2 n$, $f_2(n) = 2^{n-2}$, $f_3(n) = n \log_2 n$, $f_4(n) = n!$, and $f_5(n) = e^{n/2}$.

The growth rate of polynomial functions is less than the growth rate of exponential ones; therefore, the first position in the list of functions in order of increasing growth rate will be occupied by either $f_1(n)$, or $f_3(n)$. Let us find the limit $L = \lim\limits_{n\to\infty} (f_3(n)/f_1(n))$:

$$L = \lim_{n\to\infty} \frac{f_3(n)}{f_1(n)} = \lim_{n\to\infty} \frac{n \log_2 n}{n^2 + \log_2 n} = \lim_{n\to\infty} \frac{\log_2 n}{n + (\log_2 n)/n} = 0.$$

Based on the value $L = 0$ obtained for the limit, we conclude that the first position in the list is occupied by the function $f_3(n)$, and the second by $f_1(n)$, since $f_1(n) = O(f_2(n))$ and $f_1(n) = O(f_5(n))$.

Then, we compare the growth rates of $f_2(n)$ and $f_5(n)$:

$$L = \lim_{n\to\infty} \frac{f_5(n)}{f_2(n)} = \lim_{n\to\infty} \frac{e^{n/2}}{2^{n-2}} = \lim_{n\to\infty} 4\left(\frac{e^{1/2}}{2}\right)^n = 0,$$

since $e^{1/2} < 2$.

The function $f_4(n) = n!$, as follows from Stirling's formula, has the greatest growth rate among all the functions in this example; in the final list, $f_4(n)$ will occupy the last position.

---

[2] Guillaume François Antoine, marquis de L'Hôpital (1661–1704), French mathematician.

We finally obtain the list of functions in order of increasing growth rate:

$$n \log_2 n, \quad n^3 + \log_2 n, \quad e^{n/2}, \quad 2^{n-2}, \quad n!.$$

$\square$

Note The notation "$O(f)$" was introduced by Bachmann[3] in a textbook [4] on number theory. Sometimes the "$O(f)$" symbols are called *Landau*[4] *symbols* [26]. The modern use of "big O" notation in algorithm analysis is attributed to Knuth [13].

A.2   Asymptotic Analysis Methods

Asymptotic analysis methods are used to perform mathematically correct estimation of the execution time of algorithms and of the memory used, as a function of the size of the problem.

When analyzing algorithms, the number of *basic operations* is estimated, and it is assumed that for execution of each of the operations listed below a time $\Theta(1)$ is required [45]:

1. Binary arithmetic operations ($+$, $-$, $*$, $/$) and operations of comparison of real numbers ($<$, $\leqslant$, $>$, $\geqslant$, $=$, $\neq$).
2. Logic operations ($\vee$, $\wedge$, $^-$, $\oplus$).
3. Branching operations.
4. Calculation of the values of elementary functions for relatively small values of their arguments.

For different input data, the execution times of an algorithm may differ, in general.

Three cases are distinguished, allowing one to judge the overall efficiency of an algorithm:

1. *The best case.* The best case for an algorithm is when it has a set of input data for which the execution time is the minimum. On such a set, the number of basic operations $B(n)$ is determined by the formula

$$B(n) = \min_{\substack{\text{input} \\ \text{data}}} T(n).$$

---

[3] Paul Gustav Heinrich Bachmann (1837–1920), German mathematician.
[4] Edmund Georg Hermann Landau (1877–1938), German mathematician.

2. *The worst case.* The worst case for an algorithm is when it has a set of input data for which the execution time is the maximum:

$$W(n) = \max_{\substack{\text{input} \\ \text{data}}} T(n).$$

3. *The average case.* Analysis of the average case implies partitioning the set of all possible input data into nonintersecting classes in such a manner that for each of the classes generated the number of basic operations is the same. Then, the expectation value of the number of operations is calculated based on the probability distribution of the input data:

$$A(N) = \sum_{i=1}^{k} p_i(N) t_i(N),$$

where n is the input data size, k is the number of classes in the partition, $p_i(n)$ is the probability that the input data belong to the class with number i, and $t_i(n)$ is the number of basic operations performed by the algorithm on the input data from the class with number i.

Recall that the *probability p* of an event is a real number $0 \leqslant p \leqslant 1$. If the total number of outcomes is N and all outcomes are equally probable, then the probability of realization of each of them is $p = 1/N$ [29].

Table A.1 shows the most common asymptotic complexity values in practice, with examples of algorithms that have that complexity in the average case.

Table A.1 Asymptotic complexity of algorithms

Asymptotic complexity	Growth rate	Example of algorithm
$O(1)$	Constant, not dependent on the size of input data	Search in hash table
$O(\log_2 n)$	Logarithmic	Binary search
$O(n)$	Linear	Linear search
$O(n \log_2 n)$	*No generally accepted name*	Merge sort
$O(n^2)$	Quadratic	Insertion sort
$O(n^3)$	Cubic	Standard multiplication of matrices
$O(2^n)$	Exponential	Exhaustive search
$O(n!)$	Factorial	Generation of all permutations

Appendix B
Using the Linux Shell to Run Parallel Programs

At present, most high-performance computing systems run under the Linux operating system. According to information from the TOP500 project for June 2017, the share of this operating system was more than 99% in the ratings for the most powerful computers in the world, and since November 2017 all supercomputers in the TOP500 list have been running under Linux [75]. For this reason, this appendix offers same brief information about using the Linux operating system for running parallel programs.

B.1 The Command Interpreter of the Linux Operating System

Linux is one of the best-known freely distributed operating systems. The starting point of Linux's history is the year 1991, when Torvalds[1] started working on the kernel of a UNIX-compatible operating system. Later, this development was complemented with utilities and programs written as part of the GNU project [33]. Strictly speaking, at present, the name "Linux" means the kernel of the operating system, which, taking into account the role of the system and application programs of the GNU project, would be better called "GNU/Linux."

All Linux objects, from the user's point of view, are subdivided into two types: *files* and *processes* [33]. All data are stored in the form of files; peripheral devices are accessed via reading from and writing to special files. The functionality of the operating system is achieved via executing system or user processes. During run time, processes can read data and/or write to files.

---

[1] Linus Benedict Torvalds (b. 1969), Finnish–American researcher and software developer.

© Springer Nature Switzerland AG 2019
S. Kurgalin, S. Borzunov, *A Practical Approach to High-Performance Computing*,
https://doi.org/10.1007/978-3-030-27558-7

The *command interpreter*, or *command shell*, is the process that organizes the interaction of the user with the operating system. The most well-known is the Bash shell. The window of the command interpreter is called the *terminal* window. In the mode of remote access to a computing system, the terminal window is the only source of incoming data to the user's display.

When a user logs into the system, a *login* and *password* are requested. After the password has been entered, the terminal window displays a prompt, for example

```
bsv@main:~>
```

Here, `bsv` is the login, `main` is the name of the master computational node, `~` is the current directory, which in this case is the so-called *home* user directory, and `>` is the system prompt symbol of the command interpreter.

For security reasons, it is recommended to change the administrator-defined password during the first working session; the `passwd` command should be used for this.

Commands are entered from the keyboard and initiated by pressing the key ⌨Enter⌨. Many commands have parameters separated by a space.

Program parameters are often referred to as *keys*. Single-character parameters are usually preceded by a hyphen, and parameters of greater length by two hyphens. For example, in order to display brief information about the command `passwd`, it can be started in one of the following equivalent formats:

```
passwd -?
passwd --help
```

(here, the command line prompt has been omitted; we will do this from now on). After executing either of these commands has been executed, succinct information about the command line parameters for the program `passwd` will be displayed.

Basic users may change only their own password, while the *superuser*—the computing system administrator—may change any password and has unrestricted system management abilities.

In Linux, many commands are available, detailed information about them being provided by the command `man`. So, to call the help menu for a particular command, the name `man` is specified as a parameter. For example, one may write `man passwd` or `man man`. In the latter case, the terminal window will display the description and parameters of the command `man` itself. The help menu can be closed by pressing the key ⌨Q⌨.

In the process of typing commands, the user may edit them, navigating the terminal window with the help of the keys ⌨←⌨ and ⌨→⌨, and can also navigate the command history with the help of the keys ⌨↑⌨ and ⌨↓⌨. The control key combinations listed in Table B.1 provide additional options for working with text [36, 80].

When one is typing a command at the console, pressing the tab key ⌨⇥⌨ will result in autofill—automatic insertion of the full command name. If there are several commands beginning with the combination of letters entered, a list of suitable commands will appear. Autofill of a file name entered as a command parameter is done similarly.

The current working session is terminated by the command `exit`.

Table B.1   Control key combinations

Key combination	Command line action
Ctrl + B	Move the cursor to the left
Ctrl + F	Move the cursor to the right
Ctrl + P	Switch to the previous command entered
Ctrl + N	Switch to the next command entered
Ctrl + A	Move the cursor to the start of the line
Ctrl + E	Move the cursor to the end of the line
Alt + B	Move the cursor one word backwards
Alt + F	Move the cursor one word forwards
Ctrl + W	Delete the word before the cursor
Ctrl + K	Delete the text up to the end of the line
Ctrl + Y	Insert deleted text
Ctrl + R	Search for previously entered commands
Ctrl + G	Exit the search mode
Ctrl + _	Undo the last change
Ctrl + L	Clear the screen
Ctrl + C	Interrupt execution of the process launched

Note Access to the parameters of the command line of a program in the C language may be obtained using the following description of the function main():

```
int main( int argc, char * argv[] )
```

In the variable argc, the number of arguments transferred to the command line at the start of the program is written. Each of these arguments is available in the form of a line, addressed by the elements of the pointer array argv. According to established convention, the line argv[0] contains the program name [33].

B.2   The Linux File System

The Linux *file system* is made up of a set of files represented in the form of a hierarchical tree structure [33]. The records of the file system are divided into the files proper and directories. The name of a file defines its position in the file system tree. The *directories* (or *folders*) are a special type of file that stores a table of references to other files. Directories may contain records about files and other directories. The *root directory* has the name "/" and forms the first and highest level of the hierarchical file system. To address all other files, a *path* is used, i.e., a list of the directories that need to be passed through along the tree from the root directory in order to reach that file.

Each directory mandatorily contains the following two records: "." and "..". The record "." is a reference to the directory itself, while the record ".." refers to the *parent directory*, lying one level higher in the directory hierarchy. In the root directory, the reference to the parent directory leads to the path "/", i.e., it points to itself.

The path describing the location of a file with respect to the current directory can be *absolute* or *relative*. Absolute paths begin with the symbol "/" and contain all intermediate levels of the directory tree, starting from the root directory. Relative paths pass through the directory tree starting from the current directory, and they begin with the prefix "..".

Depending on their designation, all files in the Linux operating system are subdivided into six types [33]:

• regular files;
• directories;
• special device files;
• symbolic links;
• named pipes;
• sockets.

Let us consider briefly the peculiarities of each of these types.

Regular files contain data in a certain format. In other words, from the point of view of the operating system, they are just a sequence of bytes. It is regular files that most users usually deal with. Access to the information stored in such a file can be obtained using application programs that take into account the file format, for example text and graphics editors, or data visualization utilities.

Directories contain file names together with service information about them, *metadata*. The metadata are used for organizing the operation of the file system and contain, in particular, data about the size of files, their creation and modification times, and pointers to the data storage areas on the hard disks [33].

Special device files are designed for organizing access to physical devices in the computing system. These device files are subdivided into character and block files, depending on the type of access to the device. Character files work with data streams and are used for unbuffered access to data; block files allow the receiving and sending of data in blocks of a certain length. Character devices include terminals, printers, and mice; as examples of block devices, we can name hard disks, and drives for reading and writing data from and to optical data storage media.

A *symbolic link* points at, or, in other words, refers to another file or directory (the terms "symlink" and "soft link" are also used). In other words, symbolic links are just alternative names pointing at other names. A file specially tagged by the operating system to play the role of a symbolic link contains only the name of the destination (target) file. Since it is possible to refer in this manner to files located outside the root file system (for example, on external data storage media), symbolic links provide a convenient means of shared access to files.

For the avoidance of misunderstanding, note that in Linux the same file can exist under different equivalent names, called *hard links*. Unlike symbolic links, hard links are regular files and cannot be linked to files outside the root file system.

Named pipes are a special type of file for passing data between processes. Data can be transmitted in one direction only through a pipe established between two processes.

Sockets are used to allow interaction between processes, especially in distributed systems. Many system services use the socket mechanism in their operation. Unlike named pipes, a process can both receive and transmit information as a result of the operation of one socket.

Some restrictions are imposed on the names of files and directories. In most systems running under Linux, a file name cannot exceed 255 characters. It is also prohibited to use the symbols "/" ("slash") and the zero symbol "\0" in a file name. Remind that in Linux the *null character* "\0" is a symbol with value equals to zero, and it is used to mark the end of a string of characters [32].

Some elements from the complete set of symbols have a special meaning to the command interpreter and will not be accepted as part of a file name. When one is working in the terminal window, such special symbols should be *escaped*, by being preceded by the "backslash" symbol, "\". Note that the escape procedure is not allowed in some cases. Spaces in file names may be not escaped, but in this case the name should be enclosed in double quotes. For this reason, and for better portability of program code, it is recommended to use in file names only the following symbols from the 65-element set [33]:

- the Latin alphabet letters, a, . . . , z, A, . . . , Z;
- the decimal numbers, 0, . . . , 9;
- the dot, . ;
- the underscore, _;
- the hyphen, -.

Special attention should be paid to the fact that file names are case-sensitive. Those files whose names begin with a dot are deemed to be hidden and are not displayed by default in file managers.

B.3   Basic File System Directories

As previously noted, any absolute path in the file system begins with the root directory "/". Let us enumerate the most important directories that a user may encounter when working in Linux.

/bin contains widely used standard utilities and system programs, including the Bash command interpreter.

/boot contains the operating system kernel and its boot parameter files.

/dev contains the special device files. Because of this, the names of peripheral devices always begin with /dev.

/etc contains the system configuration files. This directory stores information about the global settings of the operating system, especially those pertaining to the initialization procedure.

/home contains the user home directories. For example, to place user files in bsv, a subdirectory /home/bsv is formed here.

/lib contains library files that can be connected to executable files.

/lib64 contains 64-bit versions of the library files.

/lost+found. The presence of files in this directory is indicative of errors in the file system. Here, data are accumulated whose identifying names were lost for some reason. This directory is usually empty in a correctly running operating system.

/mnt is used for temporary acquisition (referred to as *mounting*) of other file systems by the current root file system. Hence, data recorded on portable media, for example flash drives, are available via this directory.

/opt contains additionally installed software.

/proc contains information about all processes being executed and about the computing system as a whole.

/tmp contains temporary files.

/usr contains user programs, their documentation, and their source code.

/var is a directory that is used for storing data that changes with time: logs, reports, print system queues, etc.

B.4   Users and Groups

In the Linux operating system, users are granted rights to own files and to start the execution of programs. Each user is assigned a nonnegative integer, the *identification number* (UID, user identifier). The superuser (for whom the name "root" is usually reserved) has UID = 0 and possesses unlimited rights.

A *user group* is made up of a set of users who have common tasks from the operating system's point of view. These groups are also distinguished by an identifier (GID, group identifier). The group identifiers are nonnegative integers; the group identifier of the superuser is zero.

Lists of the users and groups are stored in files /etc/passwd and /etc/group. For security reasons, the user passwords are stored separately in a file /etc/shadow (the passwords are stored in encrypted form).

The Linux operating system allows simultaneous working of many users. For this reason, the names of the file owner and the owner's group are specified in the file metadata. Linux provides a wide range of opportunities to isolate access to different files and directories.

File attributes can be displayed with the help of the command ls with the parameter -l. For example, execution of the command

```
ls -l /home/bsv/test/test.out
```

will result in the appearance at the console (to be more exact, in the standard output stream; see Sect. B.6.1) of information about a file named `test.out` in the subdirectory `test` of the home user directory `bsv`. The following information will be displayed:

```
-rwxr-x---.  1  bsv  users  4731  Jan  20  10:00
test.out
```

The rights of access to a file are presented in the first column of these data in the following format:

$$au_1u_2u_3g_1g_2g_3o_1o_2o_3,$$

where a denotes the file type (see Sect. B.2):

-, regular file;
d, directory;
l, symbolic link;
b or c, file for a block or character device, respectively;
p, named pipe;
s, socket.

The characters $u_1u_2u_3$ (from <u>u</u>ser) denote the rights of the user who is the owner, $g_1g_2g_3$ (from <u>g</u>roup) denote the rights of the members of the owner of the user's group, and $o_1o_2o_3$ (from <u>o</u>ther) denote the rights of other users. The following designations are used:

r (from <u>r</u>ead): the right to read the file is granted;
w (from <u>w</u>rite): the right to write to the file is granted;
x (from e<u>x</u>ecute): the right to execute the file is granted;
-: there are no rights of access.

In the above example, the owner of the file `test.out` may view the contents of the file (since r is specified), change the file (w), and start its execution (x). The members of the owner's group may view the contents and execute the file, but may not change it. Finally, other users are not allowed to perform any of these actions.

The record in the first column is completed by a dot (.), which means support for the SELinux (Security-Enhanced Linux) access control technology [36, 48].

The number in the second column of the output of the command `ls -l` is the number of hard links pointing to the file (in our example it is equal to one, i.e., only one name is secured for the file).

The following columns contain information about the file owner (third column, `bsv`), the group (fourth column, `users`), and the file size in bytes (fifth column, 4731 bytes). Then follow data about the date and time it was last modified (January 20, 10:00) and, in the final column, the file name (`test.out`).

The command `chmod` is used for changing the access rights:

```
chmod t op z test.out
```

where the argument t can take the values u (change of the user's rights), g (change of the rights of the owner of the user's group, i.e., the "group-owner"), o (change of other users' rights), and a (all of these categories). The argument *op* has the following values:

+, adding rights;
-, deleting rights;
=, assigning rights.

The argument *z* can have the value r, w, or x, whose meaning is the same as that is described above.

The rights of access to a file may be changed only by the owner of that file or by the superuser.

Let us consider how the access rights are established when a new file is created. The user who has created the file becomes its owner. Its group-owner will be either the primary group of that user or the group-owner of the directory containing the file (the choice of the two options is defined by the system settings). The group-owner of the file may be changed by the command chgrp. When necessary, it is also possible to change the file owner with the command chown.

Note Links require special attention from the point of view of system security. In particular, after a file has been opened with the help of a hard or symbolic link, the access of other users to it will be blocked. If this happens, for example, with the file /etc/passwd, registration with the system will become unavailable. It should also be noted that the command ls represents, for symbolic links, the rights lrwxrwxrwx, which are dummy values not used in reality. In fact, the rights of reading, writing, and executing for a file referred to by a link are defined by the metadata of the target file. For this reason, the access rights for symbolic links contain no information about the possibility of access to the target file.

The access rights for directories have some peculiarities in comparison with regular files. In particular, the right to read a directory (when the parameter r is present) means that a user can access a list of the file names in this directory. The right to write (w) to a directory allows one to create and delete files. Note that a user may also delete the file without being its owner. The right to execute (when the parameter x is present) allows one to obtain the metadata of the files stored in the directory. In addition to this, it is possible to make a directory current only if the user has the right to execute that directory and all the overlying directories in the file system tree.

Note There exist additional file attributes that allow detailed setup of access to the file system, taking into account the requirements of administrative convenience and security [33].

B.5   Basic Operations with Files

Here, we consider the most important commands for working with files in the Linux operating system [80].

pwd
This command outputs to the screen (to be more exact, to the standard output stream) the full path from the root directory of the file system to the current directory.

cd *dir*
As a result of execution of this command, the directory *dir* is made current or, in other words, a "change" to the directory *dir* is performed. After a command of the form cd .. is executed, a change takes place along the file system tree to the level above, i.e., the parent directory. If it is called without an argument, the command cd makes the home user directory ~ current.

ls *dir*
This command outputs the contents of the directory *dir*. By default, the contents of the directory are output in alphabetical order of file names. The parameter -a causes the output to include a list of all files, including hidden ones, whose names begin with a dot. To view information about the file sizes in blocks, the parameter -s is used. As previously noted, the parameter -l is used for specification of the file properties. If the directory name is not specified, the contents of the current directory are output to the console. In the commands of the Bash interpreter, single-character keys can be combined; for example, ls -al displays detailed properties of all files in the current directory.

touch *file*
This command creates an empty file in the current directory with the name *file*. If the name of an already existing file is transferred as the parameter, then the command touch updates the metadata information about the file modification time and the file access time. By default, when a new file is created, the following rights are usually set: -rw-r--r--, i.e., the user who is the owner will be able to read and edit this file, while the users in the owner's group and all others will have only the right to view its contents.

cp *file1 file2*
This command copies the file *file1* to *file2*. If *file2* exists, it will be overwritten.

mv *file1 file2*
This command renames the file *file1* as *file2*. If, as the second argument, a directory is specified, then the file is moved to this directory. In the latter case, the call format is as follows: mv *file dir*.

mkdir *dir*
This command is used to create a new directory *dir*. For the new directory, by default, the rights drwxr-xr-x are usually set. This means that all users of the

system may view the contents of the directory created and the metadata of the files stored in it.

ln *file link*

This command creates a link *link* referring to the file *file*. By default, *link* is a hard link. The parameter - s is used to create a symbolic link.

rm *file*

This command is intended for deleting a file *file*. The call rm -r *dir* deletes the directory *dir* together with all files and subdirectories in it.

rmdir *dir*

This command deletes the subdirectory *dir* of the current directory. The subdirectory *dir* must be empty.

less *file*

This command outputs the contents of the file to the console. If the data are to big to fit on the screen, they are automatically split into parts, each of which can be displayed. It is possible to proceed to the next part by pressing the space key, and to the previous part by pressing B . Viewing of the file contents is finished by pressing the key Q .

find *dir*

This command is intended for searching for a file in the file system, starting from the directory *dir*. An example for searching file target is: find / -name target

grep *pattern file*

This command searches for strings in the file *file* that correspond to the expression *pattern*. For example, in order to print the lines from the file /etc/passwd that contain the text "test", the following should be written in the command line: grep test /etc/passwd. The expression *pattern* uses so-called *regular expressions*, templates describing the sets of lines required. The following two regular expressions are important and frequently used:

- the combination ".*" defines an arbitrary number of symbols;
- the symbol "." corresponds to exactly one arbitrary symbol.

Working with the file system is made easier by the two-panel file manager Midnight Commander [44], called by the command mc. Apart from the operations of viewing, copying, moving, and deleting files, the integrated text editor allows one to make changes in files. In addition, Midnight Commander allows many routine user operations to be performed easily, such as group renaming of files, working with archive files, and many other operations.

B.6   Processes

As previously noted, the system and user processes define the functionality of the operating system. A *process* is a program being executed [33].

Each process, at the start, receives a unique identification number (a process identifier, PID). Upon completion of operation of the process, the identifier is released and can be reassigned to the next process. In addition to the PID, the structural data of the operating system kernel also store the parent process identifier (PPID).

The resources of the operating system are distributed between processes by the *task scheduler*. Several factors are taken into account, one of them being the *relative process priority*. The relative priority—an integer n—is defined at the start of a process and satisfies the condition $n \in [-20, 19]$. By default, the standard value $n = 0$ is used. Resources are allocated to a process in accordance with the following rule: the greater the value of the relative priority, the smaller is the actual priority of the process in comparison with others. Thus, if some program has $n = 19$, the task scheduler allocates minimal resources to it (in particular, processor time) in comparison with other processes.

The start of a program by the user and, correspondingly, the creation of a process are performed by entering a command in the terminal window and then pressing the key ⏎Enter. Usually the prefix ./ is used before the name of the executable file in the current user directory in order to guarantee the starting of a user program from the current directory (and not a system file if the names coincide).

A program can be started in the *active* or the *background mode*. In the active mode, the operation of the command interpreter is suspended until the completion of the process. In the background mode, the command interpreter does not wait for the completion of the process, but continues execution of other tasks. The background operation mode is indicated by the symbol & after the name of the program and its parameters.

Let us give an example of starting a user program a.out in the background mode:

./a.out &

In response to this, the console will display a line of the form

[*N*] *PID*

where the sequential number N of the background process launched from the terminal window is shown in square brackets, and *PID* is the identifier assigned to it.

B.6.1   Redirection

The intermediate results of the execution of a command can be displayed not only on the console. For each process, the *standard input stream* is open for reading, and the *standard output stream* and *standard error stream* are open for writing [36]. The standard input stream, by default, receives data from the keyboard; the standard output and error streams are displayed on the screen.

The standard output stream can be redirected to a file with the help of the symbol >. For example, the command

```
ls /home > home.txt
```

will create in the file home.txt a list of the user home directories in the system. If a file with this name already exists, it will be overwritten.

There are some more ways of readdressing data, as follows.

The command 2> *file* redirects the error data to the file *file*; &> *file* redirects both the output data and the error data to the file *file*. If, instead of >, we specify >>, the target file will not be overwritten, and the information is instead added to the end of the file. The standard input stream can be filled from a file as follows: < *file*.

Note in this connection that the output of a command can be redirected to the input of another command with the help of a *pipe* created by specifying the symbol "|":

command1 | *command2*

To execute a chain of commands in the Bash shell, command separators are used [48]. Several commands can be executed sequentially by writing them, for brevity, on one line, separated by a semicolon ";", for example

command1; *command2*; *command3*

The results of execution of this line will coincide with the result of successive calling of each of the commands:

command1

command2

command3

The command separator && indicates that both commands should be executed, but if the first command is completed with an error (more strictly speaking, if the return code is other than zero), the second command will not be called. Similarly, if only one of the two commands should be executed, they are separated by the symbols ||. In this case, if the first command is executed correctly, the second command is not called. It should be noted that the statements && and || in the command line have the same priority.

As an illustration of working in the Bash command interpreter, let us consider a user working session consisting of several frequently used operations. In the home directory, the user executes the following sequence of commands:

```
mkdir mydirectory
cd mydirectory
touch myfile.txt
ls -l > myfile.txt
ln -s myfile.txt soft_link_to_myfile
less myfile.txt
less soft_link_to_myfile
cd .. && rm -r mydirectory
```

The first command creates a subdirectory with the name `mydirectory` in the home user directory.

The second command makes the specified directory current.

The next command creates an empty file, assigned the name `myfile.txt`.

The output stream of the command for viewing the contents of the current directory, `ls -l`, is redirected to the file created; in other words, `myfile.txt` now contains the metadata of the contents of the directory `mydirectory` (information about the only file in it, `myfile.txt`).

The next command, `ln -s`, forms a symbolic link to this file.

The next two commands display the contents of the files created.

The final line consists of two commands: a change to the parent directory and deletion of the test directory `mydirectory` together with all files stored in it.

We now consider the basic process control utilities.

`ps` inputs information about the user processes being executed: the status of the process (in progress, suspended, being launched, etc.), the identifier of the process itself and the parent process, the relative priority, the total time for process execution by the processor, etc. This utility has many parameters; traditionally, some of them are written without a preceding hyphen. For example, with the help of the command `ps ax`, we can obtain a list of all processes in the system, and not only those launched on behalf of the present user.

`nice -n` *prog* starts the program *prog* with a relative execution priority different from the default standard priority, which is equal to zero. The variable n defines the increment in comparison with the standard priority; this is an integer in the interval $[-20, 19]$. Only the administrator may raise the actual priority of a process using values $n < 0$.

`top` outputs periodically updated information about the processes launched, in decreasing order of consumption of processor resources.

`renice` *nice PID* changes the priority of the process in progress. The parameter *nice* defines a new relative priority for the process with the identifier *PID*.

`kill -`*signal PID* sends to the process with identifier *PID* a signal with the sequential number *signal*. A *signal* is the method of passing from one process to another a notification about the origination of some event. A user may only send signals to processes launched for execution by him or her. In practice, the most frequently used signal is SIGTERM, numbered *signal* $= 15$. A process that receives this signal must interrupt its operation. The SIGKILL signal, numbered *signal* $= 9$, interrupts the execution of a process, but, unlike the case for SIGTERM, the process may not ignore it. A full list of signals is available by calling the command `kill -l`.

`time` *prog* starts execution of the program *prog* and outputs the time spent on the program's operation into the standard error stream.

B.7   Bash Scripts

A *shell script* is a file containing commands to be executed sequentially by the command interpreter. The commands are read from the command file one by one. An approach based on writing scripts allows one to automate many of the routine operations of users and administrators of computing systems. Scripts in the Bash shell provide an opportunity to use variables, loops, built-in functions, and other constructs of high-level programming languages.

B.7.1   Features of Bash

The names of variables in Bash may consist of Latin alphabet characters, decimal numbers, and the underscore symbol _. The names are case-sensitive.

A peculiarity of the Bash shell programming language is the possibility of obtaining the value of a variable by adding the character $ before its name. For example, let us assign values to variables `size` and `str` and output them to the standard output stream, i.e., the terminal screen:

```
size=64
str="Message"
echo $size
echo $str
```

The following result will be displayed:

```
64
Message
```

Note that preliminary declaration of variables, as in C or Fortran, is not required.

The command `echo` *string* outputs its argument *string* to the standard output stream and then adds a line feed. This is a simple yet widely used command. The line feed at the end of the data output may be prevented by specifying the parameter -n in the command:

```
echo -n string
```

Substitution of the result of the execution of an external command is performed by placing the command in single quotes. For example, after the command

```
list=`ls -al`
```

is executed, the output of the result of executing the command `ls` with the parameters -al will be written to the variable `list`.

In order to separate the name of a variable from the following characters, the name can be placed in braces. For example, the command

```
echo ${str}123
```

will output to the terminal screen the value of the variable `str` and the variable `123`, i.e., the line "Message123".

Comments in the Bash shell begin with the character # and continue to the end of the line.

B.7.2 Conditional Statements

A branch operation in Bash is described by a *conditional statement*
```
if [[ condition ]]
    then op1
    else op2
fi
```
Here, the command *op1* will be executed if the condition *condition* takes the value true. Otherwise, the command *op2* will be executed.

For the comparison of integers, instead of the standard mathematical symbols one should use special keywords, listed in Table B.2. To establish equality and inequality of strings, the comparison symbols == and ! =, respectively, are used (Table B.3).

B.7.3 Loop Statements

We now proceed to a discussion of *loop statements*. One of the options for setting up a loop from the command shell is the following:
```
while condition
    do op
    done
```
Here, the command *op* will be executed until the condition *condition* becomes false.

Another loop statement is
```
until condition
    do op
    done
```

Table B.2 Notation for the conditions for comparison of integer variables i and j

Condition	Notation
$i = j$	i -eq j
$i \neq j$	i -ne j
$i \leqslant j$	i -le j
$i < j$	i -lt j
$i \geqslant j$	i -ge j
$i > j$	i -gt j

Table B.3 Notation for the conditions for comparison of string variables s1 and s2

Condition	Notation
Strings s1 and s2 are equal	s1 == s2
Strings s1 and s2 are not equal	s1 != s2
String s1 precedes s2 in lexicographic order	s1 < s2
String s1 follows s2 in lexicographic order	s1 > s2
String s1 has nonzero length	-n s1
Length of string s1 is equal to zero	-z s1

In this case, the command *op* will be executed in the loop until the condition *condition* becomes true.

A third method for setting up a loop is as follows:

```
for var in domain
    do op
    done
```

Here, the command *op* will be executed as many times as there are words in the string *domain*, and the variable *var* will sequentially take values coinciding with the words in this string.

B.7.4   Example of the Use of Bash

We illustrate the use of the command interpreter programming language with an example of the estimation of the speedup of a parallel program.

Example B.1   Assume that the current directory contains the texts of programs that use the OpenMP technology. We compile them and start their execution with various values of the number of threads. We then output the results to files with the extension .speedup.

Solution   We define the parameter MAX_P as the greatest number of threads in the given computational node. In order to obtain a list of the files in the current directory, we use the command ls. Then, we set up a for loop over all files.

The files, with the extension c, are compiled and started first in sequential mode and then in parallel mode, with numbers of threads $p = 2, 3, \ldots, MAX\_P$. In order to reduce the influence of random factors on the speedup, the program is started three times each time.

Operations on integer variables, such as addition, subtraction, and multiplication, are performed with the help of the command let. A considerable restriction when using the Bash shell is the impossibility of working with real variables. For this reason, we perform operations on real numbers with the help of the program bc, whose name is an abbreviation for "basic calculator." The function call

```
bc -l file
```

allows one to obtaining the result of such arithmetic operations, written in a file *file*. The parameter -l connects a mathematical library. This library defines the following functions: $\sin x$, $\cos x$, $\arctan x$, $\ln x$, e^x, and the Bessel functions $J_n(x)$ of integer order n.

To output the results into a file, we use redirection (see Sect. B.6.1). The text of the script speedup.sh is shown in Listing B.1.

```
1   #!/bin/bash
2   #
3   # Script "speedup.sh" computes the speedup
4   # depending on the number of streams p
5   #
6   # record the maximum number of streams
7   # available to the computer system
8
9   MAX_P=24
10
11  # assign the initial value to variable p
12  # for sequential execution of the program
13
14  p=1
15
16  echo -n "Maximum number of threads is equal to "
17  echo $MAX_P
18
19  # compile and start the execution of all files
20  # in the current directory with the extension "c"
21
22  for file in *.c
23  do
24    gcc -Wall -std=c99 -fopenmp -lm \
25        -o ${file}.out $file
26
27    # compute the execution time
28    # in the sequential mode
29    export OMP_NUM_THREADS=$p
30    avr_time="1.0/3.0*(" `./${file}.out` " + \
31                        " `./${file}.out` " + \
32                        " `./${file}.out` ")"
33
34    # computations with real numbers are
35    # performed with the help of the program bc
36    seq_time=`echo $avr_time | bc -l`
37
38    # fill in the first line in the resulting file
39    echo "1 1.000" >> ${file}.speedup
40
41    let p=p+1
42
43    # compute the execution time
```

```
44    # in the parallel mode
45    while [[ $p -le $MAX_P ]]
46    do
47      export OMP_NUM_THREADS=$p
48      avr_time="1.0/3.0*("`./${file}.out`" + \
49                         "`./${file}.out`" + \
50                         "`./${file}.out`")"
51      par_time=`echo $avr_time | bc -l`
52
53      # find the speedup and output it
54      # into the resulting file
55      echo -n $p" " >> ${file}.speedup
56      echo "scale=3;$seq_time/$par_time" | \
57            bc -l >> ${file}.speedup
58
59      let p=p+1
60    done
61    echo -n "The result is stored in file "
62    echo ${file}.speedup
63    p=1
64  done
```

Note that this example considers a somewhat simplified version of a script that was used for preparing the illustrative material for Chap. 6.   □

Despite its wide use and great capabilities for administering computing systems, the Bash command script programming language has some drawbacks. Among them are the complexity of working with multidimensional arrays and the impossibility of working with real variables [48]. At present, the Python language [67] is becoming increasingly popular for automation of the execution of user tasks.

B.8   The Slurm Workload Manager Scheduler

High-performance computer systems, including clusters and supercomputers, must simultaneously perform tasks for many users. The distribution of the resources of such systems and the priority of execution of user requests are organized by special *middleware*. One of the most popular representatives of the software for managing the operation of cluster systems and supercomputers is the Slurm Workload Manager, or Slurm for short [70].

Slurm is a task scheduler for clusters running under the Linux system oriented towards working with modern high-performance computer systems.

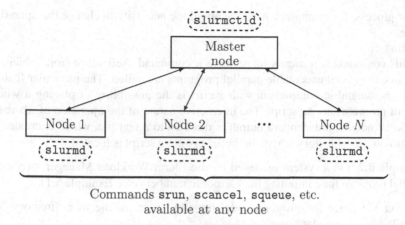

Commands `srun`, `scancel`, `squeue`, etc.
available at any node

Fig. B.1 Schematic illustration of the Slurm Workload Manager scheduler. The dashed lines indicate continuously functioning processes

The basic functions of Slurm are [5, 72]:

- organization of the access of users to the cluster's computing resources in accordance with some resource allocation policy;
- execution of parallel tasks on nodes of the system dedicated to such work;
- formation of and support for the user task queue.

The basic components of the Slurm scheduler are (Fig. B.1):

- the main process `slurmctld`, working on the cluster's master node;
- a background process `slurmd`, executed on each computational node;
- user commands `srun`, `squeue`, `scancel`, etc., available at each computational node.

There also exist other background programs, for example the user authentication module.

The resource allocation policy is quite simple: each user has the right to put a task on the queue, as well as to delete a previously put task. The Slurm configuration files are readable by all users. Only *privileged users*, specified at the initial setup of the system, may change the configuration files and abort the tasks of other users.

We now enumerate the tasks of the Slurm scheduler used for executing and monitoring user tasks.

`srun`

This command allocates computing resources to a user's task and starts its execution.

`squeue`

This task outputs to the console information about the current status of the task queue. A list of scheduled tasks and a list of the tasks being executed are displayed.

`scancel`

This task is used to abort an erroneously started task or terminate a computation whose result is no longer of interest. This command allows a signal to be sent to a user process, for example, a message about the necessity to change the operating mode.

sbatch

This command is a means for starting a command shell script from which, in turn, one or several executable parallel programs are called. The particular feature of this command in comparison with srun is the possibility of placing a whole suite of programs in one script. The interactive nature of the operation of sbatch should be noted—the standard output is directed to a text file, which is created in the current user directory where the initial program script is located.

Example B.2 On a system managed by the Slurm Workload Manager, execute a parallel program for computing the harmonic numbers (see Example 5.1).

Solution We place the program code, the file hn.c, in the user directory. We compile it in the standard way:

    gcc -Wall -fopenmp hn.c -o hn.out

Then, we create a command shell script for the task in the form of a text file hn.c. The contents of this file are shown in Listing B.2.

Listing B.2

```
 1  #!/bin/bash
 2  #
 3  #SBATCH --job-name=hn
 4  #SBATCH --output=res_hn.txt
 5  #
 6  #SBATCH --ntasks=1
 7  #SBATCH --cpus-per-task=12
 8  #SBATCH --time=100:00
 9  #SBATCH --mem-per-cpu=100
10
11  export OMP_NUM_THREADS=$SLURM_CPUS_PER_TASK
12  ./hn.out
```

Let us consider each line of the file hn.sh in more detail.

The first line of the code indicates that this file is intended for execution by the Bash command shell.

The lines beginning with the characters #SBATCH are considered by the shell as comments; these lines contain instructions for the Slurm scheduler. Line 3 states the name of the task, for identification in the common list of tasks.

Line 4 contains the file name for storing the information directed to the standard output stream, or, in other words, the results of the computation. By default, the standard output stream and the standard error stream are directed to a file slurm-j.out, where j is the task number.

Line 6 tells the Slurm scheduler the user-requested number of computational nodes for the execution of the task.

Line 7 specifies the size of the parallel team in a shared-memory system, for example for operation of the functions of the OpenMP environment.

The next two lines define the maximum operation time for the task in minutes and the required memory space per thread in megabytes. The possible formats for the time are:

- minutes,
- minutes:seconds,
- hours:minutes:seconds,
- days-hours,
- days-hours:minutes,
- days-hours:minutes:seconds.

In particular, `#SBATCH -time=100:00` here means that the limiting value of the task operation time is equal to 100 minutes.

Finally, the concluding lines are transferred for execution to the command shell. In the OpenMP environment, line 11 specifies the desired number of threads.

Line 12 starts the executable file.

Note that the execution of a parallel program with the help of the MPI technology is possible when the script file specifies a value of the parameter `ntasks` greater than one, for example

```
#SBATCH -ntasks=8
```
The execution of the script formed is started by the command
```
sbatch hn.sh
```
□

B.9   Installing Parallel Programming Environments on a Workstation

This section presents brief information about installation of the OpenMP and MPI environments on a user's workstation. The availability of parallel programming environments directly at the researcher's workplace allows the writing of code for a parallel program and initial debugging of the program without remote connection to a high-performance computing system.

As noted above, since the overwhelming majority of resource-intensive computing problems are solved on computer systems running under the Linux operating system, we will assume that the user's workstation has a Linux environment (or at least one realized by a virtual machine in some other operating system).

B.9.1   OpenMP Environment

Modern versions of the Linux operating system nearly always include the GCC compiler. In order to use the OpenMP technology, the GCC compiler must have the libgomp library, which is included in the standard distribution of Linux. For this reason, at the beginning of working with OpenMP, it is sufficient to verify the correct installation and configuration of the compiler, for example with the help of the following test program code:

```
#include <stdio.h>
int main()
{
  #ifdef _OPENMP
    printf("OpenMP technology is supported.\n");
  #endif
  return 0;
}
```

If the OpenMP environment is installed correctly on the computing system, the console will display a corresponding message. Recall that in the parameters for the compilation of the program code it is necessary to use the key -fopenmp (see Sect. 5.2).

Note that the macro _OPENMP has the value $y_1 y_2 y_3 y_4 m_1 m_2$, where $y_1 y_2 y_3 y_4$ and $m_1 m_2$ are the decimal representations of the year and the month, respectively, of the release of the OpenMP environment (see the solution to Problem 5.10).

B.9.2　MPI Environment

We consider the installation of the MPI environment using the example of the widely used implementation Open MPI [51]. The source code of this realization is available at https://www.open-mpi.org/.

Suppose that an archive file containing the source code is placed in the directory /opt. At the time of writing, the current stable version of Open MPI is 3.1.1, and so the installation package has an absolute path in the root system /opt/openmpi-3.1.1.tar.bz2.

Then, the following commands should be executed in the command interpreter:
```
cd /opt
tar xf openmpi-3.1.1.tar.gz
cd openmpi-3.1.1
./configure --prefix=path
make all install
```
The first command unpacks the archive file (for a description of the utility tar, see for example [48]). The next command makes the directory containing the files created current. Then, when the execution of the installation script configure and the command make is started, the compilation and actual installation of the software takes place (the *path* for the final placement of files is specified as a parameter of the installation script).

The compilation and starting of a user's parallel program in the Open MPI environment are performed with the help of the scripts mpicc and mpirun, respectively:

```
mpicc task.c -o task.out -g
mpirun -np N ./task.out
```

In this example, the user's parallel program, whose text is written in a file task.c in the current directory, is compiled with the addition of debugging information (parameter -g). The execution of the file task.out resulting from the compilation is started on N computational nodes, which is evidenced by the parameter -np N.

Appendix C
Introduction to the Fourier Transform

The Fourier[1] transform is one of the central methods of modern applied mathematics [23, 79].

Consider some function $s : \mathbb{R} \to \mathbb{C}$. Let $s(t)$ be absolutely integrable in the domain, i.e., $\int_{-\infty}^{\infty} |s(t)| \, dt < \infty$.

The *continuous Fourier Transform* of the function $s(t)$ is defined by the relation

$$S(f) = \int_{-\infty}^{\infty} s(t) e^{2\pi i f t} \, dt.$$

The function $S(f)$ is called an image of the original function $s(t)$. The basic properties of the image of an arbitrary function are established by the following lemma [23, 83].

Riemann[2]–Lebesgue[3] lemma. *For any absolutely integrable complex-valued function $s(t)$ on the set of real numbers, its Fourier transform $S(f)$ is a function that is bounded and continuous on $\mathbb{R}$, and tends to zero as $|f| \to \infty$.*

Note Traditionally, in physical applications $s(t)$ is considered as a *signal*, and $S(f)$ as a *signal spectrum*. The variable t has the meaning of time, and f that of a frequency. The notation $S(f) = \mathcal{F}[s(t)]$ is widely used.

If both of the functions $s(t)$ and $S(f)$ are absolutely integrable on the set of real numbers, the *inverse Fourier transform* allows one to restore the original function from the image:

$$s(t) = \int_{-\infty}^{\infty} S(f) e^{-2\pi i f t} \, df.$$

---

[1] Jean Baptiste Joseph Fourier (1786–1830), French mathematician and physicist.

[2] Georg Friedrich Bernhard Riemann (1826–1866), German mathematician and mechanician.

[3] Henri Léon Lebesgue (1875–1941), French mathematician.

© Springer Nature Switzerland AG 2019
S. Kurgalin, S. Borzunov, *A Practical Approach to High-Performance Computing*,
https://doi.org/10.1007/978-3-030-27558-7

From its definition, the Fourier transform is a linear operation. In other words, for any complex-valued functions $s_1(t)$, $s_2(t)$, defined and absolutely integrable on the set of all real numbers, and for any constant $c_1, c_2 \in \mathbb{C}$, the following equality is valid:

$$\mathcal{F}[c_1 s_1(t) + c_2 s_2(t)] = c_1 \mathcal{F}[s_1(t)] + c_2 \mathcal{F}[s_2(t)].$$

C.1   The Discrete Fourier Transform

In computational problems, the function considered is usually specified not analytically, but in the form of discrete values on some grid, usually uniform.

Let δ be the time interval between two consecutive samples of the function $s(t)$:

$$x_n = s(n\delta), \quad \text{where } n \in \mathbb{Z}.$$

For any value of δ there exists a so-called *critical frequency* f_c, or Nyquist[4] frequency, which is defined by the relation $f_c = 1/2\delta$. There exists an important result for information theory: if outside the frequency range $[-f_c, f_c]$ the spectrum of some signal is equal to zero, then this signal can be completely restored from the series of samples x_n. More formally, the following theorem is valid.

Kotelnikov's[5] Theorem (known in the English-language literature as the Nyquist–Shannon[6] theorem). *If a continuous and absolutely integrable function $s(t)$ on $\mathbb{R}$ has a nonzero Fourier transform for frequencies $-f_c \leqslant f \leqslant f_c$, then $s(t)$ is completely defined by its samples $x_n = s(n\delta)$, where $n \in \mathbb{Z}$, with a time interval δ:*

$$s(t) = \delta \sum_{n=-\infty}^{\infty} x_n \frac{\sin(2\pi f_c(t - n\delta))}{\pi(t - n\delta)}.$$

The wider the frequency band used by a communication channel, the more often samples must be taken for correct discrete coding of the signal and its restoration. The greater number of samples is compensated by the greater amount of information transferred by the signal.

In practical problems, the length of the series of samples

$$\mathbf{x} = (\ldots, x_{-2}, x_{-1}, x_0, x_1, x_2, \ldots)$$

---

[4]Harry Theodor Nyquist (1889–1976), American mathematician, specialist in information theory.

[5]Vladimir Aleksandrovich Kotelnikov (1908–2005), Soviet and Russian mathematician and radiophysicist, specialist in information theory.

[6]Claude Elwood Shannon (1916–2001), American mathematician and electrical engineer, the founder of information theory.

is usually limited, and in this connection let us consider the transition from the continuous integral transform $\mathcal{F}[s(t)]$ to an approximation of the integral by a sum:

$$(\mathcal{F}[s(t)])_n = \int_{-\infty}^{\infty} s(t)e^{2\pi i f_n t}\, dt \rightarrow \sum_{k=-\infty}^{\infty} x_k e^{2\pi i f_n t_k} \delta = \delta \sum_{k=0}^{N-1} x_k e^{2\pi i k n/N}.$$

Thus, we arrive at the definition of the *discrete Fourier transform* (DFT) N of the values x_k, where $k = 0, 1, \ldots, N-1$:

$$y_n = \sum_{k=0}^{N-1} x_k e^{2\pi i k n/N}, \quad 0 \leqslant n \leqslant N-1,$$

or, using the notation $\omega = e^{2\pi i/N}$,

$$y_n = \sum_{k=0}^{N-1} \omega^{kn} x_k, \quad 0 \leqslant n \leqslant N-1.$$

The *inverse discrete Fourier transform* is defined by the formula

$$x_n = \frac{1}{N} \sum_{k=0}^{N-1} \omega^{-kn} y_k, \quad 0 \leqslant n \leqslant N-1.$$

In vector notation, the above relations have the form $\mathbf{y} = \mathcal{F}[\mathbf{x}]$ and $\mathbf{x} = \mathcal{F}^{-1}[\mathbf{y}]$.

Sequential application of the forward and inverse DFT to an arbitrary vector $\mathbf{x}$ does not change its components: $\forall \mathbf{x} \in \mathbb{R}^n \;\; \mathcal{F}^{-1}[\mathcal{F}[\mathbf{x}]] = \mathbf{x}$ and $\mathcal{F}[\mathcal{F}^{-1}[\mathbf{x}]] = \mathbf{x}$. We can prove, for example, the first of these equalities:

$$(\mathcal{F}^{-1}[\mathcal{F}[\mathbf{x}]])_n = \frac{1}{N} \sum_{k=0}^{N-1} \omega^{-kn} (\mathcal{F}[\mathbf{x}])_k = \frac{1}{N} \sum_{k=0}^{N-1} \omega^{-kn} \sum_{i=0}^{N-1} \omega^{ik} x_i.$$

We change the order of summation:

$$(\mathcal{F}^{-1}[\mathcal{F}[\mathbf{x}]])_n = \sum_{i=0}^{N-1} x_i \left(\frac{1}{N} \sum_{k=0}^{N-1} \omega^{k(i-n)} \right).$$

We then use the following property of the variables $\omega = e^{2\pi i/N}$:

$$\frac{1}{N} \sum_{k=0}^{N-1} \omega^{k(i-n)} = \begin{cases} 1 & \text{if } i = n, \\ 0 & \text{if } i \neq n. \end{cases}$$

We finally obtain $(\mathcal{F}^{-1}[\mathcal{F}[\mathbf{x}]])_n = x_n \; \forall n = 0, 1, \ldots, N - 1$. The equality $\mathcal{F}[\mathcal{F}^{-1}[\mathbf{x}]] = \mathbf{x}$ is proved similarly.

Example C.1 Calculate the DFT of a vector $\mathbf{x}$ of length N with components equal to the binomial coefficients $x_n = C(N - 1, n)$, where $0 \leqslant n \leqslant N - 1$.

Solution In accordance with the definition of the DFT,

$$(\mathcal{F}[\mathbf{x}])_n = \sum_{k=0}^{N-1} e^{(2\pi i/N)kn} C(N - 1, n) \text{ for } 0 \leqslant n \leqslant N - 1.$$

The relation obtained for the n-th component of the vector $\mathcal{F}[\mathbf{x}]$ can be transformed using Newton's binomial formula (the binomial theorem):

$$(\mathcal{F}[\mathbf{x}])_n = \sum_{k=0}^{N-1} C(N - 1, k)\left(e^{2\pi i n/N}\right)^k = \left(1 + e^{2\pi i n/N}\right)^{N-1} = (1 + \omega^n)^{N-1}$$

for all $n = 0, 1, \ldots, N - 1$.

$\square$

The sine and cosine transforms of input data vectors are of great importance in applications.

By definition, the *sine transform* of a vector $\mathbf{x}$ of length N, when $x_0 = 0$, is a vector $(\mathcal{F}_{\sin}[\mathbf{x}])$ of the same length with the components

$$(\mathcal{F}_{\sin}[\mathbf{x}])_n = \sum_{k=0}^{N-1} x_k \sin\left(\frac{\pi kn}{N}\right).$$

Similarly, the *cosine transform* of a vector $\mathbf{x}$ of length $N + 1$ is defined as follows:

$$(\mathcal{F}_{\cos}[\mathbf{x}])_n = \frac{1}{2}\left[x_0 + (-1)^n x_N\right] + \sum_{k=1}^{N-1} x_k \cos\left(\frac{\pi kn}{N}\right).$$

Example C.2 Show that the sine and cosine transform can be reduced to the standard discrete Fourier transform.

Solution The arguments of the functions $\sin\left(\pi k/N\right)$ in the definition of the sine transform differ from the arguments of the exponents in the standard DFT by a multiplier $1/2$; for this reason, it is impossible to consider $\mathcal{F}_{\sin}[\mathbf{x}]$ as the imaginary part of $\mathcal{F}[\mathbf{x}]$. More accurate transformations are required [57].

Consider a vector $\widetilde{\mathbf{x}}$ of length $2N$ whose components satisfy the relations $\widetilde{x}[k] = x[k]$ for $0 \leqslant k \leqslant N-1$, $\widetilde{x}[k] = -x[2N-k]$ for $N+1 \leqslant k \leqslant 2N-1$, and $\widetilde{x}[N] = 0$.

In other words, $\widetilde{\mathbf{x}}$ is constructed from the source vector $\mathbf{x}$ by antisymmetric reflection of the values $x[k]$ $(0 \leqslant k \leqslant N - 1)$ with respect to $k = N$.

Let us apply the DFT to the tuple $\widetilde{x}[k]$, $k = 0, \ldots, 2N - 1$, obtained:

$$(\mathcal{F}[\widetilde{\mathbf{x}}])_n = \sum_{k=0}^{2N-1} \widetilde{x}_k e^{2\pi i k n/(2N)}.$$

We now take the part of the sum corresponding to the values $k = N, \ldots, 2N - 1$ and make the change $k' = 2N - k$ in it:

$$\sum_{k=N}^{2N-1} \widetilde{x}_k e^{2\pi i k n/(2N)} = \sum_{k'=1}^{N} \widetilde{x}_{2N-k'} e^{2\pi i (2N-k')n/(2N)}$$

$$= \sum_{k'=1}^{N} \widetilde{x}_{2N-k'} e^{2\pi i n} e^{-2\pi i k' n/(2N)} = -\sum_{k'=1}^{N} x_{k'} e^{-2\pi i k' n/(2N)}.$$

The discrete Fourier transform of the vector $\widetilde{\mathbf{x}}$ takes the form

$$(\mathcal{F}[\widetilde{\mathbf{x}}])_n = \sum_{k=0}^{N-1} x_k \left[e^{2\pi i k n/(2N)} - e^{-2\pi i k n/(2N)} \right] = 2i \sum_{k=0}^{N-1} x_k \sin\left(\frac{\pi k n}{N} \right).$$

Hence, the DFT of the vector $\widetilde{\mathbf{x}}$, apart from a multiplier $2i$, coincides with the sine transform of the vector $\mathbf{x}$.

The corresponding reasoning for the cosine transform is absolutely the same.   □

Calculation of the vector $\mathbf{y}$ from $\mathbf{x}$ in accordance with the definition requires $O(N^2)$ complex multiplications. There is, however, a way to considerably decrease the asymptotic complexity of the DFT. The *fast Fourier transform* (FFT) algorithm requires just $O(N \log_2 N)$ multiplication operations; moreover, there exist methods of parallelizing the FFT [57].

We suppose further that $N = 2^m$ for some natural number m. This limitation is not required in principle, since if it is necessary to perform the FFT algorithm for $N \neq 2^m$ one of the following approaches can be applied:

1. Fill in several cells of the array representing the signal with zeros, so that N becomes equal to the nearest power of two.
2. use one of the more complex generalizations of the FFT (see, for example, [76]).

The basis of the FFT method is that the DFT of a vector $\mathbf{x}$ of length N can be represented as a combination of transformations of two vectors, each having a length of $N/2$, and one transformation is applied to the points $\mathbf{x}$ with even indices and another is applied to the points with odd indices:

$$y_n = \sum_{k=0}^{N-1} e^{2\pi i k n/N} x_k = \sum_{k=0}^{N/2-1} e^{2\pi i (2k)n/N} x_{2k} + \sum_{k=0}^{N/2-1} e^{2\pi i (2k+1)n/N} x_{2k+1}$$

$$= \sum_{k=0}^{N/2-1} e^{2\pi i k n/(N/2)} x_{2k} + e^{2\pi i n/N} \sum_{k=0}^{N/2-1} e^{2\pi i k n/(N/2)} x_{2k+1} = y_n^{(e)} + \omega^n y_n^{(o)}.$$

In the last equality, we have introduced the notation $y_n^{(e)}$ and $y_n^{(o)}$ for the n-th components of the DFT vectors formed by the elements of the original vector $\mathbf{x}$ in even and odd positions. The relation obtained allows $\mathbf{y}$ to be calculated recursively.

Using the easy-to-check property of the variables ω

$$\omega^{n+N/2} = -\omega^n, \quad \text{where } n = 0, 1, \dots, N/2 - 1,$$

we calculate the sums $y_n^{(e)}$ and $y_n^{(o)}$. The value of $\mathbf{y}$ sought can be obtained as follows:

1. The first $N/2$ elements of $\mathbf{y}$ are equal to $y_n^{(e)} + \omega^n y_n^{(o)}$.
2. The remaining $N/2$ elements of $\mathbf{y}$ are equal to $y_n^{(e)} - \omega^n y_n^{(o)}$.

The FFT algorithm divides the calculation of a DFT vector of length N into a combination of two DFT vectors of size $N/2$. The results-combining operation has the "operations–operands" digraph shown in Fig. C.1. Such a sequence of computational operations is called a "butterfly" diagram.

A transition from a problem of size $N/2$ to a problem of size N requires $N/2$ complex multiplications and N assignment operations. Therefore, we can write a recurrence relation for the number of complex multiplication operations, $T(N)$, in the FFT algorithm:

$$\begin{cases} T(N) = 2T\left(\dfrac{N}{2}\right) + \Theta(N), & N > 1, \\ T(1) = \text{const.} \end{cases}$$

The solution of the recurrence relation obtained has the form $T(N) = \Theta(N \log_2 N)$.

Fig. C.1 "Butterfly"
computation diagram

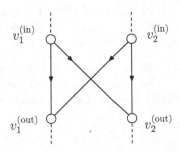

Appendix D
Answers, Hints, and Solutions to Problems

Problem 2.1: Solution

Diagrams of the hypercube Q_3 and the torus of size 4×2 are drawn in Fig. D.1. These graphs are regular; the vertex degree of each of them is equal to 3. The diameters of the graphs also coincide.

There exists a one-to-one mapping of the vertices and edges of one such graph to the vertices and edges of the other graph, where the incidence relation is preserved:

correspondence of the vertices

$1 \leftrightarrow a$	$5 \leftrightarrow d$
$2 \leftrightarrow b$	$6 \leftrightarrow c$
$3 \leftrightarrow f$	$7 \leftrightarrow g$
$4 \leftrightarrow e$	$8 \leftrightarrow h$

correspondence of the edges

$12 \leftrightarrow ab$	$23 \leftrightarrow bf$
$34 \leftrightarrow fe$	$41 \leftrightarrow fa$
$56 \leftrightarrow dc$	$67 \leftrightarrow cg$
$78 \leftrightarrow gh$	$85 \leftrightarrow hd$
$15 \leftrightarrow ad$	$26 \leftrightarrow bc$
$37 \leftrightarrow fg$	$48 \leftrightarrow eh$

Hence, the hypercube Q_3 and the 4×2 torus are isomorphic graphs.

Fig. D.1 Hypercube Q_3 and 4×2 torus in Problem 2.1

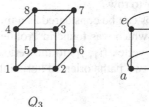
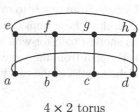

Q_3 4×2 torus

© Springer Nature Switzerland AG 2019
S. Kurgalin, S. Borzunov, *A Practical Approach to High-Performance Computing*,
https://doi.org/10.1007/978-3-030-27558-7

Fig. D.2 Hypercube Q_4

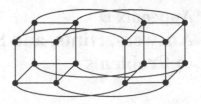

Problem 2.2: Answer
See Fig. D.2.

Problem 2.3: Hint
Similarly to the solution to Problem 2.1, construct a one-to-one correspondence between the vertices and edges of the hypercube Q_4 and the 4×4 torus where the incidence relation is preserved.

Problem 2.4: Solution
A path in an n-cycle from vertex number i to vertex number j can be constructed in two ways moving along the cycle either clockwise or anticlockwise. Hence, the length of the shortest path in $D(i, j)$ is equal to the length of the shorter of these two possible paths:

$$D(i, j) = \min(|j - i|, p - |j - i|).$$

This expression can be transformed if we apply a representation of the minimum function of two real numbers, $\min(a, b)$, using the absolute value:

$$\min(a, b) = \frac{1}{2}(a + b - |a - b|).$$

We finally obtain

$$D(i, j) = \frac{1}{2}\left(p - |p - 2|j - i||\right).$$

Problem 2.5: Solution
Assume that the two vertices between which the path is being constructed have Cartesian coordinates (i_1, j_1) and (i_2, j_2). The path is formed in two steps, first in the horizontal direction from column j_1 to column j_2, and then in the vertical direction from row i_1 to row i_2.

Each of these steps can be considered as a motion along a q-cycle, the length of the shortest path for which was found in Problem 2.4. Hence, the minimum length of the path from the vertex (i_1, j_1) to the vertex (i_2, j_2) is determined as the sum of the lengths of the two paths oriented horizontally and vertically. As a result, we obtain the answer

$$D((i_1, j_1), (i_2, j_2)) = q - \frac{1}{2}(|q - 2|i_2 - i_1|| + |q - 2|j_2 - j_1||).$$

Problem 3.1: Answer

(a) $T_p(N) = 80\tau$;
(b) $T_p(N) = 20\tau$.

Problem 3.2: Answer

(a) $T_p(N) = 2^{30}\tau$;
(b) $T_p(N) = 2^{28}\tau$.

Problem 3.3: Answer

$$(S_p)_{max} = \frac{10p}{p+9}.$$

Problem 3.4: Answer

$S_\infty = 100$.

Problem 3.5: Answer

$$S_{p'} = S_p \frac{p'(p-1)}{p(p'-1) + (p - p')S_p}.$$

Problem 3.6: Solution

Denote the execution time of the block $\mathcal{A}_1$ in the sequential mode by τ; then the execution time of $\mathcal{A}_2$ in the same mode will be $\eta\tau$. Substitute these values into the formula for the speedup S_p of the parallel algorithm on a computation system with p processors:

$$S_p = \frac{T_1}{T_p}.$$

According to the problem statement, the sequential execution time of the whole algorithm $\mathcal{A}$ is composed of the execution time of the first block and the execution time of the second block:

$$T_1 = \tau + \eta\tau = (1+\eta)\tau.$$

In the parallel mode, the times for the fractions of computation $(1 - f_1)$ in $\mathcal{A}_1$ and $(1 - f_2)$ in $\mathcal{A}_2$ will be distributed over p computational nodes. Hence, the execution time of the algorithm $\mathcal{A}$ can be estimated as

$$T_p \geqslant f_1\tau + \frac{(1-f_1)\tau}{p} + f_2\eta\tau + \frac{(1-f_2)\eta\tau}{p}$$

$$= (f_1 + \eta f_2)\tau + \frac{1 + \eta - (f_1 + \eta f_2)}{p}\tau.$$

As a result, we obtain the following expression for the maximum achievable speedup value for execution of the algorithm $\mathcal{A}$:

$$\left(S_p\right)_{\max} = \frac{(1+\eta)\tau}{(f_1 + \eta f_2)\tau + (1 + \eta - (f_1 + \eta f_2))\tau/p} = \frac{1}{\overline{f} + (1 - \overline{f})/p},$$

where the notation $\overline{f} = (f_1 + \eta f_2)/(1+\eta)$ has been introduced, meaning the average proportion of sequential operations in this algorithm.

Problem 3.7: Answer
See Fig. D.3.

Problem 3.8: Proof
Consider the "operations–operands" digraph of the algorithm $\mathcal{A}$. By virtue of the fact that a time T_∞ is required for solution of the computational problem on a paracomputer, the number of levels of the digraph is $d = T_\infty/\tau$, where τ is the execution time of one operation. We denote by n_i, $1 \leqslant i \leqslant d$, the number of nodes at the i-th level.

The algorithm $\mathcal{A}'$ will use a smaller number of processors than $\mathcal{A}$, namely p. In this case, at some level with a number i each processor takes no more than $\lceil n_i/p \rceil$ operations.

We can obtain an estimate of the execution time of the algorithm $\mathcal{A}'$ by summing the times of operation at each of the d levels of the "operations–operands" digraph:

$$T(p) \leqslant \sum_{i=1}^{d} \left\lceil \frac{n_i}{p} \right\rceil \tau.$$

Fig. D.3 Dependence of the maximum efficiency $\left(E_p\right)_{\max}$ on the number of processors p for different values of f, the proportion of sequential computations

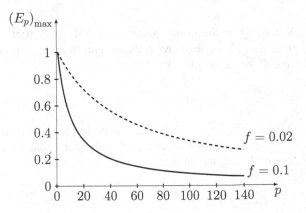

Using the property of the ceiling function $\lceil k/m \rceil \leqslant (k + m - 1)/m$, valid for all $k, m \in \mathbb{N}$, we transform this inequality into the form

$$T(p) \leqslant \sum_{i=1}^{d} \frac{n_i + p - 1}{p} \tau = \frac{1}{p} \sum_{i=1}^{d} n_i \tau + \frac{p - 1}{p} \sum_{i=1}^{d} \tau.$$

In our notation, the execution time of the algorithm $\mathcal{A}$ on a one-processor system is $\sum_{i=1}^{d} n_i \tau = T_1$. We finally obtain an estimate of the execution time of the algorithm $\mathcal{A}'$ on a PRAM with p processors:

$$T(p) \leqslant T_\infty + \frac{T_1 - T_\infty}{p}.$$

Problem 3.9: Solution

The bisection method is used for numerical solution of equations of the form $f(x) = 0$, where $x \in \mathbb{R}$ and the function $f(x)$ is defined and continuous on $[x_1, x_2]$, where the values of $f(x_1)$ and $f(x_2)$ have different signs. In this case, from the property of continuity of functions (the intermediate value theorem, or Bolzano[1]—Cauchy[2] theorem [82]), $f(x)$ has a zero in the segment (x_1, x_2).

The bisection algorithm uses the value $f(x_{mid})$, where $x_{mid} = (x_1 + x_2)/2$ is the bisection point of the segment. If $f(x_{mid}) = 0$, then the root of the equation has been found; otherwise, the algorithm is called recursively on one of the intervals (x_1, x_{mid}) or (x_{mid}, x_2). It is well known that if the above conditions for the function under consideration are satisfied, this algorithm reduces to finding a root of the equation $f(x) = 0$.

Problem 3.10: Answer

(a) $p = 128$;
(b) $p = 32$;
(c) $p = 256$.

Problem 3.11: Answer

(a) $p = 10$;
(b) $p = 15$;
(c) $p = 25$.

Problem 3.12: Answer

(a) $p = 360$;
(b) $p = 133$;
(c) $p = 88$.

---

[1]Bernhard Placidus Johann Nepomuk Bolzano (1781–1848), Czech mathematician and philosopher.

[2]Augustin-Louis Cauchy (1789–1857), French mathematician.

Problem 3.13: Solution

Consider the following pair of statements (o_1, o_2):

```
o₁:     a = a + 1;
o₂:     a = a - 1;
```

It is clear that all three of Bernstein's conditions are violated in this case. Nevertheless, the outputs of programs containing the sequences (o_1, o_2) and (o_2, o_1) will be the same for all possible values of the variable a. Thus, Bernstein's conditions are not necessary conditions for the commutativity of two statements.

Problem 3.14: Solution

We write out the output object sets $W(o_i)$ and input object sets $R(o_i)$ for $i = 1, 2, 3, 4$:

$$W(o_1) = \{a\}, \qquad R(o_1) = \{c\};$$

$$W(o_2) = \{b\}, \qquad R(o_2) = \{a\};$$

$$W(o_3) = \{c\}, \qquad R(o_3) = \{b, c\};$$

$$W(o_4) = \{b\}, \qquad R(o_4) = \{a, c\}.$$

For each pair of statements (o_i, o_j), where $i, j = 1, 2, 3, 4$ and $i < j$, we construct intersections of the form $W(o_i) \cap W(o_j)$, $W(o_i) \cap R(o_j)$, and $R(o_i) \cap W(o_j)$. The intersections that contain any elements lead to dependencies between the respective statements:

$$(o_1, o_2): \quad W(o_1) \cap R(o_2) = \{a\};$$

$$(o_1, o_3): \quad R(o_1) \cap W(o_3) = \{c\};$$

$$(o_1, o_4): \quad W(o_1) \cap R(o_4) = \{a\};$$

$$(o_2, o_3): \quad W(o_2) \cap R(o_3) = \{b\};$$

$$(o_2, o_4): \quad W(o_2) \cap W(o_4) = \{b\};$$

$$(o_3, o_4): \quad W(o_3) \cap R(o_4) = \{c\},$$

$$\qquad\qquad R(o_3) \cap W(o_4) = \{b\}.$$

As a result, we find that the following dependencies are present in the program code section considered:

$$o_1 \delta o_2, \quad o_1 \bar{\delta} o_3, \quad o_1 \delta o_4, \quad o_2 \delta o_3, \quad o_2 \delta^0 o_4, \quad o_3 \delta o_4, \quad o_3 \bar{\delta} o_4.$$

Problem 3.15: Proof

In order to prove the theorem, we use the method of mathematical induction on the number of statements in the program (we will call the number of statements in any program code section the *size* of that section).

Consider an arbitrary program consisting of n statements. We introduce a variable k, which is the size of the coincident part $\mathbf{U}^0 = (u_1, u_2, \ldots, u_k)$ of the vectors $\mathbf{U}$ and $\mathbf{V} = (v_1, v_2, \ldots, v_n)$: $\forall i \leqslant k \ (u_i = v_i)$. The vector $\mathbf{U}^0$ will also be referred to as the common prefix. The variable k can take values from the set $\{0, 1, \ldots, n\}$.

Basis step For the minimum possible value of $n = 2$, we obtain the result that permutation of statements u_1 and u_2 is possible if they are independent. Bernstein's conditions for the pair (u_1, u_2) are fulfilled, and the memory content history is hence preserved.

Inductive step Take the number of components of the vector $\mathbf{U}$ equal to $n > 2$. Since the size of the common prefix is k, then the statement u_{k+1}, after permutation, will occupy a position in $\mathbf{V}$ with index i, where $i > k + 1$. The statement v_{i-1} positioned before v_i in $\mathbf{U}$ must be characterized by an index j, where $j > k + 1$. In the ordered sequences $\mathbf{U}$ and $\mathbf{V}$, the statements $u_{k+1} = v_i$ and $u_j = v_{i-1}$ appear to be positioned in reverse order. Hence, they cannot be in a dependency relationship, since the condition of preservation of the relative order of statements is not fulfilled in this case. Hence, v_i and v_{i-1} can be swapped, and the memory content history will not change.

After that, repeating similar reasoning, we can swap v_{i-1} and v_{i-2} and so on, thus relocating v_i to a position with index $k + 1$. Thus, the size of the common prefix will increase by one and will become equal to $k + 1$. The process described above is repeated until the size of the coincident part of $\mathbf{U}$ and $\mathbf{V}$ takes the value n.

As a result, keeping the memory content history unchanged at each permutation of statements, we come to the statement of the theorem. The statement permutation theorem is proved.

Problem 4.1: Solution

Yes, in the MPI environment, a communicator's process may send a message to any process belonging to the same communicator, including itself. However, it is desirable to avoid this possibility, since in this case a deadlock situation may arise.

Problem 4.2: Answer

(a) $\texttt{rank} \in \{0, 1, \ldots, N - 1\} \cup \{\texttt{MPI\_PROC\_NULL}\}$;
(b) $\texttt{rank} \in \{0, 1, \ldots, N - 1\} \cup \{\texttt{MPI\_PROC\_NULL}\} \cup \{\texttt{MPI\_ANY\_SOURCE}\}$.

Problem 4.3: Solution

In order to measure a time interval, one variable of type double is enough, as shown in the following section of program code:

```
double t;
t = MPI_Wtime();
... // computational part of the program
t = MPI_Wtime() - t;
printf("Computation time is %lf sec.", t);
```

Problem 4.4: Solution

In order to execute the required message-passing operation, the following can be done. The sending of a message in the form of a string constant "testtesttesttest" from a process with rank size − 1 to a process with rank 0 is organized with the help of the standard functions for pairwise message exchange MPI_Send() and MPI_Recv().

The data are placed in the array buf[NMAX]; the size of the string being sent is equal to the value strlen(buf)+1, since in computing this size, the end-of-line character "\0" needs to be taken into consideration.

As can be seen from the program text below, the process with rank size − 1 calls the function MPI_Send(), and the process with rank 0 calls the function MPI_Recv() and, by doing so, stores the data obtained in the array buf. The variable status contains information about the result of execution of the data transfer operation, in particular the actual size of the string received by the process with rank 0. Then, the contents of the array buf[] and the size of the received message are output to the console.

```
#include <stdio.h>
#include <string.h>
#include <mpi.h>

#define NMAX 25

int main( int argc, char * argv[] )
{
    char buf[NMAX];        // array for placement
                           // of the data being sent
    int L;                 // actual size of the line
                           // received by the receiving process
    int rank, size;        // process rank and
                           // the total number
                           // of running processes
    int tag = 1;           // message identifier
    MPI_Status status;     // structure containing
                           // some parameters of
                           // the received message
```

```
MPI_Init(&argc, &argv);

// determining the rank of the process and
// the total number of processes
MPI_Comm_size(MPI_COMM_WORLD, &size);
MPI_Comm_rank(MPI_COMM_WORLD, &rank);

// executing data send and receive operations
if ( rank == size - 1 )
  {
      strcpy(buf, "testtesttesttest");
      MPI_Send(buf, strlen(buf)+1, MPI_CHAR, 0, tag, \
              MPI_COMM_WORLD);
  }
else if ( rank == 0)
      {
          MPI_Recv(buf, NMAX, MPI_CHAR, size-1, tag, \
                  MPI_COMM_WORLD, &status);
          MPI_Get_count(&status, MPI_CHAR, &L);
          printf("Message received: ");
          printf("%s\n", buf);
          printf("Its size - %d characters", L);
      }

MPI_Finalize();
return 0;
}
```

Problem 4.5: Solution

In the program code suggested by the student, all the processes of the global communicator call the function MPI_Send(). Most implementations of the MPI standard use a system buffer (usually of relatively small size) for storing messages, and when this system buffer is full or too small, the synchronous message-passing mode is used. Hence, a situation is possible where all the processes will be blocked by a call of a synchronous option of the message-passing function, i.e., a deadlock situation.

The correct solution to this problem using the standard-message passing function MPI_Send() consists in permutation of the order of the operations MPI_Send() and MPI_Recv(), called in processes with odd ranks. We present the appropriate program code below.

Listing 7.1

```
1 #include <stdio.h>
2 #include <mpi.h>
3
4 #define N 25
```

```
 5
 6    // user function fill_buffer() places
 7    // into array buf[] the data to be sent
 8    void fill_buffer(char buffer[]);
 9
10    int main(int argc, char * argv[])
11    {
12      char buf[N];              // buffer for placement
13                                // of the data being sent
14      int rank, size;          // process rank and
15                                // total number of
16                                processes
17      int next, prev;          // ranks of the next
18                                // clockwise process and
19                                // the previous process
20      int tag = 1;             // message identifier
21      MPI_Status status;       // structure containing
22                                // some parameters of
23                                // the received message
24
25      MPI_Init(&argc, &argv);
26
27      MPI_Comm_rank(MPI_COMM_WORLD, &rank);
28      MPI_Comm_size(MPI_COMM_WORLD, &size);
29
30      // computing the ranks of the next and previous
31          processes
32      next = rank + 1;
33      prev = rank - 1;
34      if (prev < 0)
35        prev = size - 1;
36      if (next >= size)
37        next = 0;
38
39      // the data to be sent are placed into the buffer
40      fill_buffer(buf);
41
42      // organizing message exchange
43      if ( rank%2 != 0 )
44        {
45           MPI_Recv(buf, N, MPI_CHAR, prev, tag,
46                    MPI_COMM_WORLD, &status);
47           MPI_Send(buf, N, MPI_CHAR, next, tag,
48                    MPI_COMM_WORLD);
```

```
49      }
50    else
51    {
52          MPI_Send(buf, N, MPI_CHAR, next, tag,
53                  MPI_COMM_WORLD);
54          MPI_Recv(buf, N, MPI_CHAR, prev, tag,
55                  MPI_COMM_WORLD, &status);
56    }
57
58    MPI_Finalize();
59    return 0;
60 }
```

The user function fill_buffer() places into the array buf[N] the data that will form the message to be sent.

Note that the computation of the ranks of the next and previous processes in lines 30–35 of the program can be written more succinctly, for example as follows:

```
next = (rank + 1) % rank;
prev = (rank - 1 + size) % size;
```

As an alternative solution, we can offer an option using nonblocking data-passing operations (see Sect. 4.5 and following pages).

Problem 4.7: Solution

Let the number of processors used for solution of this problem be size. We represent the set [Nmin, Nmax] in the form of a union of nonintersecting segments of length chunk:

$$\text{chunk} = \left\lceil \frac{\text{Nmax} - \text{Nmin} + 1}{\text{size}} \right\rceil.$$

If size does not divide (Nmax − Nmin + 1) exactly, then the last segment will have a length less than chunk.

On each of the specified intervals, the search for prime numbers can be performed with the help of the following sufficient condition: if a natural number $k \geqslant 2$ is not divisible exactly by any of the numbers from the set $\{2, 3, 4, \ldots, \lfloor\sqrt{k}\rfloor\}$, then k is prime. We check this condition with the help of the function is_prime(k):

```
bool is_prime( int k )

{
  int i;
  int i_max = (int)sqrt(k);
  for ( i=2; i<=i_max; i++ )
    if ( k%i == 0)
      return false;
  return true;
}
```

Allocation of memory for storing the prime numbers obtained requires estimation of the quantity of prime numbers in the segment [Nmin, Nmax]. We can obtain such an estimate based on Chebyshev's[3] inequality for the function $\pi(x)$, the number of primes not exceeding the argument x:

$$a\frac{x}{\ln x} < \pi(x) < b\frac{x}{\ln x} \quad \forall x > x_0,$$

where a, b, and x_0 are constants [21]. In [62], it was shown that for $x_0 > 17$ we can take $a = 1.0$ and $b = 1.25506$. In our program, we choose $a = 0.8$ and $b = 1.3$ for the purpose of taking into account the points at the boundaries of the segment under investigation. From the inequality for $\pi(x)$ it follows that the interval [Nmin, Nmax] being investigated contains no more than

$$\left\lfloor b\frac{\text{Nmax}}{\ln \text{Nmax}} \right\rfloor - \left\lceil a\frac{\text{Nmin}}{\ln \text{Nmin}} \right\rceil$$

prime numbers.

The program code that solves this problem is presented below:

```c
#include <stdio.h>
#include <stdlib.h>
#include <stdbool.h>
#include <math.h>
#include <mpi.h>

const double a = 0.8;
const double b = 1.3;

bool is_prime( int k );

int main( int argc, char * argv[] )
{
  int k;
  int input_check;        // variable used for verifying
                          // the correctness of the input
                          // data received

  int Nmin, Nmax;         // limits of the interval
                          // under investigation
  int Nmin_loc, Nmax_loc; // limits of the local intervals
  int count;              // quantity of prime numbers
                          // found at each computing node
```

---

[3]Pafnutiy Lvovich Chebyshev (1821–1894), Russian mathematician and mechanician.

```
int chunk;                    // quantity of numbers
                              // under investigation
                              // falling within each process

int buf[3];                   // temporary buffer for passing
                              // the local parameters
                              // to all processes

int number_of_primes, max_number_of_primes;

int * p, * p_loc;             // in arrays p[] and p_loc[]
                              // are stored the prime
                              // numbers found
int * counts_array;           // array counts_array[]
                              // contains the quantity
                              // of prime numbers determined
                              // in each process
int * displs;                 // auxiliary array for
                              // function MPI_Gatherv()

int rank, size;               // process rank and
                              // the total number
                              // of running processes

int root = 0;

FILE * fp;


MPI_Init(&argc, &argv);
MPI_Comm_rank(MPI_COMM_WORLD, &rank);
MPI_Comm_size(MPI_COMM_WORLD, &size);

if ( rank == 0 )
  {
    if ((fp = fopen("input.txt","r")) == NULL)
      {
          perror("\nError opening initial file "
                "\"input.txt\"");
          fclose(fp);
          MPI_Abort(MPI_COMM_WORLD, MPI_ERR_OTHER);
      }
    input_check = 0;
    if ((input_check = fscanf(fp, "%d %d", \
```

```
                              &Nmin,  &Nmax)) !=2)
    {
        perror("\nError reading parameters " \
               "Nmin and Nmax");
        fclose(fp);
        MPI_Abort(MPI_COMM_WORLD, MPI_ERR_OTHER);
    };
    fclose(fp);

    // upper bound for the quantity of prime numbers
    // on segment [Nmin,Nmax]
    if ( Nmin != 1 )
       max_number_of_primes = floor(b*Nmax/log(Nmax)) - \
                              ceil(a*Nmin/log(Nmin));
    else
       max_number_of_primes = floor(b*Nmax/log(Nmax));
    buf[0] = Nmin;
    buf[1] = Nmax;
    buf[2] = max_number_of_primes;
  }

MPI_Bcast(buf, 3, MPI_INT, root, MPI_COMM_WORLD);
Nmin = buf[0];
Nmax = buf[1];
max_number_of_primes = buf[2];

// small arguments case
if ( Nmax <= 17 )
  {
    if ( rank == 0 )
      {
        if ((fp = fopen("output.txt","w")) == NULL)
          {
            perror("\nError opening file "
                   "\"output.txt\"");
            fclose(fp);
            MPI_Abort(MPI_COMM_WORLD, MPI_ERR_OTHER);
          }
        for ( k = Nmin; k <= Nmax; k++ )
          if ((k==2)||(k==3)||(k==5)||(k==7)||(k==11) \
                 ||(k==13)||(k==17))
            fprintf(fp, "%d ", k);
        printf("\nThe result is written " \
               "to file \"output.txt\"");
        fclose(fp);
```

```
        }

    MPI_Finalize();
    return 0;
  }

if ((p_loc = \
    (int *)malloc(max_number_of_primes*sizeof(int)))==NULL)
  {

    perror("\nError allocating memory "
            "to array p_loc[]");
    MPI_Abort(MPI_COMM_WORLD, MPI_ERR_OTHER);
  }

chunk = ceil((double)((Nmax-Nmin+1)/size));
Nmin_loc = Nmin + chunk*rank;
Nmax_loc = Nmin - 1 + chunk*(rank+1);

count = 0;
// number 1 is not prime
if ( Nmin_loc == 1 )
  Nmin_loc++;
// number 2 is prime
if ( Nmin_loc == 2 )
  {
    p_loc[count++]=2;
    Nmin_loc++;
  }
// an even number greater than 2 cannot be prime
if ( (Nmin_loc%2) == 0 )
  Nmin_loc++;

if ( Nmax_loc > Nmax )
  Nmax_loc = Nmax;

for ( k=Nmin_loc; k<=Nmax_loc; k+=2 )
  if ( is_prime(k) )
    p_loc[count++] = k;

if ( rank == 0 )
  {
    if ((counts_array = \
          (int *)malloc(size*sizeof(int)))==NULL)
      {
        perror("\nError allocating memory to array " \
```

```
                                "counts_array[]");
                 MPI_Abort(MPI_COMM_WORLD, MPI_ERR_OTHER);
             }
         if ((displs = (int *)malloc(size*sizeof(int)))==NULL)
            {
                perror("\nError allocating memory to array " \
                        "displs[]");
                MPI_Abort(MPI_COMM_WORLD, MPI_ERR_OTHER);
            }
     }

MPI_Gather(&count, 1, MPI_INT, counts_array, 1, MPI_INT, \
           root, MPI_COMM_WORLD);

if ( rank == 0 )
   {
       // forming the displacement array
       // for function MPI_Gatherv()
       displs[0] = 0;
       for ( k = 1; k <= size ; k++ )
         displs[k] = displs[k-1] + counts_array[k-1];

       number_of_primes = 0;
       for ( k = 0; k < size ; k++ )
         number_of_primes += counts_array[k];

       if ((p = \
           (int *)malloc(number_of_primes*sizeof(int)))==NULL)
          {
              perror("\nError allocating memory to array p[]");
              MPI_Abort(MPI_COMM_WORLD, MPI_ERR_OTHER);
          }
   }

MPI_Gatherv(p_loc, count, MPI_INT, p, counts_array, \
            displs, MPI_INT, root, MPI_COMM_WORLD);

free(p_loc);

if ( rank == 0 )
  {
      free(counts_array);
      free(displs);

      if ((fp = fopen("output.txt","w")) == NULL)
```

```
        {
            perror("\nError opening file " \
                    "\"output.txt\"");
            fclose(fp);
            MPI_Abort(MPI_COMM_WORLD, MPI_ERR_OTHER);
        }

        for ( k=0; k < number_of_primes; k++ )
            fprintf(fp, "%d ", p[k]);
        printf("\nThe result is written to file " \
                "\"output.txt\"\n");

        free(p);
        fclose(fp);
    }

    MPI_Finalize();
    return 0;
}

bool is_prime( int k )
{
    int i;
    int i_max = (int)sqrt(k);
    for ( i=3; i<=i_max; i+=2 )
        if ( k%i == 0)
            return false;
    return true;
}
```

As is well known, no even number except 2 is prime. For this reason, the function
is_prime(k) is only called in the program for odd arguments, and hence the
check of the condition k%i == 0 for even values of i is redundant. Writing the
main computation cycle of the function is_prime() in the form
for (i=3; i<=i_max; i+=2)
decreases the number of comparisons, but the procedure of checking the odd number
k for primality remains correct.

Let us estimate the program's running time, considering the case of execution on
a computing system with a number of processors equal to size. The running time
of the function is_prime() is $\Theta(\lfloor\sqrt{k}\rfloor/2) = \Theta(\sqrt{k})$. Since k ⩽ Nmax, the full
running time T_{size} satisfies the relation

$$T_{size}(Nmin, Nmax) = O\left(\frac{\sqrt{Nmax}(Nmax - Nmin)}{size}\right).$$

Problem 4.8: Solution

We denote the integer vector of input data by $\mathbf{a}$:

$$\mathbf{a} = (11, 21, 31, 41, 51).$$

(a) The function MPI_MAX determines the maximum number among the components of the vector $\mathbf{a}$. It is clear that MPI_MAX($\mathbf{a}$) $= 51$.

(b) The function MPI_MIN computes the minimum number among the components of $\mathbf{a}$; therefore, MPI_MIN($\mathbf{a}$) $= 11$.

(c) Since the predefined function MPI_SUM computes the sum of its arguments, then

$$\text{MPI\_SUM}(\mathbf{a}) = 11 + 21 + 31 + 41 + 51 = 155.$$

(d) The function MPI_PROD computes the product of the arguments; therefore,

$$\text{MPI\_PROD}(\mathbf{a}) = 11 \times 21 \times 31 \times 41 \times 51 = 14,973,651.$$

(e) In this case, the arguments are viewed as logical values, and the function MPI_LAND computes the conjunction of its arguments. Recall that in the C language the numerical value of a logical expression is something other than zero if the expression is true, and is equal to zero if it is false.

Since the conjunction of several variables takes the value true if and only if all the arguments take the value true, then

$$\text{MPI\_LAND}(\mathbf{a}) = 1.$$

(f) The function MPI_BAND calculates a bitwise conjunction. In order to compute the value of this function, we write the components of the vector $\mathbf{a}$ in a binary representation. As is well known, in most modern computing systems, four bytes of memory are allocated for storing a variable of type int. Hence, the binary representation of an arbitrary integer of this type contains $4 \times 8 = 32$ bits.

In the case of the vector $\mathbf{a}$, the three high-order bytes of all components contain only bits that are equal to zero. For brevity, we denote the high-order bytes by an ellipsis:

$$11 = 8 + 2 + 1 \qquad\qquad = (\ldots 0000\,1011)_2,$$
$$21 = 16 + 4 + 1 \qquad\qquad = (\ldots 0001\,0101)_2,$$
$$31 = 16 + 8 + 4 + 2 + 1 \quad = (\ldots 0001\,1111)_2,$$
$$41 = 32 + 8 + 1 \qquad\qquad = (\ldots 0010\,1001)_2,$$
$$51 = 32 + 16 + 2 + 1 \quad = (\ldots 0011\,0011)_2.$$

By applying a bitwise conjunction to these bit strings, we find the value of the function:

$$\text{MPI\_BAND}(\mathbf{a}) = (\dots 0000\,0001)_2 = 1.$$

(g) The function MPI_LOR calculates the disjunction of the arguments considered as logical values. The disjunction of several variables takes the value true if and only if at least one of the arguments takes the value true. Hence, MPI_LOR(**a**) = 1.

(h) We use the binary representation of the arguments of the vector **a**. In this case, the bitwise disjunction is equal to

$$\text{MPI\_BOR}(\mathbf{a}) = (\dots 0011\,1111)_2 = 63.$$

(i) The function MPI_LXOR performs the logical operation of "exclusive OR": MPI_LXOR(**a**) = 1, since all the arguments have the value true and the number of them is odd.

(j) The function MPI_BXOR is used to compute a bitwise "exclusive OR". Computation shows that

$$\text{MPI\_BXOR}(\mathbf{a}) = (\dots 0001\,1011)_2 = 27.$$

To validate the solution obtained, we may use the program code presented below:

```c
#include <stdio.h>
#include <stdlib.h>
#include <mpi.h>

#define N 5                    // input data vector size

int main( int argc, char * argv[] )
{
  int rank, size;            // process rank and
                             // the total number
                             // of running processes

  int a;                     // data to which the reduction
                             // operation is applied
  int res;                   // result of the reduction operation

  int root = 0;

  MPI_Init(&argc, &argv);
  MPI_Comm_rank(MPI_COMM_WORLD, &rank);
  MPI_Comm_size(MPI_COMM_WORLD, &size);
```

```
if ( size != N )
  {
    if ( rank == root )
      perror("\nThe number of running processes " \
             "should be equal to 5");
    MPI_Abort(MPI_COMM_WORLD, MPI_ERR_OTHER);
  }

// forming the input data vector
switch ( rank )
  {
    case 0:
             a = 11;
             break;
    case 1:
             a = 21;
             break;
    case 2:
             a = 31;
             break;
    case 3:
             a = 41;
             break;
    case 4:
             a = 51;
             break;
  }


MPI_Reduce(&a, &res, 1, MPI_INT, MPI_MAX, root, \
           MPI_COMM_WORLD);
if ( rank == root )
  printf("MAX = %d\n", res);

MPI_Reduce(&a, &res, 1, MPI_INT, MPI_MIN, root, \
           MPI_COMM_WORLD);
if ( rank == root )
  printf("MIN = %d\n", res);

MPI_Reduce(&a, &res, 1, MPI_INT, MPI_SUM, root, \
           MPI_COMM_WORLD);
if ( rank == root )
  printf("SUM = %d\n", res);

// ... further, similar for operations MPI_LAND,
// MPI_BAND, MPI_LOR, MPI_BOR, MPI_LXOR
```

```
// and MPI_BXOR

MPI_Finalize();
return 0;
}
```

Problem 4.9: Answer
The result of execution of the reduction operation changes in part (d) only. Because the product of the components of the input data vector exceeds the upper bound of the type `short int` in the C language, arithmetic overflow occurs. In a program prepared with the help of the GCC compiler, the number

$$11 \times 21 \times 31 \times 41 \times 51 \bmod 2^{16} = 31,443$$

will be written in the variable `res` (see the program code on pages 171–173 in Appendix D).

The results do not change in the remaining parts of the problem.

Problem 4.10: Solution
According to the MPI standard, the function `MPI_Reduce()`, used for computing the maximum of the numbers and its position in the source file, returns the *lexicographic maximum* (see Sect. 4.6). This means that the smallest of the possible values of the index of such an element will be written in the answer.

Problem 4.11: Hint
Computing the standard deviation $D(\mathbf{x})$ by the specified formula requires knowledge of the mean value $E(\mathbf{x})$. For parallel computing of these values, it is convenient to use the auxiliary sums $U = \sum_{i=1}^{N} x_i$ and $V = \sum_{i=1}^{N} x_i^2$. The sought values can be expressed with the help of the following easily verifiable relations, linking the sums U and V to $E(\mathbf{x})$ and $D(\mathbf{x})$:

$$E(\mathbf{x}) = \frac{V}{N},$$

$$D(\mathbf{x}) = \frac{1}{N-1}\left(NU - V^2\right).$$

Problem 4.12: Solution
In order to compute the number of prime twins, i.e. pairs of prime numbers of the form $(p, p + 2)$, we use a reduction operation with the predefined function `MPI_SUM`. The program code is provided below:

```
#include <stdio.h>
#include <stdlib.h>
#include <stdbool.h>
#include <math.h>
#include <mpi.h>
```

```
bool is_prime( int k );

int main( int argc, char * argv[] )
{
  int k;
  int input_check;          // variable used for verifying
                            // the correctness of the input
                            // data received

  int N;                    // upper bound of the interval
                            // under investigation
  int Nmin_loc, Nmax_loc;   // limits of the local intervals
  int count;                // number of pairs of twins
                            // found by the process
  int chunk;                // quantity of the numbers
                            // under investigation falling
                            // within each process
  int res;                  // total number of pairs of twins

  int rank, size;           // process rank and
                            // the total number
                            // of running processes
  int root = 0;

  FILE * fp;

  MPI_Init(&argc, &argv);
  MPI_Comm_rank(MPI_COMM_WORLD, &rank);
  MPI_Comm_size(MPI_COMM_WORLD, &size);

  if ( rank == 0 )
    {
        if ((fp = fopen("input.txt","r")) == NULL)
          {
              perror("\nError opening initial file " \
                     "\"input.txt\"");
              fclose(fp);
              MPI_Abort(MPI_COMM_WORLD, MPI_ERR_OTHER);
          }
        input_check = 0;
        if ((input_check = fscanf(fp, "%d", &N))!=1)
          {
              perror("\nError reading parameter N");
              fclose(fp);
              MPI_Abort(MPI_COMM_WORLD, MPI_ERR_OTHER);
```

```
        };
      fclose(fp);
   }


MPI_Bcast(&N, 1, MPI_INT, root, MPI_COMM_WORLD);


// initializing the variable accumulating
// the total number of pairs of twins
res = 0;


// small arguments case
if ( N <= 6 )
   {
      if ( rank == 0 )
        {
            if ((fp = fopen("output.txt","w")) == NULL)
              {
                  perror("\nError opening file " \
                         "\"output.txt\"");
                  fclose(fp);
                  MPI_Abort(MPI_COMM_WORLD, MPI_ERR_OTHER);
              }
            fprintf(fp, "%d", 1);
            printf("\nThe result is written " \
                   "\nto file \"output.txt\"");
            fclose(fp);
        }

      MPI_Finalize();
      return 0;
   }


chunk = ceil((double)(N/size));
Nmin_loc = 1 + chunk*rank;
Nmax_loc = chunk*(rank+1);


count = 0;


if ( Nmin_loc <= 2 )
  Nmin_loc = 3;


// an even number greater than 2 cannot be prime
if ( (Nmin_loc%2) == 0 )
  Nmin_loc++;
```

```
if ( Nmax_loc > N-2 )
  Nmax_loc = N-2;


for ( k=Nmin_loc; k<=Nmax_loc; k+=2 )
  if ( is_prime(k) && is_prime(k+2) )
    count++;


MPI_Reduce(&count, &res, 1, MPI_INT, MPI_SUM, root, \
           MPI_COMM_WORLD);


if ( rank == 0 )
  {
      if ((fp = fopen("output.txt","w")) == NULL)
        {
            perror("\nError opening file \"output.txt\"");
            fclose(fp);
            MPI_Abort(MPI_COMM_WORLD, MPI_ERR_OTHER);
        }

      fprintf(fp, "%d", res);
      printf("\nThe result is written to file " \
             "\"output.txt\"\n");

      fclose(fp);
  }

MPI_Finalize();
return 0;
}


bool is_prime( int k )
{
  int i;
  int i_max = (int)sqrt(k);
  for ( i=3; i<=i_max; i+=2 )
    if ( k%i == 0)
      return false;
  return true;
}
```

The resulting computations show that, for example, in the first 10^9 natural numbers the number of prime twins is equal to 3,424,506.

Problem 5.1: Answer

(a) The loop allows parallelization; the corresponding directive is

```
#pragma omp parallel for
```
(b) The loop allows parallelization; the corresponding directive is
```
#pragma omp parallel for reduction(+:res)
```
(c) The presence of the operator break does not allow the use of parallelization directives.
(d) For $N > 4k$ there is a dependency between loop iterations, and therefore one cannot apply OpenMP directives.

Problem 5.2: Solution

(a) The compiler will ignore the second directive owing to a syntax error – the omission in the line #pragma single of the reserved word omp. The correct version of this line is
```
#pragma omp single
```
(b) The directive #pragma omp parallel starts a parallel region, and the loop will be executed by each thread separately. The correct directive is
```
#pragma omp parallel for.
```
(c) The scope of the parameter ordered is not specified. The correct option is, instead of the line res[i]=func(1.0/(i+1)), to put the lines

```
{
    #pragma omp ordered
        res[i]=func(1.0/(i+1));
}
```

In addition, there is one more inaccuracy in the code. The function ceil returns a double value, and therefore the loop continuation condition must be written as i<(int)ceil(log2(N)).
(d) A common resource, in this case the external file associated with the pointer fp, cannot be used simultaneously by different threads. One must add the directive #pragma omp critical immediately before calling the function fprintf().

Problem 5.3: Answer
$k = (i$ div $p)$ mod (mp).

Problem 5.4: Solution
According to the rules of combinatorics, the number of options for distributing the students among the enterprises is equal to the number of combinations with repetition of $k = 62$ from $N = 6$, or $(n + k - 1)!/k!(n - 1)! = 67!/62!5! = 9,657,648$.

The following program provides an opportunity to obtain this answer by an exhaustive search. Parallelization is implemented in a standard way by applying the directive parallel for to the outer loop. Note that parallelization of inner loops greatly increases the overhead during program execution and is therefore rarely used. The counters of the inner loops should be declared as local variables. It is easy to combine the results obtained from different threads using a reduction operation.

```
#include <stdio.h>

#define K 62        // number of students

int main ( void )
{
  unsigned short int i1,i2,i3,i4,i5,i6;

  // the number of ways of distributing
  // students to enterprises, or
  // the number of combinations of K from 6
  unsigned long count = 0;

  #pragma omp parallel for \
  private(i2,i3,i4,i5,i6)   \
  reduction(+:count)
  for (i1=0; i1<=K; i1++)
    for (i2=0; i2<=K; i2++)
      for (i3=0; i3<=K; i3++)
        for (i4=0; i4<=K; i4++)
          for (i5=0; i5<=K; i5++)
            for (i6=0; i6<=K; i6++)
              if (i1+i2+i3+i4+i5+i6==K)
                count++;

  printf("The number of ways = %lu", count);
  return 0;
}
```

Problem 5.5: Solution

As a combinatorial calculation shows, the number of ways to select eight of the company's employees in this case is equal to

$$L = C(35, 8) - (C(24, 8) + C(20, 8) + C(26, 8))$$
$$+ (C(9, 8) + C(15, 8) + C(11, 8)) = 21,118,713,$$

where $C(n, k) = n!/(k!(n - k)!)$ is the number of combinations of k elements from n, or a binomial coefficient [2, 60].

In the following program, the value of L is obtained with the help of an exhaustive search of the possible options. As the basis, we take a simple algorithm that lists all subsets of the set of the company's employees. In C, it is especially easy to implement such an enumeration using a binary representation of nonnegative integers.

We consider a 64-bit number k, the first 35 bits of which, with the numbers $i = 0, 1, \ldots, 34$, reflect the inclusion of the i-th employee in a list. All ways to select several employees are enumerated in a loop in which k runs from 0 to $2^{35} - 1$. The program code is as follows:

```c
#include <stdio.h>
#include <stdint.h>

#define N        35    // the total number
                       // of employees

#define N_eng  11      // the number of engineers
#define N_prog 15      // the number of programmers
#define N_test  9      // the number of testing
                       // specialists

int main ( void )
{
  uint64_t k;

  unsigned long int i;
  unsigned long int sum;
  unsigned long int sum_eng, sum_prog, sum_test;
  unsigned long int count = 0;

  // in the main computational cycle
  // the search of all possible combinations
  // of employees occurs
  #pragma omp parallel for \
  private(i,k,sum,sum_eng,sum_prog,sum_test) \
  reduction(+:count)
  for (k=0; k<((uint64_t)1<<N); k++)
    {
      // bit string b[N] forms
      // the current combination
      unsigned short int b[N];

      sum = sum_eng = sum_prog = sum_test = 0;

      for (i=0; i<N; i++)
        {
          b[i] = (k>>i)&1;
          sum += b[i];
        }

      // calculating the number of engineers,
      // programmers, and testing specialists
```

```
// in this combination
for(i=0;i<N_eng;i++)
    sum_eng += b[i];
for(i=N_eng;i<N_eng+N_prog;i++)
    sum_prog += b[i];
for(i=N_eng+N_prog;i<N_eng+N_prog+N_test;i++)
    sum_test += b[i];

if ( (sum==8)&&(sum_eng>0) \
        && (sum_prog>0)&&(sum_test>0) )
    count++;
    }

    printf("Number of ways = %ld", count);
    return 0;
}
```

An exhaustive list of combinatorial algorithms for solving problems of this type is given in [35].

Problem 5.8: Answer

With an absolute error not exceeding μ, we have:

(a) $\mathcal{I} = 0.7447989188$;
(b) $\mathcal{I} = 0.6394221546$;
(c) $\mathcal{I} = 2.6020169324$;
(d) $\mathcal{I} = 3.1415925567$.

Problem 5.9: Solution

To perform numerical integration, we use a method based on the application of the midpoint quadrature formula (see Example 5.3):

$$\mathcal{I} = \iint\limits_{\mathcal{D}} f(x, y)\, dx\, dy = \delta_1 \delta_2 \sum_{i=1}^{N_1} \sum_{j=1}^{N_2} f(x_i, y_j) + R,$$

where $f(x, y) = \ln(x^2 + y^2 + 1)$ and R is the error of the quadrature formula.

Let us estimate the absolute error of the midpoint quadrature formula. For this purpose, we calculate the maximum absolute values of the second-order partial derivatives of the function $f(x, y)$,

$$M_{2x} = \max_{(x,y)\in\mathcal{D}} \left| \frac{\partial^2 f(x, y)}{\partial x^2} \right|, \quad M_{2y} = \max_{(x,y)\in\mathcal{D}} \left| \frac{\partial^2 f(x, y)}{\partial y^2} \right|.$$

To determine M_{2x}, we introduce the function $u(x, y) = \left| \partial^2 f(x, y)/\partial x^2 \right|$ and examine it for a maximum. As the domain of definition of $u(x, y)$ we assume the entire real plane $\mathbb{R}^2$, in order to take into account possible critical points of this function. By double differentiation of $f(x, y)$, we obtain an analytical expression for the function $u(x, y)$:

$$\frac{\partial f(x, y)}{\partial x} = 2\frac{x}{x^2 + y^2 + 1}, \quad \frac{\partial^2 f(x, y)}{\partial x^2} = 2\frac{y^2 - x^2 + 1}{(x^2 + y^2 + 1)^2};$$

consequently,

$$u(x, y) = \left|\frac{\partial^2 f(x, y)}{\partial x^2}\right| = 2\frac{|y^2 - x^2 + 1|}{(x^2 + y^2 + 1)^2}.$$

The function $u(x, y)$ is defined on the whole real plane $\mathbb{R}^2$. As is well known, a necessary condition for an extremum of a function of two variables is that the partial derivatives with respect to each of these variables are equal to zero:

$$\begin{cases} \dfrac{\partial}{\partial x}u(x, y) = 0, \\[2mm] \dfrac{\partial}{\partial y}u(x, y) = 0. \end{cases}$$

In order to differentiate the absolute value of a function $\mathcal{F}(x)$, we can use the defining formula for the modulus of a real number:

$$\frac{d}{dx}|\mathcal{F}(x)| = \frac{d}{dx}\begin{cases} \mathcal{F}(x) \text{ if } \mathcal{F}(x) > 0, \\ -\mathcal{F}(x) \text{ if } \mathcal{F}(x) < 0 \end{cases}$$

$$= \begin{cases} \dfrac{d}{dx}\mathcal{F}(x) \text{ if } \mathcal{F}(x) > 0, \\[2mm] -\dfrac{d}{dx}\mathcal{F}(x) \text{ if } \mathcal{F}(x) < 0 \end{cases} = \frac{d\mathcal{F}(x)}{dx}\,\text{sign}(\mathcal{F}(x)), \quad \mathcal{F}(x) \neq 0,$$

where $\text{sign}(x)$ is the sign of the number $x \in \mathbb{R}$. We draw attention to the fact that the case $\mathcal{F}(x) = 0$ requires separate consideration, since at the zeros of the function $\mathcal{F}(x)$ the derivative of the modulus of this function may not exist, even if the function itself is differentiable over the entire domain of definition.

After some algebraic transformations, we obtain

$$\frac{\partial}{\partial x}\left|\frac{\partial^2 f(x,y)}{\partial x^2}\right| = 4x\,\frac{x^2 - 3y^2 - 3}{(x^2 + y^2 + 1)^3}\,\mathrm{sign}(y^2 - x^2 + 1), \quad y^2 - x^2 + 1 \neq 0.$$

At the points of the plane $\mathbb{R}^2$ on the hyperbola

$$\Gamma = \{(x,y)\colon y^2 - x^2 + 1 = 0\},$$

we have $u(x,y)|_\Gamma = \left|\partial^2 f(x,y)/\partial x^2\right|\big|_\Gamma \equiv 0$. It is easy to see that at such points the smallest value of a nonnegatively defined function $u(x,y)$ is equal to zero.

Similarly, for a derivative with respect to the variable y, we obtain

$$\frac{\partial}{\partial y}\left|\frac{\partial^2 f(x,y)}{\partial x^2}\right| = 4y\,\frac{3x^2 - y^2 - 1}{(x^2 + y^2 + 1)^3}\,\mathrm{sign}(y^2 - x^2 + 1), \quad y^2 - x^2 + 1 \neq 0.$$

At the points where the equality $y^2 - x^2 + 1 = 0$, holds, the maximum of the function $u(x,y)$ cannot be achieved, for the above reason.

We can write the necessary conditions for an extremum in the form of a system of algebraic equations,

$$\begin{cases} \dfrac{\partial}{\partial x}\left|\dfrac{\partial^2 f(x,y)}{\partial x^2}\right| = 0, \\[3mm] \dfrac{\partial}{\partial y}\left|\dfrac{\partial^2 f(x,y)}{\partial x^2}\right| = 0, \end{cases}$$

provided that $y^2 - x^2 + 1 \neq 0$. Elementary algebraic calculations make it possible to obtain a set of solutions to the above system:

$$A = \{(0,0), (-\sqrt{3},0), (\sqrt{3},0)\}.$$

From among the possible points of a local extremum, we select only those at which $u(x,y)$ takes its maximum value. We use a sufficient condition for an extremum of a twice differentiable function $u(x,y)$ of two variables: (x_0, y_0) is a point of a possible extremum, and at this point the following condition holds:

$$\frac{\partial^2 u}{\partial x^2}\frac{\partial^2 u}{\partial y^2} - \left(\frac{\partial^2 u}{\partial x\,\partial y}\right)^2 > 0,$$

Then the function $u(x,y)$ has a local extremum at (x_0, y_0), namely, a maximum for $\partial^2 u(x,y)/\partial x^2\big|_{(x_0,y_0)} < 0$ and a minimum for $\partial^2 u(x,y)/\partial x^2\big|_{(x_0,y_0)} > 0$. If at

(x_0, y_0) the inequality

$$\frac{\partial^2 u}{\partial x^2}\frac{\partial^2 u}{\partial y^2} - \left(\frac{\partial^2 u}{\partial x\,\partial y}\right)^2 < 0$$

holds, then $u(x, y)$ does not have an extremum at this point.

We now verify the fulfillment of this sufficient condition for an extremum at each of the points in the set A. To this end, we compute the second-order partial derivatives of the function $u(x, y)$:

$$\frac{\partial^2 u}{\partial x^2} = -12\,\frac{x^4 - 6x^2(y^2 + 1) + (y^2 + 1)^2}{(x^2 + y^2 + 1)^4}\,\mathrm{sign}(y^2 - x^2 + 1),\quad y^2 - x^2 + 1 \neq 0,$$

$$\frac{\partial^2 u}{\partial x\,\partial y} = -48\,xy\,\frac{x^2 - y^2 - 1}{(x^2 + y^2 + 1)^4}\,\mathrm{sign}(y^2 - x^2 + 1),\quad y^2 - x^2 + 1 \neq 0,$$

$$\frac{\partial^2 u}{\partial y^2} = 4\,\frac{3x^4 + 3y^4 - 18x^2 y^2 + 2x^2 + 2y^2 - 1}{(x^2 + y^2 + 1)^4}\,\mathrm{sign}(y^2 - x^2 + 1),\quad y^2 - x^2 + 1 \neq 0.$$

1. Let $x_0 = 0$, $y_0 = 0$. Then

$$\left.\frac{\partial^2 u}{\partial x^2}\right|_{(0,0)} = -12,\quad \left.\frac{\partial^2 u}{\partial x\,\partial y}\right|_{(0,0)} = 0,\quad \left.\frac{\partial^2 u}{\partial y^2}\right|_{(0,0)} = -4.$$

The sufficient condition for the extremum takes the form $(-12)\times(-4) - 0^2 > 0$. Consequently, at the point $(0, 0)$ the function $\left|\partial^2 f(x, y)/\partial x^2\right|$ has a local maximum.

2. Let $x_0 = -\sqrt{3}$, $y_0 = 0$. In this case

$$\left.\frac{\partial^2 u}{\partial x^2}\right|_{(-\sqrt{3},0)} = -\frac{3}{8},\quad \left.\frac{\partial^2 u}{\partial x\,\partial y}\right|_{(-\sqrt{3},0)} = 0,\quad \left.\frac{\partial^2 u}{\partial y^2}\right|_{(-\sqrt{3},0)} = -\frac{1}{2}.$$

Consequently, at the point $(-\sqrt{3}, 0)$ the function $\left|\partial^2 f(x, y)/\partial x^2\right|$ has a local maximum.

3. Let $x_0 = \sqrt{3}$, $y_0 = 0$. Then

$$\left.\frac{\partial^2 u}{\partial x^2}\right|_{(\sqrt{3},0)} = -\frac{3}{8},\quad \left.\frac{\partial^2 u}{\partial x\,\partial y}\right|_{(\sqrt{3},0)} = 0,\quad \left.\frac{\partial^2 u}{\partial y^2}\right|_{(\sqrt{3},0)} = -\frac{1}{2}.$$

As in the previous two cases, at the point $(\sqrt{3}, 0)$ the function $\left|\partial^2 f(x, y)/\partial x^2\right|$ has a local maximum.

Calculating the values of the function $u(x, y)$ at the points $(x_0, y_0) \in A$, we obtain

$$u\Big|_{(0,0)} = 2, \quad u\Big|_{(-\sqrt{3},0)} = \frac{1}{4}, \quad u\Big|_{(\sqrt{3},0)} = \frac{1}{4}.$$

Hence it follows that the maximum of the function $u(x, y)$, defined at the interior points of the rectangle $\mathcal{D}$, is reached at the point $(0, 0)$.

Using the methods of the differential calculus of functions of one variable, we can show that on the boundary of the rectangle

$$\partial \mathcal{D} = \{(x, y) \colon (a_1 \leqslant x \leqslant b_1 \text{ and } y = a_2) \text{ or } (a_1 \leqslant x \leqslant b_1 \text{ and } y = b_2) \text{ or}$$

$$\text{or } (x = a_1 \text{ and } a_2 \leqslant y \leqslant b_2) \text{ or } (x = b_1 \text{ and } a_2 \leqslant y \leqslant b_2)\},$$

the values of $u(x, y)\Big|_{\partial \mathcal{D}}$ do not exceed $u(0, 0) = 2$. Graphs of the functions $\partial^2 f(x, y)/\partial x^2$ and $u(x, y) = \left|\partial^2 f(x, y)/\partial x^2\right|$ are shown in Fig. D.4.

Thus, $M_{2x} = \max\limits_{(x,y)\in\mathcal{D}} \left|\partial^2 f(x, y)/\partial x^2\right| = 2$.

The symmetry of an integrable function with respect to its variables x and y allows us to conclude that $M_{2y} = M_{2x}$. As a result, we obtain an estimate of the error in the form

$$R \leqslant \frac{(b_1 - a_1)(b_2 - a_2)}{24}\left(\delta_1^2 M_{2x} + \delta_2^2 M_{2y}\right) = \frac{(b_1 - a_1)(b_2 - a_2)}{12}\left(\delta_1^2 + \delta_2^2\right).$$

For example, for the rectangle $\mathcal{D} = [-1, 1] \times [-1, 1]$ we have

$$R \leqslant \frac{1}{3}(\delta_1^2 + \delta_2^2),$$

and to achieve an accuracy of $\mu = 10^{-10}$ it suffices to choose, $\delta_1^2 = \delta_2^2 = 10^{-5}$.

As a result of numerical calculations, we obtain the result that with an absolute error not exceeding μ the double integral $\mathcal{I}$ is equal to:

(a) 1.9158485731;
(b) 0.4902816524;
(c) 7.4087458136;
(d) 18.8927259031.

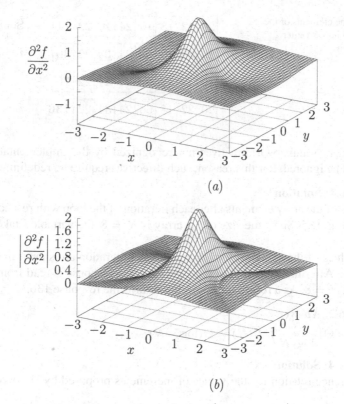

(a)

(b)

Fig. D.4 Graphs of the functions $\partial^2 f(x,y)/\partial x^2$ (a) and $\left| \partial^2 f(x,y)/\partial x^2 \right|$ (b)

Problem 5.10: Solution
The functions and environment variables of the OpenMP environment may be conditionally defined with the help of preprocessor directives. For this, the macro _OPENMP is used, which has the value $y_1 y_2 y_3 y_4 m_1 m_2$, where $y_1 y_2 y_3 y_4$ and $m_1 m_2$ are the decimal representations of the year and month, respectively, of the release of the OpenMP environment. For example, if a parallel program uses the functions for defining the number of threads in a team and the sequential number of a thread, then, in the program preamble, the line #include <omp.h> should be replaced with the following sequence of lines:

```
#ifdef _OPENMP
  #include <omp.h>
#else
  int omp_get_num_threads() { return 1; }
  int omp_get_thread_num()  { return 0; }
#enfif
```

Note that directives beginning with #pragma omp in the sequential-program compilation mode (without the key -fopenmp) will be considered by

Fig. D.5 The elements of the array in Problem 6.1 after each iteration

| 20 | 12 | 18 | 16 | 24 | 10 | 22 | 14 | Source data |

| 20 | **32** | 18 | **34** | 24 | **34** | 22 | **36** | $i = 1$ |

| 20 | 32 | 18 | **66** | 24 | 34 | 22 | **70** | $i = 2$ |

| 20 | 32 | 18 | 66 | 24 | 34 | 22 | **136** | $i = 3$ |

the compiler as unknown directives not recognized by the implementation, and hence will be ignored. For this reason, such directives require no redefinition.

Problem 6.1: Solution
The values of the array elements after each iteration of the loop with respect to i are shown in Fig. D.5. Since the size of the array is $N = 8$, the variable i takes values $1, 2, 3$.

The values of the elements that change at each iteration are shown in bold and underlined. After the execution of the algorithm, the response is read from the cell numbered $N = 8$. As a result, the algorithm returns the response 136.

Problem 6.2: Answer
$$S(N) = \Theta\left(\frac{N}{\log_2 N}\right), \quad E(N) = \Theta(\log_2^{-1} N).$$

Problem 6.4: Solution
The recurrence relation for the values of increments proposed by Hibbard has the form

$$\begin{cases} h_s = 2h_{s-1} + 1, & s \geqslant 1, \\ h_0 = 1. \end{cases}$$

This relation is satisfied by the sequence $h_s = 2^{s+1} - 1$ for all nonnegative integers s. Therefore, the procedure for filling the array h can be organized in this way:

```
void parhfill(int * h, int L)
{
    #pragma omp parallel for
        for (int s=0; s<L; s++)
            h[s] = (1 << (s+1)) - 1;
}
```

Here, the operation of raising the number 2 to the power $s + 1$ is replaced by a bit construction `(1 << (s+1))`.

One iteration of this loop takes time $\Theta(1)$, and the total number of iterations is $L = \Theta(\log_2 N)$. Consequently, the time for the `parhfill` operation is $\Theta(p^{-1} \log_2 N)$, where p is the size of the team.

For the increments in parts (b)–(d), the procedure `parhfill` is written similarly.

Problem 6.6: Answer
With an absolute error not exceeding μ, we have:

(a) $\mathcal{J} = 3.332307$;
(b) $\mathcal{J} = 0.357242$;
(c) $\mathcal{J} = 2.380980$;
(d) $\mathcal{J} = 2.873681$.

Note In the four cases listed above, it is possible to obtain analytical expressions for the values of the integrals, which can be useful for testing and debugging the program. For example, in part (b), a transformation to a cylindrical coordinate system defined by the equalities

$$\begin{cases} x_1 = r\cos\varphi, \\ x_2 = r\sin\varphi, \\ x_3 = z, \end{cases}$$

where $0 \leqslant r \leqslant \sqrt{1 - z^2/2}$, $0 \leqslant \varphi < 2\pi$, and $-\sqrt{2} \leqslant z \leqslant \sqrt{2}$, leads to the answer
$\mathcal{J} = \pi^{3/2}\left(\text{erf}(\sqrt{2}) - (\sqrt{2}/e)\text{erf}(1)\right) = 2.873681227143\ldots$

Problem 6.7: Hint
Reduce the improper integral $\mathcal{K} = \int_1^\infty \sqrt{x}\, e^{-x^2} dx$ to $\int_0^1 x^{-5/2} e^{-1/t^2} dt$ by making the change of variable $t = \dfrac{1}{x}$. Applying the Monte Carlo method to the integral obtained will make it possible to obtain an answer with an absolute error not exceeding $\mu = 10^{-5}$: $\mathcal{K} = 0.159316$.

Problem 6.9: Solution
We denote the probability of the event $A = $ "at least two files out of N have the same size" by $p(N)$. We compute the probability $\overline{p}(N)$ of the opposite event $B = $ "the sizes of all N files differ"; then the answer to the problem will be the variable $p(N) = 1 - \overline{p}(N)$.

In order to compute $\overline{p}(N)$, consider the cases of small values of $N = 1, 2, \ldots$
If $N = 1$, then $\overline{p}(1) = 1$, since the file is the only one, and it is clear that there is no second file of the same size.

If $N = 2$, then, since the file size is a uniformly distributed random variable $V \in (0, V_{max}]$, the favorable outcomes for the event B will be $(V_{max} - 1)$ outcomes out of V_{max} possible outcomes. Hence,

$$\overline{p}(2) = \frac{V_{max} - 1}{V_{max}} = \overline{p}(1)\left(1 - \frac{1}{V_{max}}\right).$$

If $N = 3$, then the number of outcomes that are favorable for the event B will decrease in comparison with the previous case to $(V_{max} - 2)$:

$$\overline{p}(3) = \overline{p}(2)\frac{V_{max} - 2}{V_{max}} = \overline{p}(2)\left(1 - \frac{2}{V_{max}}\right).$$

It is easy to notice the following regularity:

$$\overline{p}(N) = \overline{p}(N-1)\left(1 - \frac{N-1}{V_{\max}}\right) \text{ for } N \leqslant V_{\max}.$$

By mathematical induction, we can prove that for all N satisfying the condition $N \leqslant V_{\max}$, the following equality is satisfied:

$$\overline{p}(N) = 1 \times \left(1 - \frac{1}{V_{\max}}\right)\left(1 - \frac{2}{V_{\max}}\right) \cdots \left(1 - \frac{N-1}{V_{\max}}\right) = \prod_{i=0}^{N-1}\left(1 - \frac{i}{V_{\max}}\right).$$

If $N > V_{\max}$, we have $\overline{p}(N) = 1$.

Finally, the probability of the event $A = $ "at least two files out of N have the same size," namely $p(N)$, is determined by the relation

$$p(N) = 1 - \prod_{i=0}^{N-1}\left(1 - \frac{i}{V_{\max}}\right), \quad N \leqslant V_{\max}.$$

We now perform a numerical estimate of the variable $p(N)$ for the parameters specified in the problem statement. Reduction operations are used in the program code. The answer is written in the file `output.txt`.

```c
#include <stdio.h>
#include <stdlib.h>
#include <omp.h>

int main(void)
{
    int i;
    double N, VMAX;  // task parameters
    double p = 1.0;  // probability of occurrence
                     // of event B for case N=1
    FILE * fp;

    if ((fp = fopen("input.txt","r")) == NULL)
      {
        perror("\nError opening file "
               "\"input.txt\"");
        exit(EXIT_FAILURE);
      }
    fscanf(fp, "%lf %lf", &N, &VMAX);
    fclose(fp);

    #pragma omp parallel
```

```
{
    #pragma omp for schedule(static) reduction(*:p)
        for( i=0; i<(int)N; i++ )
            p *= (1.0 - i/VMAX);
}

if ((fp = fopen("output.txt","w")) == NULL)
    {
        perror("\nError opening file " \
               "\"output.txt\"");
        exit(EXIT_FAILURE);
    }
else
    // the sought probability of occurrence
    // of event A is equal to (1-p)
    if (fprintf(fp, "%.8lf", 1-p)<=0)
        {
            perror("\nError writing to file " \
                   "\"output.txt\"");
            fclose(fp);
            exit(EXIT_FAILURE);
        }
    fclose(fp);
    printf("The result is written to file " \
           "\"output.txt\"");
    return 0;
}
```

As a result, with an absolute error not exceeding $\mu = 10^{-8}$, we have for $V_{max} = 10^{10}$ $p(5 \times 10^5) = 0.99999627$.

Problem 6.10: Answer
With an absolute error no greater than $\mu = 10^{-8}$, for $V_{max} = 10^{15}$ we obtain $p(1.5 \times 10^8) = 0.99998699$.

Problem 6.11: Answer
$N = 37,234$.

Problem 6.12: Answer
$N = 117,742$.

Problem 6.13: Hint
Make use of the following equality obtained from the expansion of the exponential function $f(x) = e^{-\alpha x}$ into a Taylor series about the point $x = 0$:

$$1 - \alpha x = e^{-\alpha x} + O\big((\alpha x)^2\big).$$

Problem 6.14: Hint
Use the information about the Fourier transform given in Appendix C.

Problem 6.15: Hint
Rewrite the result for the two-dimensional Fourier transform as a sequential application of the one-dimensional transformation first to the rows of the matrix x and then to the columns of this matrix.

Problem 6.16: Solution
The check of the "$3N+1$" conjecture for $1 \leqslant a_0 \leqslant L$ consists in the construction of the sequence $\{a_n\}$ until the first occurrence of the value 1. For example, for $a_0 = 10$ we obtain the following sequence:

$$a_f$$

$$10 \quad 5 \quad 16 \quad 8 \quad 4 \quad 2 \quad \textcircled{1} \quad 4 \quad 2 \quad 1 \quad 4 \quad \ldots$$

As is easy to see, the members of the sequence then begin to cycle.

In the program, we include a parallel loop over the natural numbers not exceeding L, in whose body the maximum path length to one is accumulated in a variable `length`. The threads of the parallel team preserve their private values of the variable `length` in an array `length_array[]`, and the values of a_0 corresponding to them in an array `a_array[]`.

In the final stage of the program; the global maximum is computed of the elements of the array `length_array[]`. Into the output file `output.txt` are output the maximum path length to one, the initial value of a_0, and the maximum member of the sequence beginning with that a_0.

We present the full code of the program below:

```
#include <stdio.h>
#include <stdlib.h>
#include <omp.h>

int main ( void )
{
  int a, k, L;
  int a_extr;            // initial value of a0,
                         // for which the path length
                         // to one is maximum
  int max_value;         // the maximum term
                         // of sequence
  int length=0, length_max=1; // current path length
                         // and its maximum value
  int length_local_max=1;     // maximum value for
                         // the given thread of
                         // the team
  int * length_array, * a_array;
                         // local data
```

```
                                        // storage arrays
  int size, p;              // number of threads
                            // in the team and ordinal
                            // number of the thread


  FILE * fp;

  if ((fp = fopen("input.txt","r")) == NULL)
    {
       perror("\nError opening initial file " \
               "\"input.txt\"");
       exit(EXIT_FAILURE);
    }
  if (fscanf(fp, "%d", &L)!=1)
    {
       perror("\nError reading parameter L");
       fclose(fp);
       exit(EXIT_FAILURE);
    };
  fclose(fp);

  #pragma omp parallel
    #pragma omp single
      size = omp_get_num_threads();

  if ((length_array = \
     (int *)malloc(size*sizeof(int))) == NULL)
       {
          perror("\nError allocating memory "
                  "to length_array[]");
          exit(EXIT_FAILURE);
       }
  if ((a_array = \
     (int *)malloc(size*sizeof(int))) == NULL)
       {
          perror("\nError allocating memory "
                  "to a_array[]");
          exit(EXIT_FAILURE);
       }

  #pragma omp parallel \
            shared(length_array, a_array, size) \
            private(p, k, a, length, length_local_max)
  {
     p = omp_get_thread_num();
```

```
        length_local_max = 1;

    // main computation cycle
    #pragma omp for
      for (k=1; k<=L; k++)
        {
            a = k;
            length = 0;
            while (a!=1)
              {
                  if ( a%2==0 )
                    a = a/2;
                  else
                    a = 3*a+1;
                  length++;
              }
            if (length>length_local_max)
              {
                  length_array[p] = length;
                  length_local_max = length;
                  a_array[p] = k;
              }
        }
    }

// computing the maximum among
// the local values of the path length to one
length_max = 1;
for (k=0; k<size; k++)
  if (length_array[k]>length_max)
    {
        length_max = length_array[k];
        a_extr = a_array[k];
    }

// computing the maximum term
// of the sequence a1, a2, ..., af
max_value = a = a_extr;
while (a!=1)
  {
      if ( a%2==0 )
        a = a/2;
      else
        a = 3*a+1;
      if (a>max_value)
```

```
        max_value = a;
  }

  if ((fp = fopen("output.txt","w")) == NULL)
  {
      perror("\nError opening file \"output.txt\"");
      fclose(fp);
      exit(EXIT_FAILURE);
  }

  fprintf(fp, "The maximum path length to one "      \
              "among the first %d numbers is "       \
              "equal to %d and is achieved for "     \
              "a0 = %d,\n"                            \
              "the maximum term of this sequence " \
              "is equal to %d",                      \
              L, length_max, a_extr, max_value);
  printf("The result is written to file " \
         "\"output.txt\"\n");
  fclose(fp);

  free(length_array);
  free(a_array);

  return 0;
}
```

Note that for computation of the maximum path length to one without the variable a_0 corresponding to it, it is sufficient to use a reduction operation of the form

```
reduction(max : length)
```

Application of this reduction allows one to compute the maximum value of the variable length by means of the OpenMP environment.

Figure D.6 shows the elements of the sequence $\{a_n\}$ for the initial condition $a_0 = 97$. It can be seen from this figure that segments of rapid growth of the values of the members of the sequence members' values alternate with segments of rapid decrease. At some step, the variable a_n becomes equal to an integer power of two, and then it falls rapidly to the value $a_f = 1$.

The "$3N + 1$" conjecture states that such behavior of the variables a_n is typical for any initial variable a_0. We note one more time that the question of the validity of this conjecture remains open [39].

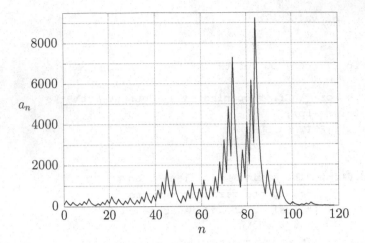

Fig. D.6 The Collatz sequence $\{a_n\}$ with initial condition $a_0 = 97$. The path length to one is equal to 118. For visual clarity, the points on the graph have been connected by a continuous line

Bibliography

1. Akl, S.G.: The Design and Analysis of Parallel Algorithms. Prentice Hall, Upper Saddle River (1989)
2. Anderson, J.A.: Discrete Mathematics with Combinatorics. Prentice Hall, Upper Saddle River (2003)
3. Andrews, G.R.: Foundations of Multithreaded, Parallel, and Distributed Programming. Pearson, London (1999)
4. Bachmann, P.G.H.: Die Analytische Zahlenthcoric. B. G. Teubner, Leipzig (1894)
5. Balle, S.M., Palermo, D.J.: Enhancing an open source resource manager with multi-core/multi-threaded support. In: Frachtenberg, E., Schwiegelsohn, U. (eds.) Job Scheduling Strategies for Parallel Processing, pp. 37–50. Springer, Berlin (2008)
6. Bang-Jensen, J., Gutin, G.: Digraphs: Theory, Algorithms and Applications, 2nd edn. Springer Monographs in Mathematics. Springer, London (2008)
7. Bernstein, A.J.: Analysis of programs for parallel processing. IEEE Trans. Electromagn. Compat. **EC-15**(5), 757–763 (1966)
8. Bertsekas, D.P., Tsitsiklis, J.N.: Parallel and Distributed Computation: Numerical Methods. Optimization and Neural Computation, vol. 7. Athena Scientific, Nashua (1997)
9. Brent, R.P.: The parallel evaluation of general arithmetic expressions. J. Assoc. Comput. Mach. **21**(2), 201–206 (1974)
10. Breshears, C.: The Art of Concurrency. O'Reilly, Beijing (2009)
11. Casanova, H., Legrand, A., Robert, Y.: Parallel Algorithms. Chapman & Hall/CRC Numerical Analysis and Scientific Computing Series. CRC Press, Boca Raton (2008)
12. Chapman, B., Jost, G., van der Pas, R.: Using OpenMP: Portable Shared Memory Parallel Programming. Scientific and Engineering Computation. MIT Press, Cambridge (2008)
13. Cormen, T.H., Leiserson, C.E., Rivest, R.L., Stein, C.: Introduction to Algorithms, 3rd edn. MIT Press, Cambridge (2009)
14. Deitel, P.J., Deitel, H.: C for Programmers: With an Introduction to C11. Deitel Developer Series. Pearson Education, Upper Saddle River (2013)
15. Desikan, S., Ramesh, G.: Software Testing: Principles and Practices. Pearson Education, Upper Saddle River (2006)
16. Diestel, R.: Graph Theory. Graduate Texts in Mathematics, 5th edn., vol. 173. Springer, Berlin (2017)
17. Dongarra, J., Foster, I., Fox, G., Gropp, W., Kennedy, K., Torczon, L., White, A.: The Sourcebook of Parallel Computing. Morgan Kaufmann, Amsterdam (2003)
18. Dow, M.: Transposing a matrix on a vector computer. Parallel Comput. **21**, 1997–2005 (1995)

© Springer Nature Switzerland AG 2019
S. Kurgalin, S. Borzunov, *A Practical Approach to High-Performance Computing*,
https://doi.org/10.1007/978-3-030-27558-7

19. Feautrier, P.: Bernstein's conditions. In: Padua, D. (ed.) Encyclopedia of Parallel Computing. Springer Reference. Springer, Boston (2011)
20. Feautrier, P.: Dependences. In: Padua, D. (ed.) Encyclopedia of Parallel Computing. Springer Reference. Springer, Boston (2011)
21. Fine, B., Rosenberger, G.: Number Theory: An Introduction via the Density of Primes, 2nd edn. Birkhäuser, Basel (2016)
22. Gonnet, G.H., Baeza-Yates, R.: Handbook of Algorithms and Data Structures: In Pascal and C, 2nd edn. International Computer Science Series. Addison-Wesley, Boston (1991)
23. Grafakos, L.: Classical Fourier Analysis. Graduate Texts in Mathematics, 2nd edn., vol. 249. Springer, Berlin (2008)
24. Graham, R.L., Knuth, D.E., Patashnik, O.: Concrete Mathematics: A Foundation for Computer Science, 2nd edn. Addison-Wesley, Boston (1994)
25. Grama, A., Kumar, V., Gupta, A., Karypis, G.: Introduction to Parallel Computing, 2nd edn. Addison-Wesley, Boston (2003)
26. Grimaldi, R.P.: Discrete and Combinatorial Mathematics: An Applied Introduction, 5th edn. Pearson Education, Upper Saddle River (2004)
27. Hamacher, V.C., Vranesic, Z.G., Zaky, S.G.: Computer Organization, 5th edn. McGraw-Hill Series in Computer Science. McGraw-Hill, New York (2002)
28. Harary, F.: Graph Theory. Addison-Wesley, Reading (1969)
29. Hazewinkel, M. (ed.): Encyclopaedia of Mathematics. Springer, Berlin (1994)
30. Hibbard, T.N.: An empirical study of minimal storage sorting. Commun. ACM **6**(5), 206–213 (1963)
31. Hockney, R.W., Jesshope, C.R.: Parallel Computers: Architecture, Programming and Algorithms. Adam Hilger, Bristol (1987)
32. Kernighan, B.W., Ritchie, D.M.: The C Programming Language, 3rd edn. Prentice Hall, Englewood Cliffs (1988)
33. Kerrisk, M.: The Linux Programming Interface. No Starch Press, San Francisco (2010)
34. Knuth, D.E.: The Art of Computer Programming, vol. 3. Seminumerical Algorithms, 2nd edn. Addison-Wesley, Boston (1998)
35. Knuth, D.E.: The Art of Computer Programming, vol. 4A. Combinatorial Algorithms, Part 1. Pearson Education, Upper Saddle River (2013)
36. Kofler, M.: Linux: Installation, Configuration, and Use, 2nd edn. Addison-Wesley, Boston (2000)
37. Kruskal, C.P., Rudolph, L., Snir, M.: A complexity theory of efficient parallel algorithms. Theor. Comput. Sci. **71**(1), 95–132 (1990)
38. Kurgalin, S., Borzunov, S.: The Discrete Math Workbook: A Companion Manual for Practical Study. Texts in Computer Science. Springer, Berlin (2018)
39. Lagarias, J.C. (ed.): The Ultimate Challenge: The $3x+1$ Problem. American Mathematical Society, Providence (2010)
40. Levitin, A.: Introduction to the Design and Analysis of Algorithms, 3rd edn. Pearson, London (2012)
41. Linux Man-Pages Project: Linux Programmer's Manual, Drand48_r(3) (2018). http://man7.org/linux/man-pages/man3/drand48_r.3.html
42. McConnell, J.J.: Analysis of Algorithms: An Active Learning Approach, 2nd edn. Jones and Bartlett, Burlington (2008)
43. McCool, M., Robison, A.D., Reinders, J.: Structured Parallel Programming: Patterns for Efficient Computation. Elsevier, Amsterdam (2012)
44. Midnight commander: home page (2018). https://www.midnight-commander.org/
45. Miller, R., Boxer, L.: Algorithms Sequential and Parallel: A Unified Approach, 3rd edn. Cengage Learning, Boston (2013)
46. MPI Forum: home page (2018). http://www.mpi-forum.org/
47. MPICH: home page (2018). http://www.mpich.org/
48. Nemeth, E., Snyder, G., Hein, T., Whaley, B., Mackin, D.: UNIX and Linux System Administration Handbook, 5th edn. Addison-Wesley, Boston (2017)

49. Olver, F.W.J., Lozier, D.W., Boisvert, R.F., Clark, C.W. (eds.): NIST Handbook of Mathematical Functions. Cambridge University Press, Cambridge (2010)
50. OpenMP: home page (2018). http://www.openmp.org/
51. Open MPI: Open Source High Performance Computing (2018). http://www.open-mpi.org/
52. Ortega, J.M.: Introduction to Parallel and Vector Solution of Linear Systems. Frontiers in Computer Science. Springer, Berlin (1988)
53. Pacheco, P.S.: An Introduction to Parallel Programming. Elsevier, Amsterdam (2011)
54. Padua, D.A., Wolfe, M.J.: Advanced compiler optimizations for supercomputers. Commun. ACM **29**(12), 1184–1201 (1986)
55. Patton, R.: Software Testing, 2nd edn. Sams Publishing, Indianapolis (2005)
56. Pratt, V.R.: Shellsort and Sorting Networks. Outstanding Dissertations in the Computer Sciences. Garland, New York (1979)
57. Press, W.H., Teukolsky, S.A., Vetterling, W.T., Flannery, B.P.: Numerical Recipes: The Art of Scientific Computing, 3rd edn. Cambridge University Press, Cambridge (2007)
58. Quinn, M.J.: Parallel Programming in C with MPI and OpenMP. McGraw-Hill Higher Education, Boston (2004)
59. Rauber, T., Rünger, G.: Parallel Programming for Multicore and Cluster Systems, 2nd edn. Springer, Berlin (2013)
60. Rosen, K.H.: Discrete Mathematics and Its Applications, 7th edn. McGraw-Hill, New York (2012)
61. Rosen, K.H., Michaels, J.G., Gross, J.L., et al. (eds.): Handbook of Discrete and Combinatorial Mathematics. Discrete Mathematics and Its Applications. CRC Press, Boca Raton (2000)
62. Rosser, J.B., Schoenfeld, L.: Approximate formulas for some functions of prime numbers. Ill. J. Math. **6**(1), 64–94 (1962)
63. Ruetsch, G., Fatica, M.: CUDA Fortran for Scientists and Engineers: Best Practices for Efficient CUDA Fortran Programming. Morgan Kaufmann, Burlington (2014)
64. Sanders, J., Kandrot, E.: CUDA by Example: An Introduction to General-Purpose GPU Programming. Addison-Wesley, Boston (2011)
65. Sedgewick, R.: A new upper bound for shellsort. J. Algorithms **7**(2), 159–173 (1986)
66. Sedgewick, R.: Algorithms in C, 3rd edn. Addison-Wesley, Boston (1998)
67. Sedgewick, R., Wayne, K., Dondero, R.: Introduction to Programming in Python: An Interdisciplinary Approach. Pearson, London (2015)
68. Shell, D.L.: A high-speed sorting procedure. Commun. ACM **2**(7), 30–32 (1959)
69. Shen, A., Vereshchagin, N.K.: Computable Functions. Student Mathematical Library, vol. 19. American Mathematical Society, Providence (2003)
70. Slurm: Slurm Workload Manager (2018). https://slurm.schedmd.com/
71. Smith, J.R.: The Design and Analysis of Parallel Algorithms. Oxford University Press, New York (1993)
72. Sterling, T., Anderson, M., Brodowicz, M.: High Performance Computing: Modern Systems and Practices. Elsevier, Amsterdam (2018)
73. Tanenbaum, A.S., Austin, T.: Structured Computer Organization, 6th edn. Prentice Hall, Boston (2013)
74. Tanenbaum, A.S., Wetherall, D.J.: Computer Networks, 5th edn. Pearson Custom Library. Prentice Hall, Boston (2011)
75. TOP500: home page (2018). http://www.top500.org/
76. Van Loan, C.: Computational Frameworks for the Fast Fourier Transform. Frontiers in Applied Mathematics. Society for Industrial and Applied Mathematics, Philadelphia (1992)
77. Voevodin, V.V.: Mathematical Foundations of Parallel Computing. World Scientific Series in Computer Science, vol. 33. World Scientific, Singapore (1992)
78. von Hagen, W.: The Definitive Guide to GCC, 2nd edn. Apress, New York City (2006)
79. Vretblad, A.: Fourier Analysis and Its Applications. Graduate Texts in Mathematics, vol. 223. Springer, Berlin (2003)
80. Ward, B.: How Linux Works: What Every Superuser Should Know, 2nd edn. No Starch Press, San Francisco (2015)

81. Wilkinson, B., Allen, M.: Parallel Programming Techniques and Applications Using Net-worked Workstations and Parallel Computers, 2nd edn. Pearson Prentice Hall, Upper Saddle River (2004)
82. Zorich, V.A.: Mathematical Analysis I. Universitext, 2nd edn. Springer, Berlin (2015)
83. Zorich, V.A.: Mathematical Analysis II. Universitext, 2nd edn. Springer, Berlin (2016)

Name Index

© Springer Nature Switzerland AG 2019   199
S. Kurgalin, S. Borzunov, *A Practical Approach to High-Performance Computing*,
https://doi.org/10.1007/978-3-030-27558-7

Subject Index

A

Access conflict, 79
Adjacent vertices, 8
Algorithm
    for calculating sum, 93, 94, 113
    cost-optimal (*see* cost-optimal algorithm)
    fast Fourier transform, 152
    for matrix multiplication, 109, 111, 112
    for matrix transposition, 109–112
    sorting (*see* sorting)
Algorithm efficiency, 117
    average case, 122
    best case, 121
    worst case, 122
Amdahl's law, 22, 23, 33, 34
Antidependency, 29
Arc, 8, 27
Array, 59, 82, 93–101, 109, 113, 114
    h-ordered (*see* h-ordered array)
    ordered, 96, 98
Asymptotic behavior, *see* growth rate

B

Base of natural logarithms, 119
Bash shell, 124, 127, 134, 136
    drawbacks, 140
Basic operation, 117, 121, 122
Bernstein's conditions, 28, 29, 31, 32
Big O notation, 118, 121
Bisection method, *see* method, bisection
Bit, 41
Bit string, 10
Blocks in file system, 131
Brent's lemma, 22, 34

"Butterfly" diagram, 152
Byte, 41

C

C programming language, 41, 57, 59, 67, 69,
        109, 125, 136
    C99 standard, 67, 69
C+ programming language, 67, 69
Cache memory, 32, 111
Ceiling function, *see* function, ceiling
Chunk, 74
Circuit, 27
Class of functions
    $O(g(n))$, 117
    $\Theta(g(n))$, 118
    $\Omega(g(n))$, 118
Co-array Fortran (specialized programming
        language), 38
Collective communication, 52–58
    allgather, 52, 54, 55
    alltoall, 52, 54, 55
    broadcast, 52, 65
    gather, 52, 54, 55
    reduction, 52, 55, 59
        generalized, 52, 58
    scatter, 52, 54, 55
Command interpreter, *see* command shell
Command shell, 124, 127, 136
Communication line, 7
    bidirectional, 8
    unidirectional, 8
Communication network, 7, 13
Communicator, 40, 52, 54, 58
    global, 40, 48, 64

© Springer Nature Switzerland AG 2019
S. Kurgalin, S. Borzunov, *A Practical Approach to High-Performance Computing*,
https://doi.org/10.1007/978-3-030-27558-7

Printed in the United States
By Bookmasters

Printed in the United States
By Bookmasters